WE DES ARGUMENTS

How Presuppositional Apologetics Empowers the Believer to Refute Unbelief

STEPHEN FEINSTEIN

We Destroy Arguments by Stephen Feinstein
Copyright © 2015 by Stephen Feinstein
All Rights Reserved.

ISBN: 978-1-59755-062-8

Published by: ADVANTAGE BOOKS™
Longwood, Florida, USA
www.advbookstore.com

Scripture quotations are from the ESV® Bible (The Holy Bible, English Standard Version®), copyright © 2001 by Crossway, a publishing ministry of Good News Publishers. Used by permission. All rights reserved."

Library of Congress Catalog Number: 2014959590

First Printing: August 2015
15 16 17 18 19 20 21   10 9 8 7 6 5 4 3 2
Printed in the United States of America

Table of Contents

Stephen Feinstein

Acknowledgements

Any given book represents the work, thoughts, and grit of many people. This book is no different. First and foremost, I acknowledge the God who saved me from the penalty and power of sin and adopted me into His family of saints. I thank God for placing the burden and weight of this book upon my heart and equipping me to write it for the sake of His kingdom.

I also am thankful for the people that the Lord used in my life to make this book possible. First on that list is Jim Kathan, a friend and coworker in Christ. He is the one who opened me to the world of presuppositional apologetics. He continued to press me for years until I finally came to understand what he was pressing upon me. The Scriptures themselves provide much guidance on how we are to defend the faith against all forms of unbelief. Jim opened the door for me to see this, and the content of this book is the result of all of the research and studying that I have done after entering through that door.

Second, I am thankful for my family. My wife Bonny has been very patient with me as this book is the product of five years of work. My daughter Rachel has been a great encouragement to me throughout the process. My daughter Hadassah inspires me to continue to write so as to leave for her a solid theology of apologetics when she comes of age.

Third I am thankful for my church family at Sovereign Way Christian Church, in Hesperia, CA. They have given me the privilege of being their pastor ever since the church's founding in 2010. Before the content of this book was put in this form, I previously taught it as a class to the saints at Sovereign Way. I received much encouragement in doing so, and was pleased to see Christians learning to think God's thoughts after Him. Many within the church strongly urged me to put the content of the class into the form of a book. The pastors that labor with me in the ministry were also great encouragements to me throughout the process of both teaching the class and writing the book. So to Mohammed Khazaal and Ryan Felton, I say thank you.

Fourth, I am thankful for one of the deacons at Sovereign Way Christian Church, Brian Orr. Brian is an amazing grammarian and spent many hours editing this book, thus ensuring its flow. His suggestions truly made this book far better than it would have been without his input.

Finally, I am thankful for the men that have gone before me in writing on this subject. For the last five to six years, I have been in the minds of true geniuses, men like Corneilus Van Til, Greg Bahnsen, John Frame, Francis Schaeffer, Jason Lisle, just to name a few. I have read their books again and again, absorbing into my mind the wonderful world of presuppositional apologetics. I hope to add to their work for the kingdom by bringing forth a volume that focuses both on knowledge and application. May God use this work for His glory. Thanks be to Him.

Introduction

The Biblical Way

Three thousand years ago, a man after God's own heart walked this earth. The Lord took this person from being a relatively unimportant shepherd for his father's sheep and raised him up to be king over the people of God. His name was David. For much of his life, he only sought to please the Lord. He cared so little for his own life that he alone, as a young inexperienced teenager, traversed the treacherous battlefield to confront an almost ten-foot-tall giant. His only concern was that this pagan insulted the God of Israel, and that was enough for him to act. Someone had to defend the honor of God, even if it meant certain death. Yet, God was with the boy, and with a mere stone and sling, the blaspheming giant fell on his face, smitten by the shepherd boy of Israel.

God grew this boy into a man, and eventually made him king over Israel. Although David had his run-ins with sin, for the most part his heart was seeking the glory of God. One only needs to look at the psalms penned by this man of God to see this is true. However, when examining the life of this hero of the faith, a very clear truth becomes evident. It is not enough to merely have the right motive of seeking God's will, but instead something more is necessary.

Such a statement may be shocking at first glance, but consider with me an important event early from David's kingship. In 1 Chronicles 13:3-13, we read the following:

> Then let us bring again the ark of our God to us, for we did not seek it in the days of Saul." All the assembly agreed to do so, for the thing was right in the eyes of all the people. So David assembled all Israel from the Nile of Egypt to Lebo-hamath, to bring the ark of God from Kiriath-jearim. And David and all Israel went up to Baalah, that is, to Kiriath-jearim that belongs to Judah, to bring up from there the ark of God, which is called by the name of the LORD who sits enthroned above the cherubim. And they carried the ark of God on a new cart, from the house of Abinadab, and Uzzah and Ahio were driving the cart. And David and all Israel were

1

rejoicing before God with all their might, with song and lyres and harps and tambourines and cymbals and trumpets. And when they came to the threshing floor of Chidon, Uzzah put out his hand to take hold of the ark, for the oxen stumbled. And the anger of the LORD was kindled against Uzzah, and he struck him down because he put out his hand to the ark, and he died there before God. And David was angry because the LORD had broken out against Uzzah. And that place is called Perez-uzza to this day. And David was afraid of God that day, and he said, "How can I bring the ark of God home to me?" So David did not take the ark home into the city of David, but took it aside to the house of Obed-edom the Gittite.

Through this event, David learned exactly who God is. David had previously seen God's favor, mercy, and grace, but now David was reminded of God's holiness. Please do notice a few crucial points from this passage. First, David had a most excellent and noble desire. He wanted to bring the ark of God to the city that God had chosen. He was rightly upset over the fact that the ark was not sought out during the days of his predecessor. Thus, his goal was to start his reign off the right way through obedience to God by the honoring of His name. However, David did not bother to seek the mind of God from God's written revelation. God prescribed the manner in how he wanted the ark moved from place to place. David, however, copied the world's method of moving the ark, for the Philistines were the first ones to ever transport it on a cart.

Even though David had a pure motive to honor God, and even though he sought to obey a command of God, he went about it in the wrong way, and someone died because of it. Fortunately, David learned his lesson, repented of taking God's holiness for granted, and a few months later he retrieved the ark the right way. In 1 Chronicles 15:3, David said to the Levites, "Because you did not carry it the first time, the LORD our God broke out against us, because we did not seek him according to the rule." What was the key truth that David learned here? The Lord broke out against us "because we did not seek him according to the rule."

So why begin an apologetics book with the lesson that David learned about God's holiness? It is rather simple. Many Christians engaging in apologetics act as David did before he inquired of the Lord. They have pure motives. After all, they are seeking to defend God, Christ, and the Bible against the sneering of unbelievers. They also understand that the Bible commands them to do apologetics, thus leading to their obedience of this command. Yet, at the end of the day, they are moving the ark of God on a cart pulled by oxen. Rather than "seeking according to the rule," they use the world's methods, thoughts, and tactics in an attempt to obey this command. In so doing, like David, they dishonor God each and every time they defend the faith.

These are strong words and are offensive to many, but the truth is the truth. Method matters! At the church that I pastor, I have one overarching goal for the saints: I desire that Sovereign Way Christian Church would be a church of biblical people, doing biblical things, in a biblical way. My desire that they would be biblical people simply means that they would be gospel-centered people who adore God and His Word, and therefore, live as people after His own heart. My desire that they would be doing biblical things would have them consistently obey God's commands. He commands much of His saints: evangelism, discipleship, apologetics, counseling, encouraging, edifying, loving one another, etc. Correct doctrine should lead to an overflow of obedient living. Thus, orthodoxy must necessarily lead to orthopraxy.

I believe that many churches—even some of the churches that appear to be worldly in their practice—honestly believe themselves to be comprised of biblical people doing biblical things. The problem is they do not always seek from God's Word the biblical way to do biblical things. There are many examples. The Bible commands that we evangelize, but it also tells us how to do it. Christians are to go into the world, preach the gospel, and bring the saved into the body of fellowship for the sake of discipleship and holiness. The Great Commission statements of all four Gospels command the disciples to *go*, for they are *sent* by Christ out into the world. Never once does the Bible command Christians to invite unbelievers to Sunday worship for the purpose of mass evangelism. Yet, in many churches the pastor will give the same milky, evangelistic message time and again in order to fatten the invited goats while the poor neglected sheep starve. Too many churches obey the command to evangelize by using this method, but in doing so their obedience is contrary to how God commanded it to be done. There are consequences for this. The saints fail to grow in their knowledge and churches begin to care more about entertaining goats than feeding sheep. Obedience of a command is *not* enough; the command must also be obeyed in an obedient fashion, meaning that it must be obeyed in the manner that God prescribes.

Other examples include counseling, worship, and preaching. The Bible teaches us how to counsel, and yet so few Christians are instructed in biblical or nouthetic counseling. Instead, they integrate modern psychology with the church, sprinkle Jesus on top, and expect to empower people through the enhancement of self-esteem rather than the mortification of sin. Many of the men whose methods they employ believe we are evolved animals with only a material body, and the ultimate goal for us is the restoration of a wounded inner child. Yet, the Scriptures teach that we are a fallen race, living under the curse, comprised of a physical body and immaterial soul, and that the source of our problems is sin. We need repentance, not self-esteem. So here we see again, like with evangelism, Christians attempt to obey the command, but they do so in an unbiblical manner.

Preaching and worship are in a similar state. The Bible commands that when we gather we are to sing songs, hymns, and spiritual songs, and there is to be a public reading of the Scriptures and a devotion to the Apostles' doctrine.[2] Yet, all across the land, songs with hardly any biblical theology are sung with the goal of facilitating the man-centered theology of so many churches and the goats they entertain. Additionally, the Apostles' doctrine has been replaced with twenty-minute sermonettes that are self-help messages with Scriptures carelessly stitched together in order to make the human message seem divine. What are we left with? We are left with a landscape of decade-old infants in Christ, with a spiritual immaturity that is indistinguishable from the world's. Furthermore, unbelievers all across the globe consider Christianity to be one of the largest jokes in history.

Ultimately, you cannot be a biblical person doing biblical things, if you are not also doing them in the biblical way. For a second time I say method matters! Many people will fight bitterly against everything said here, but at the Bema Seat,[3] their work will be judged by a holy God. That should cause the majority of pastors to shudder.

In getting back to the issue of apologetics, what are the implications of doing biblical things in the biblical way for apologists? Quite honestly, the implications are enormous. To demonstrate this, I will ask the apologist a few questions. First, have you done a thorough study of apologetics in the Bible? I am not asking if you have studied apologetics, but instead, have you looked specifically at how the Bible defends itself and how heroes of the faith within the Bible engaged in apologetic discourse? If not, then you should not be trying to defend the faith. Not yet, at least. The simple truth is you have no idea of how to do this biblical thing in the biblical way if you have not first studied to see if there even is a biblical way to begin with. Second, does your method of defending the faith consist of you learning numerous secular facts and arguments, and then through secular means trying to prove the Bible is true? If so, have you ever considered that you might be moving the ark with the cart of the Philistines? Third, in your apologetic endeavors, what carries the greatest authority in your arguments? Do you place more weight on secular history

---

[2] Acts 2:42; Ephesians 5:19; Colossians 3:16; 1 Timothy 4:13.
[3] Romans 14:10, 1 Corinthians 3:13, and 2 Corinthians 5:10.

and science than on the Scriptures? Do you rest your case on the authority of man, or on the authority of God?

The last question is paramount. Please, I beg you, think through the implications. If the Bible can be demonstrated as true only if you can prove it with history and science, then does that not mean that the Bible is under their authority? Does it not mean that the Word of God only gets to remain as such as long as it passes the tests of the word of man? Every apologist will answer with a loud, "No," but actions speak louder than words. A man can profess love for his wife all day long, but if he physically abuses her, has numerous affairs with other women, and endlessly neglects her, then his actions disprove his words. As Christians, we may say that we value God's Word above that of man, but if we act as though the Bible needs the word of man as authentication, then our actions demonstrate that we intrinsically do not believe the 3,000 statements within the Scriptures that declare it to be the Word of God.

The bottom line is if you use the reasoning of fallen man—reasoning built on the suppression of the truth due to a hatred of God—and you place that reasoning in a higher court than the Bible (meaning you judge the Bible by such reasoning rather than judging such reasoning by the Bible), then you are guilty of blasphemy. The frightening fact is most apologists do not know this. The Lord knows that for over a decade I practiced apologetics in such a manner, but by His grace He showed me a different way—a biblical way.

I do not want my words to be misconstrued, however. I am not saying that secular learning has no place, but its place must be in submission to the Scripture. Many pages of this book are dedicated to proving this. So if you find yourself in great disagreement, please be patient. Before you get one-third of the way in, my point shall be made.

The truth of the matter is that apologetics is often done incorrectly because apologists do not take into consideration biblical and systematic theology. Doctrine should inform how we do everything: evangelize, worship, counsel, preach, etc. What the Bible teaches about man, sin, and salvation has enormous implications for both evangelism and apologetics. When these subjects are ignored, and we merely attempt to defend the faith with facts and arguments, we are often counterproductive, and we dishonor God by allowing fallen man to assume the place of judge over God and His claims.

This book seeks to demonstrate what apologetics looks like when it is informed by the Bible. And in doing so, evangelicals will be doing the biblical thing of apologetics, but doing so in the biblical way. Given the fact that there is no chapter in the Bible dedicated to how one defends the faith against unbelievers, a biblical apologetic must be derived from a holistic understanding of the doctrines of Scripture. This is to be done in conjunction with scriptural examples of men of God engaging in apologetics. When this is followed, presuppositional apologetics is the outcome.

Purpose

As all introductions aim to inform the reader as to where the author is heading, this introduction is no different. By now, a predictable thesis should be discernible. If doing the biblical things in the biblical way is so important, then there must be a biblical way to do apologetics. In the 20th century, certain theologians of the Reformed community, beginning with Cornelius Van Til, began to stress the importance of submitting our apologetic methodology to the Christian theology of the Bible. When all doctrines are taken into consideration, when the examples of Scripture are brought to light, and when a Christian truly is in a place in which he is thinking God's own thoughts after Him, then a particular type of apologetic defense should emerge.

Among the various schools of apologetics, the most common name for this form of apologetics is presuppositionalism. It is my contention that presuppositional apologetics is the biblical way to do apologetics, and it glorifies God above any other methodology. It takes into account the full scope of Christian theology, it challenges unbelievers directly where they need to be challenged, it harmonizes with all apologetic examples in Scripture, and when used correctly it is irrefutable.

Secondary to this thesis is a plea for evangelicals to embrace, adopt, and utilize this method of apologetics in defending the faith. Allowing fallen mankind to sit in judgment over God, appealing to their tests, methods, and interpretations in order to vindicate God, and embracing the myth of neutrality[4] will always be the wrong way to do this. Unbelievers continue to lose more and more respect for Christianity in general, and for the most part the classical and evidential arguments do not impact them too much.

There are many critics of presuppositional apologetics, but most of the criticisms demonstrate a misunderstanding of what presuppositionalism is and is not. The purpose of this book is to teach the reader what presuppositionalism is, how a Christian should engage in apologetic discourse, and why presuppositionalism should truly be for everyone. There is no reason why this should be the best kept

---

[4] The myth of neutrality will be explained in Chapter One.

secret of Reformed apologists. Instead, biblical apologetics, like biblical evangelism and counseling should be spreading fast among true evangelicals. Hopefully this book can assist in this process.

As a brief definition, presuppositional apologetics is a biblical method of defending the faith. It takes into account what the Scriptures teach about fallen humanity, and it builds an apologetic defense consistent with this. Due to the fact that fallen humanity rejects the biblical God due to a suppression of the truth in unrighteousness,[5] they will not submit to Christ by the mere presentation of logical arguments or evidential reasoning. Instead, their very presuppositions (their underlying assumptions of reality) will dictate how they interpret evidence and use logic. Since their presuppositions are those that suppress the truth in unrighteousness, it is here at the presuppositional level that they must be challenged. When it is demonstrated that their presuppositions are impossible since they fail to meet all necessary preconditions of intelligibility, then all of their alleged evidence becomes moot. Much more will be said on presuppositional reasoning in Chapter Two.

Contrary to various misrepresentations of presuppositional apologetics, presuppositionalists do in fact use evidence and certainly use logic. Where we part ways with classical and evidential apologists is in the manner of how we use evidence and logic. We never use them in a manner that appeals to the false autonomy of mankind by which they think they sit in judgment over God's claims. Instead, we use logic to prove to the unbeliever that the God of the Bible is the necessary precondition of logic. We also use the laws of logic to demonstrate to the unbeliever that his worldview is inconsistent. Likewise, evidence is not used in a manner that assumes the unbeliever only needs more information. According to Romans 1:18-32, fallen humanity has plenty of information, and in their heart of hearts they already know that the biblical God exists. If we truly believe what the Bible says, then the manner in which we appeal to the unbeliever should reflect that. The way a presuppositionalist utilizes evidence is designed to demonstrate to the unbeliever that he is arbitrary in the evidence he ignores versus the evidence he accepts, and that Christianity is not blind, but is instead very reasonable. Furthermore, we can point to the intelligibility of evidence as one more item of the real world that requires the biblical God as its necessary precondition. As the pages of this book unfold, this shall be fleshed out in more detail.

Many fantastic books have been written about presuppositional apologetics. Any presuppositional books found in my footnotes are highly recommended. However, this book is not intended to focus on Van Til nor is it intended to discuss the

---

[5] Romans 1:18.

differences of opinion among presuppositionalists, for I will leave that subject to the scholars. Instead, the goal is to present the most powerful form of apologetics and to demonstrate through many examples how it tears to tatters all forms of unbelief. Ultimately, this book is designed to equip the saints for the work of the ministry.[6]

In order to create a meaningful introduction for apologetics, a short discussion on the importance of apologetics, Christian responsibility in apologetics, and a quick look at some of the key passages that speak directly of apologetics are necessary to review.

Christian Apologetics and Responsibility

The need for apologetics cannot be underestimated, yet many Christians neglect the responsibility. Like other works commanded of us by the Lord, apologetics is avoided as many believers create excuses to avoid responsibility in defending the faith. However, I want call our attention to two passages: 1 Peter 3:15 and Philippians 1:7:

> But in your hearts honor Christ the Lord as holy, *always being prepared to make a defense to anyone* who asks you for a reason for the hope that is in you; yet do it with gentleness and respect,[7]

> It is right for me to feel this way about you all, because I hold you in my heart, for you are all partakers with me of grace, both in my imprisonment and *in the defense and confirmation of the gospel.*[8]

Notice what is italicized. Peter commands that we honor Christ, in part, by always being prepared to make a defense to anyone. Perhaps one wonders if this verse should be universally applied to all believers, and the answer is yes. In 1 Peter 1:1, he addresses the letter to the "elect," which refers to all of the Christians in the regions he wrote to. Then in chapter three, they are commanded to always be prepared to make a defense to anyone who questions the hope (which is the gospel) that is in them. Likewise, in Philippians 1:7, the apostle Paul commends his Christian brothers and sisters in Philippi and says of them that they are partakers in the defense of the gospel. In this letter too, the first verse shows universal application since it is addressed to the saints of Philippi, rather than to the pastors only.

---

[6] Ephesians 4:11-14.
[7] 1 Peter 3:13 (emphasis mine).
[8] Philippians 1:7 (emphasis mine).

The reason for laying out the texts in this way is to dispel the idea that apologetics is only for the professionals (i.e., pastors).[9] No. Like evangelism, apologetics is the task and duty of all Christians. We are obligated to defend the faith, which obligates us to always be prepared. At times, people misapply Matthew 10:19 where Jesus says not to worry about what to say, but to instead rely on the Holy Spirit to give us the right words. Contextually, however, this verse is speaking to the apostles with specific regard to them being arrested and brought before kings. In those moments, when great fear would possibly overcome them, the Holy Spirit would give them the strength and wisdom to speak His Word. It is somewhat ironic that many who would deny the need for all Christians to engage in apologetics would on one hand deny the commands of verses universally applied to the whole church, but then take shelter under verses that only referred to the apostles' unique situation. Let us be better stewards of God's Word.

Apologetics is important for more than just the sake of silencing the critics of Christ. It strengthens our evangelism. Undoubtedly, if we are preaching the gospel to the lost, many will object and challenge the truth. If we truly care for their souls, then apologetics is a key ingredient in removing their man-made barriers to the faith. Another reason that apologetics is important is it builds up Christians who may be suffering from doubt. Our dedication to defending the faith can be priceless to the brother or sister who currently struggles with doubt. Is this not the heart of fellowship? Finally, apologetics can make you more confident in the faith that you hold, which only will increase your boldness, fruitfulness, and effectiveness in the Lord.

Do not be confused, however. God does not need us to defend Him anymore than a lion needs protection from a rabbit. The Bible offers its own rationale and its own defensive thought patterns. Furthermore, God is not one who can be surrounded by man and put on trial. If all men said that God does not exist, this would not automatically make Him vanish from existence. So we are not needed by God to do apologetics. Likewise, we are not needed by God to evangelize. Yet, rest assured, this does not remove the responsibility from us. There is a big difference between what God needs from us and what God requires from us. He needs nothing from us, but in His sovereignty He requires much of His people. In other words, God has ordained both the ends and the means. He determined the ends of who would be saved and how it would come to pass, but He also declared that we His people would be the means of this through evangelism and apologetics. Thus, the fact that He does

---

[9] Richard L. Pratt, *Every Thought Captive: A Study Manuel for the Defense of Christian Truth* (Phillipsburg, NJ.: Presbyterian and Reformed Publishing Co., 1979), 7.

not need us will not relieve us of the responsibility to do what he has commanded of us.

Final Considerations

In Matthew 7:24-27, Jesus Christ tells us that if we put His words into practice, we are like a wise man who builds a house on a solid foundation that can withstand all sorts of torrential pressures. Yet, if we do not put His words into practice, we are like a fool who builds a house on the sand. One gust of wind and the building is gone! This is true in all aspects of our Christian faith. Apologetics is no exception. Our apologetic foundation needs to be the words of Christ, which ultimately means the entire Bible (both the Old and New Testaments). All too often, apologists do not use the Bible as their foundation, but instead they start with reason, logic, historical evidence, scientific facts, psychology, etc. And with these, they try to build a house of defense for the Lord. However, doing so is to build on the sand. Hopefully as you continue to read through this book, you will see clearly why this is so.

One of the key foundational verses for apologetics is 1 Peter 3:15-16. Let us look at it again but much closer this time.

> But in your hearts honor Christ the Lord as holy, always being prepared to make a defense to anyone who asks you for a reason for the hope that is in you; yet do it with gentleness and respect, having a good conscience, so that, when you are slandered, those who revile your good behavior in Christ may be put to shame.

Apologists often focus on the clause that tells us to make a defense, but rarely is there a focus on the other fundamental aspects of this passage. The very first words in the English Standard Version are, *"In your hearts* honor Christ the Lord as holy" (emphasis added). Other translations render it as "sanctify" Christ as Lord in your hearts.[10] The thrust of this is that even before we make a defense, Christ must be set apart as Lord in our hearts. What does that mean? The word Lord[11] means that He is completely sovereign and in total mastery over us, and we are 100% dependent upon Him.

If you put this together with the next clause, *"always be prepared to make a defense to anyone who asks you for a reason for the hope that is in you,"* it becomes

---

[10] E.G., King James Version, New King James Version, New American Standard Bible, New Revised Standard Version.

[11] *Kurios* in the Greek. I highly recommend the reader do a word study on the Greek Old Testament and New Testament usage of this word.

crystal clear that this defense that you are required to make must be made from the foundation of Christ being Lord in your heart. This means that making a defense that is founded upon any other premise than that of Christ being Lord is unbiblical. If your premise is that Christ has to first be proven as Lord by man-centered logic and reasoning before He can be sanctified in the heart as Lord, then your apologetic is backward.

Of course, there is even more for us to consider from this passage. As we make the defense, we are also to do so *"with gentleness and respect."* In other words, we are not to demean, insult, or be contentious against those who question the Lord. In fact, the word "respect" is the Greek word for "reverence." We are to show reverence to those who question us, namely because they too are created in the image of God and deserve the dignity and respect that goes along with that status. A contentious heart jumps into arguments with nonbelievers for the sake of the fight, carrying prideful intentions to flex intellectual muscles. This is to be rebuked for sure. If we treat people correctly, and defend the Lord with the correct scriptural foundation, then according to verse 16 we shall have a *"good conscience."* Associated with the good conscience is a godly life. We are called to live above reproach. If our lives are a mess and betray evidence of blatant hypocrisy, then our message from God loses credibility and persuasive value. Yet, if we live in accordance with Scripture and have a good reputation with those outside of the church due to our Christ-like living, then those *"who revile your good behavior in Christ may be put to shame."*

Thus, apologetics is not arrogant, but it is gentle and respectful. Furthermore, it must be accompanied by righteous living, or the unbeliever will not take it seriously. Also, setting Christ apart as Lord in your heart means that your apologetic is not to be compromised with worldly wisdom. At times, Christians will tell unbelievers what they want to hear, or even apologize for what the Bible clearly teaches, in the hopes that unregenerate hearts might find Christianity more acceptable. This is to be avoided at all costs. It will become clear later that there is no neutrality between the wisdom of God and the wisdom of the world. It is actually sinful to drown out God's clear claims in order to appeal to unbelieving wisdom. Doing so reveals that you are actually ashamed of the gospel. The only recourse then is to repent.

The final introductory comment is that we must know what the Bible says and teaches. How can you defend something that you do not know? Furthermore, how can you set Christ apart as Lord in your heart if you do not know much about Him? God has revealed Himself to us in the Bible. In it, we learn of His attributes, expectations, and our responsibilities. We learn of the world, man, sin, and everything else needed to explain all of what is seen in this world. You cannot defend what you do not know. So read and study the Bible as your highest priority. Remember, God calls and commands all believers to evangelize and defend the faith. Doing so requires an extensive knowledge of God's Word, a foundational commitment to Christ as Lord, and a godly lifestyle to further convict the world of its rebellion. With these introductory considerations aside, I have only one more subject to address.

Organization of this Book

Many wiser men have written on presuppositional apologetics. Men with far greater intelligence and education have dedicated their lives to this subject and have written wonderful books about it. I am indebted to these men, for they are my teachers, and I am not attempting to surpass them. Even if I wanted to, I could not at this stage of my life. Instead, my purpose with this book is far different. I cannot add some new philosophical teaching nor can I improve upon the epistemological considerations offered in those other books.

However, what I can do is write this book from the perspective of a pastor seeking to equip the saints for the work of the ministry. As such, this book will be organized far differently than other books of presuppositional apologetics. The intent is to create a single volume that can build presuppositional apologetics from the ground up and then demonstrate its use against a large variety of common unbelieving worldviews.

To be honest, my heroes in apologetics were quite lacking towards this end. Concerning the necessity of presuppositional apologetics, they wrote majestically, but they neglected its application. I found myself convinced of the need of presuppositionalism, and I wanted to immediately go out and defend the Lord correctly; however, I had no idea of how to actually use it. After many months of research and contemplation, I created a class on presuppositional apologetics that I taught to my local church. In order to make it usable for them, there had to be as much content on application as there was on theology, philosophy, and epistemology. As I constructed the curriculum for the class, I realized that my presentational design of the content was exactly what I felt was lacking in the books from which I learned this most excellent form of apologetics. Thus, it made sense for me to take the design of that class and forge it into this book.

The organization of this book, therefore, reflects the design of that class. As a result, it is tailored to the reader to not only convince him of the necessity and importance of presuppositional apologetics but also to teach him how to use it day to day. Therefore, the book is divided into two sections.

The first section, covering chapters one through four, contains the building of the defense. In this section, building a biblical apologetic will be compared to building a shed. Ultimately, the builder will need detailed instructions, appropriate tools, and the right type of door. Proper theology is the single most important factor in constructing a God-honoring defense of the faith. Once the Christian possesses a strong grasp of what the Bible teaches, especially as it relates to apologetics, the tools of philosophy become useful. When the Christian understands the role and strength of Christian philosophy and the weaknesses of worldly philosophy, then a particular type of argument, a transcendental argument, becomes available by which the Christian can evaluate unbelieving presuppositions.

After the apologetic is built, then begins the second section of the book, which is the application of presuppositional apologetics. The motif for these chapters is martial arts combat since apologetics is a form of the spiritual war mentioned by Paul in 2 Corinthians 10:3-5. Thus, it makes an appropriate analogy. In this section, I will offer practical guidelines in terms of preparation and also refute the following worldviews and arguments: Atheism, Macroevolution, Problem of Evil, Secular Dualism, Hinduism, Confucianism, Buddhism, Islam, and Mormonism. It is through these chapters that the reader will see all that was taught in the first section be applied to these very common forms of opposition to Christ.

The practical nature of this book, then, is designed to teach all Christians who read it how to construct and utilize an apologetic defense that honors God and casts down all opinions raised against the knowledge of God. Truly, the goal and purpose of my effort is to glorify God by providing one crucial service for biblical people attempting to do the biblical thing of apologetics—the biblical way of doing so.

Stephen Feinstein

Section One

Building the Apologetic

Chapter One

Theology of Apologetics

Introduction

Let us imagine that a man went to the local hardware store and purchased a 400 square-foot shed for his backyard. To save money, he decided to put it together himself. Before he began the work, he had two simple options from which to choose. He could either open up the instructions and study them thoroughly, or he could assume that he knew enough about construction and therefore begin the assembly right away. Which option is the better one? Many of us have learned from experience that not following the instructions can lead to wasted time and potential disaster. Many of us husbands have foolishly declared a construction project as done only to have our wives point to a really large piece on the floor and ask, "Where does this part go?" Often in pride, our answer is, "Oh, that is an extra piece that is unimportant." After seeing the skeptical look on their faces, we attempt to assure them that the contraption is fine and sturdy. It does not take long before the thing begins to fall apart.

Studying the instructions solves this problem. No pieces get left out, the building project gets properly assembled, and it ends up sturdy enough to pass the test of time. Therefore, the man who purchased the shed would be wise to read the instructions thoroughly. After all, it will instruct him on everything from laying a proper foundation to putting each section up in its correct order. Although this concept is fairly simple, too many Christians engaging in apologetics do not follow it. They simply assume they know what is necessary to defend the faith, and so they go and do so. Yet, could it be possible that in their attempts they have a false foundation? If they do, will this not create a shaky building that in the end only dishonors God? I am convinced so.

So many Christians quote 2 Timothy 3:16-17 often, thus insisting upon their belief in it. The passage is quite clear.

All Scripture is breathed out by God and profitable for teaching, *for reproof, for correction,* and *for training in righteousness,* that the man of God *may be competent,* equipped *for every good work* (emphasis added).

All scripture is given by God and it is profitable for reproof, training in righteousness, making us competent, and equipping us for every good work. Yet, too many of the Christians that say they believe this deny it with their actions. For counseling, they rely on modern psychology built on a foundation of evolutionary theory. Yet, they say with their mouths that Scripture is sufficient. Others "evangelize" people using manipulation and theatrical gimmicks, drawing them in with means that are far from biblical, yet they say with their mouths that they believe Scripture is sufficient. My point is simple. If the Bible is sufficient for "every good work," then all Christian works should be practiced in a manner informed by our theology from Scripture. Apologetics is no different. It too is a good work that should be informed by our theology.

Many lay apologists do not even attempt to study the theology of apologetics. Instead, they rush into debates immediately engaging in scientific, historical, and philosophical argumentation, but all the while, scriptural guidelines are ignored. If the Bible is sufficient for every good work, then what it says *must* be the leading force of how we engage in apologetics. Do you think that what the Bible says about God, the world, man, sin, knowledge, reason, and argumentation is irrelevant to apologetics? Perish the thought! What the Bible says about the effects of sin on man's intellect speaks volumes as to how we must engage in apologetics. What the Bible teaches us about God compels us to defend Him in a manner that does not insult His very attributes. The point is real simple. Just as our theology should inform everything else we do, it must also inform our apologetics. It cannot be divorced from it.

To practice apologetics separate from theology is to try to build the shed without looking at the instructions. The designers of the shed know better than anyone else how to put it together. The God of the universe, and His revealed Word, knows more about apologetics than any philosopher or scientist.

Therefore, this first chapter is dedicated to the theology of apologetics. This is where we learn how to lay the foundation and how our Designer expects us to build a defense. The subjects that will be covered are as follows: basic systematic theology, the nature of divine revelation, the difference between unregenerate (unbelieving) and regenerate (believing) humans, the biblical fact that there can be no neutrality, the cause of the Fall, and the theology of the fool. With an adequate understanding of the instructions, the Christian will then be ready to move on towards the phase of construction.

Christian Theology as a Whole

Cornelius Van Til correctly argued that when defending the faith, Christian theism should be presented and defended as a unit.[1] Arminian and Catholic apologists often break Christianity into smaller pieces and through so-called autonomous reasoning attempt to prove the existence of a god and then later the Christian God. Truly, this makes little sense. Every fact of the Christian worldview bears witness to, depends upon, and works synergistically with every other fact of the Christian worldview. Christians are not out there to prove that a god exists, but instead that the biblical God exists. We are to prove that this biblical God has made Himself clearly known to all people at all times with clear distinct revelation that has left people without excuse. You cannot accomplish this by using piecemeal arguments that only demonstrate one sliver of the Christian worldview at a time. Instead, the Christian worldview as a whole is what is to be presented. Yet, it is even more than this. Christianity must be presented not only as an entire system, but as the only system of truth that is even possible.

In order to defend Christianity as a worldview (a philosophy of life that accounts for and explains all things), people need to understand what Christianity teaches as a collective unit. It is for this reason that I recommend that prior to studying apologetics in any depth, the Christian first needs to study systematic theology in order to understand exactly what he is defending. A person cannot defend what he does not know. In fact, it can be embarrassing to see a Christian that has learned very little biblical doctrine attempt to defend the faith against a witty unbeliever. The Bible speaks with authority about all things, and so it is the foundation of our worldview. Yet if a person does not know what the Bible says about most subjects, how can he present and defend the Christian worldview?

Therefore, I find it beneficial to quickly go through the doctrines of the Bible in order to lay the Christian worldview out on the table. By no means is this exhaustive. Godly men have written thousands of pages on the doctrines of the Bible. And therefore, what exists here is but a summary of the following doctrines: God, Man, Christ, Salvation, the Church, and the Last Things.[2]

---

[1] Cornelius Van Til, *Defense of the Faith:* (P & R Publishing, 1980), 114.
[2] It is also relevant to study these doctrines: Bible, the Holy Spirit, Sin, Israel, and Angels. It could be argued that these subjects can be covered under the broader subjects mentioned in this chapter, but I prefer systematic theology books that are broken down into ten or more doctrines.

Concerning the doctrine of God, He exists with both incommunicable and communicable attributes. Incommunicable attributes are attributes that are unique to God in that nothing in creation shares these particular attributes. Among these are independence, immutability, infinity, and unity. By independence, I mean that God is completely independent of all things and depends upon nothing (the world) and no one (creatures), but instead He is self-existent.[3] Due to immutability, God is unchanging and unchangeable.[4] The only thing that accounts for change in the first place is dependence, something that can never apply to God. By infinity, it is meant that God bears the various omni characteristics (omniscience, omnipresence, omnipotence, omnibenevolence),[5] which also relates to His independence. In terms of unity, the Scripture presents the existence of only one God.[6] Since God is independent, He is what we would call a necessary being (self-existent), whereas all other things are contingent beings (dependent on causation). The Bible presents to us only one God, and even philosophical reasoning can show that if a necessary being exists, there can only be one.[7] These are the incommunicable attributes of God. Nothing in creation shares in these attributes.

There are also communicable attributes of God, such as light, holiness, and sovereignty. These are considered communicable because we can relate to and partake of them, just not to the infinite degree that God does. All three of these communicable attributes are related to God's genuineness, veracity, justice, mercy, love, grace, faithfulness, righteousness, integrity, reliability, and purity.[8] All of these exist in humanity in lesser forms, but in God they exist in their perfect infinite forms. Because God is who He is (the divine, independent, and infinite creator), He is

---

[3] Acts 17:24-25; John 5:26

[4] Psalm 102-26-27; Psalm 33:11; Malachi 3:6.

[5] Psalm 139:7-12; Psalm 90:2; Psalm 147:5; Jeremiah 32:17.

[6] Deuteronomy 6:4; Mark 12:29.

[7] By definition, a necessary being is unlimited since it is uncaused, unsustained by anything outside of itself, and undetermined by outside factors. A necessary being is also totally independent of all other things. If a being meets these characteristics, there cannot be more than one. If two things had the exact same properties, they would actually be one thing, not two. For example, two "identical" pens are not really identical because they both occupy different spatial coordinates. Thus, they are not really identical. Well, if a necessary being exists, and is unlimited, thus occupying all spatial coordinates and possesses all omni-characteristics, then a second or third being of the exact same description would not differ or constitute another necessary being, but instead they would be in fact, a single necessary being. This philosophical truth not only proves God must be monotheistic, but it also philosophically explains why it is possible for three persons (Father, Son, and Holy Spirit) to be in fact one God.

[8] Isaiah 6:1-4; Hebrews 1:13; Psalm 19:7-9; Romans 6:23; Jeremiah 10:10; 1 Samuel 15:29; Titus 1:2; Exodus 34:6-7; Psalm 86:15.

sovereign. He is in control of all things in the universe and has the right to declare what is true and what is not true. He has the right to declare what ought to be done and what ought not to be done. He is original; we are derivative. He is the final arbitrator of truth. There is no higher authority that we can take God to. He is the Most High!

God's incommunicable attributes show Him to be transcendent, that is, completely not of this world, but entirely beyond it. Yet, His communicable attributes show him to be immanent—He interacts with the world and is present everywhere within it (this does not mean God is the world as some try to stretch it). In addition to these points, the Scriptures attest to the absolute personality of God. He is not an impersonal *it*, but a personal *He* who is self-aware and absolute. Since God is original and we are derivative, our personhood has its basis in His personhood. We are not absolute persons because we are not necessary or independently existent. Thus we are derivative.

Another fact to consider is that God is Triune. There is only one God, but as mysterious as it seems, He exists as three persons: the Father, Son, and Holy Spirit. Each are 100% equally God.[9] In fact, it can be argued that in order for a monotheistic God to exist, He must be Triune. This will be elaborated upon in the next chapter.

As for the doctrine of God, much more could be said. I suggest that the reader open up a systematic theology book,[10] and look up each of these attributes mentioned here in order to see and appreciate the number of scriptures that attest to each attribute of God. They permeate throughout the entire Bible.

We move next to the doctrine of man. According to the Bible, man was created in the image of God,[11] which means we were like God in every way that a creature can be like Him. Originally, Adam had all of the communicable attributes of God in a perfect, yet finite capacity. Yet, the incommunicable attributes of God remind us that even in perfection we could never outgrow our creature-hood, but instead would always be dependent on God. Man, being created by God from the dust of the ground, is physically related to the universe around him. Reformed theologians often point out that Adam as vice-regent of the earth was to be a prophet, priest, and king for all of creation. Being in God's image and having direct revelation from God, Adam would then care for the creation with the revelation, wisdom, and authority given to him by God. Yet, man today is not as he was originally created. Then came

---

[9] Matthew 28:19

[10] Make sure it is written by a conservative Christian scholar with a high view of Scripture. The best systematic theologies are written by scholars who believe the doctrines of grace, or are Calvinistic in their doctrinal leanings.

[11] Genesis 1:26-28.

the Fall of man, in which Adam and his wife Eve disobeyed God and brought sin into the universe, leading to the cursing of both man and the rest of creation.[12] In so doing, man rejected dependence on God, which was a refusal to admit creature-hood. All humans since then are born into the world with a sin nature,[13] seeking independence from God, and are unable do any good before the Holy Creator.[14]

Jesus Christ came into the world and bridged the impassable gap between God and man. Thus, the doctrine of Christ, or Christology, is the study of our Lord and His work. The second person of the Trinity, at a specific point in history, added humanity to His nature by incarnating Himself in the form of a man in the womb of a virgin.[15] And through His perfect union of the two natures (God and man), He was able to reconcile man to God in a way that allowed for God to be both just and merciful at the same time. Being a perfect man as Adam was prior to the Fall, Christ fulfilled all of the divine requirements perfectly and executed the intended role of prophet, priest, and king without error, and thereby earned for His people a true and human righteousness. By then substituting His innocent Son in the place of guilty sinners, God laid upon Christ the punishment earned by His sheep and laid upon the sheep the righteousness earned by Christ.[16] In so doing, God judged the sin of the saved by inflicting wrath upon Christ and granted mercy to the saved by imputing Christ's righteousness to them. All men not in Christ are still in Adam and will be judged eternally for their sin. Through the person of Christ, man witnesses and beholds all of God's attributes. Also, Christ rose from the dead and currently is at the right hand of the Father making intercession for His people.

The doctrine of salvation then tells us of how Christ's work was imputed into our accounts. The Bible speaks of God in eternity past predestining the saints for salvation,[17] sending Christ in real time to purchase it with His substitutionary atonement, and then enacting it in our lives through the work of the Holy Spirit. To counteract the spiritual death caused by the Fall,[18] the Holy Spirit gives us a new birth from above, or regeneration,[19] enabling us to come to Christ in faith from a

---

[12] Genesis 3:14-24.

[13] Psalm 51:5.

[14] Isaiah 64:6.

[15] Philippians 2:5-8; Colossians 2:9.

[16] 2 Corinthians 5:21; 1 Peter 2:24.

[17] Romans 8:29-20; Ephesians 1:3-8; 2 Timothy 2:9; etc.

[18] Genesis 2:17; Ephesians 2:1,5, Colossians 2:13; 1Peter 4:6.

[19] John 1:13; John 3:3-8; Titus 3:5; 1 John 5:1 (please study the Greek grammar); Romans 8:5-8.

special inward call.[20] Upon faith, we are justified,[21] which simply means Christ's earned righteousness is given to us and our sin is forever paid for by Christ's atonement on the cross.[22] We are then indwelt with the Holy Spirit who sanctifies us and serves as our guarantee of salvation upon the return of Christ.[23] When Christ returns, we will be made into glorified beings as Christ is,[24] and we will possess immortality for all eternity.

The doctrine of the church is the Scripture's teaching that upon justification, we become part of the church, which is the spiritual body of Christ. This body represents Him before the world and is assigned with the task of continuing His work through evangelism, discipleship, and apologetics. As such, we are the people of God, the bride of Christ, and the sheep of the true shepherd. The church collectively (the invisible church) is the whole number of the elect.

We can then end with the doctrine of the last things. God in His sovereignty has just as much control over the end as He had of the beginning. He demonstrates His sovereign control over history and time through predictive prophecy. Such prophecies teach us that Christ will return, the creation will be redeemed, the wicked will be judged, the righteous will be rewarded, and the curse will be forever ended.[25] It is under this doctrine that we learn much about the judgment to come.

Thus, in a nutshell, this is the unit of Christian theism. This is the guiding worldview and the ultimate presupposition by which we as Christians interpret all things. Unbelievers reject this worldview. They reject the notion that God is independent and sovereign. Instead, they substitute it with a view that makes the universe impersonal (to avoid the judgment to come) and man independent (so that we can be a law unto ourselves). You cannot be successful in apologetics if you only seek to prove bits and pieces of the worldview. It is a total-packaged deal. You either take it or leave it. The Jesus you preach to people is the Jesus you convert them to. If it is anything less than the biblical Jesus, then their faith and allegiance are still to themselves rather than to the true God.

Now that you know in a general way what we are defending as apologists, we can move on specifically to God's two books of revelation.

---

[20] Romans 8:30 (being called precedes being justified, which means it precedes faith); John 5:25 (they hear Christ's voice while dead).

[21] Romans 5:1; Galatians 2:16.

[22] 1 Corinthians 5:21.

[23] Ephesians 1:13-14; Philippians 1:6; Romans 8:9-27.

[24] Philippians 3:21; 1 John 3:2

[25] I recognize that within Christian circles there is disagreement over the details of the last things, but the list included in the above text are basic truths that all Christians agree upon.

General and Special Revelation

God left two different types of revelation of Himself for mankind. General revelation (sometimes called natural revelation) refers to the creation itself. When one looks at the complexity of the universe, the actual structure of the galaxies, the uniformity of the laws of physics, the nature of man, the complexity of both the micro and macro-creation, it is clear that a God with omni characteristics created it all. Denying this is more absurd than looking at a painting and saying there was no painter. The first chapter of the book of Romans makes it clear that all men intrinsically know the truth:

> For the wrath of God *is revealed from heaven* against all ungodliness and unrighteousness of men, who by their unrighteousness *suppress the truth.* For *what can be known about God is plain to them, because God has shown it to them.* For his invisible attributes, namely, his eternal power and divine nature, *have been clearly perceived,* ever since the creation of the world, in the things that have been made. *So they are without excuse.* For although they knew God, they did not honor him as God or give thanks to him, but *they became futile in their thinking, and their foolish hearts were darkened.*[26]

The text insists that God has clearly revealed Himself by what He has created, but men actively suppress this truth, convince themselves of a lie, and live with darkened hearts. Thus, it is not an intellectual problem that fallen man suffers from but a moral one.

General revelation has never been, nor was it ever intended to be, enough revelation for man to fulfill his duty before God. Even prior to the Fall, Adam did not have omniscience over the universe. Adam was created with the attribute of finitude and as such could not have had exhaustive knowledge of anything. It was for this reason that general revelation was supplemented by special revelation, which is the direct Word of God. We are told in the second chapter of Genesis that God conversed with Adam in the Garden of Eden. God gave him commands to upkeep the Garden, to name the creatures, and to not eat of the tree of the knowledge of good and evil. This all serves to imply that God walked with Adam explaining things to him and giving him the proper guidelines of interpreting the created order. When Adam and Eve sinned in Genesis's third chapter, they chose to interpret the world independently of God, thus introducing sin. Since mankind was now spiritually

---

[26] Romans 1:18-21 (emphasis added).

separated from God after this point, they were in need of more special revelation. Thus, over the centuries God, by the Holy Spirit, revealed more and more to His prophets, servants, and apostles, which culminated in the entire canon of Scripture known as the Bible.

This special revelation is totally necessary because the knowledge gained from general revelation is only enough to leave men without excuse. General revelation can tell us that God is righteous, infinite, and holy. It can tell us that we are sinners since we all violate the conscience deep inside of us, and if we are consistent, we should expect wrath and judgment. Of course, sinful man tries to convince himself of everything but these truths to make the prospect of judgment go away. However, even if a sinful man did not suppress the witness of general revelation, he would still realize there is nothing in general revelation that speaks or points to a solution to man's dilemma before God. Thus, special revelation is necessary to let us know specifically what His holy standards require of us and what must happen to atone for our violations of those standards. Thus, the story of redemption unfolds in the Bible as we learn more about God, man, the world around us, sin, and salvation.

So, here, we are left with what many call the two books of revelation: nature and Scripture.[27] Both are God's Word, but special revelation must take priority. The reason for this is pretty clear. If mankind's natural tendency is to attempt to think independently of God and suppress what general revelation is actually meant to teach them, then it follows that fallen humanity will reach a number of false conclusions. This is not to say that scientific experimentation will not yield true knowledge, as it often does. However, this is not because of man's rebellion, but instead is in spite of it. In later chapters, it will become clear that unbelieving scientists do not operate consistently on the presuppositions of their worldview, but instead borrow extensively from ours to do science. With that said, the unbeliever, left to his own devices, will only misinterpret and misapply the meaning of general revelation. Therefore, humans need to rely on special revelation to interpret general revelation.

Simply put, this is very logical. None of us truly are independent existences, but we are dependent on numerous causes outside of us. Since by our nature we are dependent beings, we also have dependent knowledge. When mankind acts as though we have an independent knowledge, they are inconsistent. God is the one who created all things and is the only one who knows His creation exhaustively. As such, we are dependent upon His interpretation of general revelation. He gives us such interpretation in the Bible, which is His special revelation. It is only out of

---

[27] John M. Frame, *Apologetics to the Glory of God: An Introduction* (P & R Publishing, 1994), 24.

sinful rebellion that man rejects this. We must look at the world through the spectacles of faith.

Fallen man will never accept this for two reasons. First, it contradicts his fundamental assumption that he is independent. Acknowledgement of dependence would logically demand obedience to whoever we depend upon. Second, it means he would have to accept the Bible without the ability to question or judge it. After all, if it is God's Word, then it is self-sufficient and self-attesting. Furthermore, it is authoritative and binding since it comes directly from God to whom there is no higher authority. This would mean that there is no human standard by which he can bring the Bible to trial. He would dependently have to accept it as the final word. Man's commitment to his own independence will not tolerate this. He would cry that to do so is to reason in circles since he would have to automatically presuppose the Bible as truth. Yet, he fails to realize that he already reasons in circles by automatically presupposing his independence. Much more will be said on this when I get to philosophy and epistemology in upcoming chapters.

The Bible does attest within itself many times that it is God's Word. Over 3,000 times, the speakers and authors of the Bible claim their word is from God. Expressions such as, "Thus says the Lord," appear over 1,700 times in the Old Testament alone. If a written book was the Word of God, we would expect to see this, and so we do. God leaves His autograph all over the place. Furthermore, the Bible uses prophecy as means to show its supernatural character. Men are constrained by time and therefore cannot accurately predict the future. Yet the Bible has well over 1,000 prophecies in it. Just with the person of Jesus Christ alone, it makes over 300 prophecies. When the repetitions are taken into account we are left with 109 distinct prophecies about the first coming of Christ. All 109 were fulfilled in Him. The Bible also makes prophecies concerning empires, destruction of certain cities, timelines, etc., of which the evidence clearly attests as being literally fulfilled. Of course, the fallen man does not accept the reality of his dependence, and so he looks at these facts through the spectacles of his own assumptions and arbitrarily decides what is possible and impossible. By deciding that future predicting is impossible, fallen man then concludes these prophecies were written after the fact, even though textual critical studies show otherwise. Thus, he ignores the clear signs of God's autograph within the Scriptures.

It is also worthy to note that the Bible has changed millions of lives throughout history and has been the most printed and purchased book in history. Yet, at the exact same time, it is the most persecuted and hated book in history. Also consider that the Bible had at least thirty-six authors who wrote its sixty-six books over a period of 1,600 years (circa 1440 B.C. to A.D. 100). These writers came from a diversity of occupations and geographical locations (stretching 2,000 miles from Babylon to Rome). To top it off, the Bible was written in three different languages on three different continents. If the Bible was merely a human book, you would find no unified theme and a multitude of contradictions. Keep in mind, the authors did not know they were compiling an anthology. They simply wrote what they were inspired by God to write. After thousands of years and each piece being composed, they were brought together and found to be in perfect unity. This is impossible if the Bible is not the Word of God. It is through the dual authorship of Scripture by both God and man that this unity is possible. It is in this unity that the drama of salvation history unfolds in perfection. What the world tries to call contradictions usually betrays the fact that they do not look closely at what certain texts are actually saying.

Be clear on one thing. All of this is not being presented to *prove* the Bible is God's special revelation. The Bible is God's special revelation regardless of what Christians or its critics claim. There is no standard higher than the Bible that we can judge it by. Instead, I brought these things up to show that the Bible indeed is consistent with what we would expect in a message from the independent, absolute, and infinite God.

Therefore, as Christians, we are people who dependently submit to God's interpretation of all things. With that fact in mind, it seems unfaithful to engage in apologetic methods that rely on fallen humanity's interpretation of things. Yet this is exactly what the other apologetic systems do. In terms of methodology, classical apologetics[28] treats autonomous reason as though it is a standard independent of God by which we as finite humans can judge whether or not God exists.[29] They will not

---

[28] Classical Apologetics was the method of defending the faith created by the medieval scholastics. It uses logic in an attempt to prove that God exists, or that there is a high probability that God exists. The better known classical arguments are the cosmological argument (reasons back to God via causation), teleological argument (reasons that God exists by appealing to design in nature), and the ontological argument (reasons that since God is the highest concept we can conceive of, He must exist).

[29] In all fairness, many classical apologists would not openly state this, but from my perspective as a presuppositionalist, this is exactly what they are doing. In March 2014 a movie came out titled "God's Not Dead," where a young college student debates an atheist philosophy professor using a typical classical approach. The student's opening premise was that they were going to put God on trial, and the philosophy class gets to be the jury. In the scenario, the individuals in the class would decide whether or not God exists based on their independent reasoning. Another example is William Lane Craig's critique of Gary Habermas evidential arguments in *Five Views of Apologetics* (pgs. 125-128). Craig uses Bayes' Theorem to show that with a classical approach you can show that the probability of the resurrection is above 50%. Not only does this posit the possibility the resurrection did not happen, but it used autonomous human

rely on the Bible until they first determine with fallen presuppositions that there might be a God who might have inspired a Bible.

Evidentialists[30] appeal to historical and scientific evidence that is extra-biblical because many fallen men will not respect the Bible. Yet, they fail to see that the reasons fallen humanity disrespects the Bible are the same reasons men have devised their interpretive schemes in the first place. They did so to escape their responsibility to God. Remember, the Bible tells us they are suppressing the truth. Why give in to their darkened demands of interpretation? We should instead challenge their whole interpretive scheme at the outset.

Cumulative Case[31] admittedly uses tests that unbelievers have created, which lends it to the same weakness as the other two systems.[32] Reformed Epistemology[33] also is guilty since it relies on independent reasoning from the field of epistemology

---

logical reasoning alone to derive the conclusion of $Pr > 0.5$. Thus, in practice, many classical apologists do treat autonomous human reason as a standard independent of God, by which they can judge the probability of His existence. Lest anyone accuse me of only citing Arminian attempts at classical argumentation, I will also state here that the Reformed classical apologists at Ligonier have the same problem. John Frame in *Apologetics to the Glory of God* (pgs. 224-238) reviews their book *Classical Apologetics* and rightly points out that they begin with man as a starting point rather than God. They also begin apologetic discourse with the autonomous use of certain logical laws such as non-contradiction.

[30] Evidential Apologetics was a response against the Enlightenment philosophers' refutation of classical arguments. Since Enlightenment thinkers favored empiricism and inductive reasoning (as opposed to the deductive reasoning used by the scholastics), evidential apologists used the same type of argumentation to *prove* the Bible is true. For example, they would use historical evidence to make an argument for the reliability of the Bible and the resurrection of Christ. They also will use scientific evidence to disprove the theory of evolution. This form of apologetics is still highly popular in our day.

[31] Cumulative Case Apologetics is a relatively new apologetic methodology. Rather than try to prove Christianity is true by appealing to a single argument, they instead present Christianity as an entire worldview and then make a total case (much like a legal brief) showing that Christianity is the strongest worldview. On the surface, it sounds like evidential apologetics, but it is distinct and unique since it focuses on entire worldviews rather than single arguments.

[32] Paul Feinberg, "Evidential Apologetics," in *Five Views On Apologetics* ed. Steven Cowan (Grand Rapids, MI.: Zondervan, 2000), 156. On this page, Feinberg writes, "These are tests that scientists, historians, and others—not just theists—would use in settling conflicting truth claims."

[33] Reformed Epistemology does not attempt to prove Christianity is true, but instead it uses epistemology (study of knowledge) to prove that all humans hold most of their beliefs on faith alone. We appear to be designed to accept things on authority. No one empirically checks out everything he reads in a textbook in order to verify it. Yet, he will repeat the things he reads as though he knows they are true. Is that any different than a Christian treating the Bible the same way? Thus, Reformed Epistemology is mainly the defense of the Christian's right to claim he is still rational even with his faith.

to justify faith in the Bible.[34] Christians, why not engage in apologetics the same way we engage in evangelism, preaching, and teaching? We engage in these by dependently submitting to what God has revealed. Much more will be said on this in succeeding chapters.

We should be convicted in our hearts if we realize that we are not consistent with our theology when engaging in apologetics. In theology, we let God's Word speak and define our beliefs and actions. It should also be this way in apologetics. With that being the case, we must let God interpret the world for us, in order that we may defend the faith with God's absolute, unquestionable perspective.

Apologetics is a part of spiritual warfare, and every wise student of war understands the necessity of knowing one's enemy. Since as finite humans we cannot exhaustively know anything, we should once again lean on God's exhaustive knowledge and absolute interpretations of our enemy. With regard to apologetics, our enemy is fallen humanity. Let us see what the Bible teaches us about fallen men so that we may know how to challenge them.

The Affects of Sin Contrasted with Regeneration

After the Fall, mankind was affected by sin in a variety of ways. Psalm 51:5 says we are conceived in sin and are therefore sinners at birth. Ephesians 2:3 says that fallen man is enslaved to fleshly passions. In fact, when surveying a variety of passages from the Bible, fallen man is said to be darkened, hostile to God, unable to understand spiritual truth, unwise, and futile. He worships the creature instead of the creator, has a corrupted intellect, conscience, heart, and lives in a state of spiritual death.[35] In short, the Fall affected all parts of all men. This is known in Calvinist circles as the doctrine of total depravity. Often misunderstood, total depravity does not mean man is as bad as he can be. The common grace of God actually restrains man from being as bad as possible. Instead, total depravity simply means all parts of a man are affected by sin. The Roman Catholic apologists of a past era taught that the Fall only affected our moral capacities, but our intellectual and rational capacities, as well as our free will were unaffected.[36] Total depravity corrects this and agrees with the Scripture that sin affects our moral, intellectual, rational,

---

[34] This, I believe, can be seen in the way that Kelly James Clark argues in favor of this position in *Five Views on Apologetics*. On pages 269-270 he makes some rather brilliant observations that prove most human beliefs are not derived from evidence. As useful as this is, his reasoning did not begin from the Scriptures, but instead from his own epistemological prowess.

[35] Romans 1:18-32; Romans 8:7; 1 Corinthians 2:14; Jeremiah 8:9; 2 Corinthians 4:4; 1 Timothy 4:2; Ephesians 4:18.

[36] Their position was that of semi-pelagianism.

emotional, volitional (will), and physical capacities; hence the depravity is total. There is no part of us that was unaffected by the Fall. Many theologians call this the noetic effects of sin.

Since sin has claimed every aspect of a man, even his reasoning and logical abilities are darkened. He is not neutral. Thus, we should not immediately appeal to a fallen man's reasoning skills since his very nature causes him to suppress the truth about God. Man's fallen reasoning often convinces him in a logically circular fashion that he is independent; as such, his reasoning will always start from a presupposition of epistemological independence from God, rather than dependence. As a result, he will use logic to discount what the Bible says. By independently and arbitrarily determining what is impossible, he will logically conclude many accounts from the Bible are mythical. The Christian, in contrast, presupposes dependence on an absolute and sovereign God. As such, he lets God determine what is possible, and in so doing, he still obeys all of the laws of logic when affirming the accounts in the Bible. This demonstrates that both the Christian and the fallen man reason with a broad circularity. In other words, we all reason from our presuppositions. This should be expected since the Bible tells us that fallen man suppresses the truth for a lie; that is, he creates a false presupposition. Whenever he reasons, he does so beginning from his false presupposition and therefore makes conclusions that allegedly confirm that very presupposition.

Apart from the sovereign miraculous regeneration of the Holy Spirit, Christians would be in the same boat as the unbelievers. When we are born again, the Holy Spirit gives us eyes to see and hearts to understand the Bible, which then leads us to accept the wisdom of God.[37] This leads us to declare Jesus as Lord, thus declaring His lordship and sovereignty over our lives.[38] We then deny the false notion of human independence but instead begin to love God with all our heart, mind, and body, and we bring every thought captive to His word.[39] With our new commitments, we exist as a new creation.[40] We cease to conform to the foolish thinking patterns of the world. Instead, according to Scripture, we are transformed by the renewal of our minds and can then think God's thoughts after him.[41] From this vantage point, we then reason with both proper and dependent presuppositions.

---

[37] 1 Corinthians 2:4-5, 12-16.
[38] 1 Corinthians 12:3; Romans 10:9-10.
[39] Matthew 22:37; 2 Corinthians 10:5.
[40] 2 Corinthians 5:17.
[41] Romans 12:1-2.

Furthermore, we have a subjective[42] certainty inside of us that the fallen man could never understand. Romans 8:16 tells us that the Holy Spirit dwells within us and personally bears witness to us that we are sons of God. Since the unbeliever does not have the indwelling of the Holy Spirit, he cannot understand this certitude that the believer has. As our commitments change, our understanding of the world radically shifts as we begin to see the world through the lens of Christian theism. We cease to arbitrarily decide what is possible and impossible, but instead, we trust God's declaration concerning possibility.

All of this is important for one chief reason: Neutrality is now impossible between the believer and unbeliever. Reason, logic, history, and science are not neutral. Instead, these things are understood from within our presuppositions. With the unbeliever having opposite presuppositions from the believer (e.g., dedication to the myth of independence) he will come to different conclusions when looking at the same facts. For example, the believer and unbeliever can look at the facts regarding the American Civil War and after sifting through the evidence can come to general agreement. But when the exact same process is followed with the resurrection of Christ, the believer and unbeliever come to two entirely different conclusions, even though there is an enormously strong case from historical documentation for the resurrection of Christ. Why? The fallen man presupposes that a resurrection is impossible, Jesus was just a normal man rather than God, and the Bible is unscientific. From that starting point, the unbeliever radically reinterprets the evidence. After all, to him, evidence could not possibly confirm something that the he has already presupposed to be impossible.

It is for this reason that there is no neutral ground on which we can agreeably argue with the unbeliever. The entire universe is God's whether the fallen man accepts it or not, so all ground is God's ground. None of it is neutral, ever! The main thing we have in common with the unbeliever is we are both made in the image of God. He suppresses the truth and reasons away from God, yet he does so inconsistently. We, in contrast, accept the truth and reason through God, yet we too can be inconsistent since we still have the sin nature. However, with our Christian worldview, we have the possibility to be completely consistent, something that an unbeliever can never attain. Yet, given the fact that both of us exist in God's creation bearing His image deep inside, we can appeal to that as the common ground by

---

[42] This is not to be confused with relativism. By subjective certainty, I refer to something that is personally experienced and, therefore, is not objectively apparent for all to see. It is a personal witness of the Holy Spirit to one's own heart. It conveys an objective reality but through a subjective means.

which we reason with the unbeliever. However, this means we have to start at the presuppositional level since that is where we can expose his inconsistency of interpretation. This will have to be elaborated upon much more when we move to the chapters focused on application. For now, it suffices that it has been shown that there is no neutrality. In fact, the next section addresses this topic with more clarity.

The Myth of Neutrality

Christians, we are at war. Is this not what the Bible declares of us? Consider the following passages:

> *This charge* I entrust to you, Timothy, my child, in accordance with the prophecies previously made about you, that by them *you may wage the good warfare,* ... (emphasis added).[43]

> For though we walk in the flesh, *we are not waging war according to the flesh.* For the *weapons of our warfare* are not of the flesh but have *divine power to destroy strongholds. We destroy arguments and every lofty opinion raised against the knowledge of God,* and *take every thought captive to obey Christ,*... (emphasis added).[44]

These passages are very clear. Paul charged Timothy to wage the good warfare, and in 2 Corinthians he described us as people who are "waging war" in which we destroy arguments and opinions raised against the knowledge of God. Our goal is to take thoughts captive to obey Christ the Lord.

What does this mean for you and me? To put it bluntly, there is a massive global war going on between Christ and Satan, and *all* people are combatants whether they admit it or not. All people are either for God, or they are against Him; no one is without a military uniform. As Christians, our commitment to the Prince of Peace is also a formal declaration of war on the world. Bear in mind that 2 Corinthians 10:3-5 makes it clear that we are not waging a war of flesh with guns, tanks, swords, or the like. Our war is spiritual in which we oppose Satan and storm the gates of Hell in order to win converts to the love of God in Christ. It is only in this way that the lost have a chance to be at peace with the Prince of Peace. Unlike the warfare of man, our warfare causes the dead to come to life eternally. It is a warfare designed upon peace. We love our enemies to such a point that we desire to see them live eternally with God.

---

[43] 1Timothy 1:18.
[44] 2Corinthians 10:3-5.

Participation in this war is not optional. Any Christians who try to sit on the sideline and avoid the war are actually sinning. By not engaging in war, they actually are serving the side of Satan since their slothfulness and cowardice serves to keep more people in bondage to sin and death. There is no need to belabor this point. Therefore, the remainder of this section is written to those who actually will obey God's commands. To the rest, only one thing can be said—repent, I beg you.

So we are all warriors. We are Christian soldiers moving forward. What does this mean? In warfare, there is no neutrality. You are either on one side or the other. The fact that we are at war exposes the notion of neutrality as a myth. The myth of neutrality is the idea that there is neutral ground in which believer and unbeliever have a common standing and can converse with each other. Belief in this myth causes classical apologists of all sorts to try to reason with unbelievers from a neutral standpoint. They act as though reason, logic, science, and evidence are neutral territories in which the two warring sides can rest and converse in peace. Like in modern warfare, they see these fields of thought as though they were a type of Switzerland.[45] In reality, there is no neutrality. There is little in common between believer and unbeliever since we both see the world from completely different presuppositions and commitments.[46] The reality of the situation is blunt. In the global spiritual war there is no Switzerland, but instead there is only "No Man's Land." Anytime you step out of the trench into the open ground, thousands of artillery shells and tens of thousands of bullets are flying directly at you.

The truth be told, we must accept the fact that reason, logic, science, and evidence are part of the weapons used in the warfare. We use these tools to proclaim that Christian theism is true, but the unbelievers use the same fields of thought to declare that Christian theism cannot be true. What happened to the neutrality? It was never there to begin with. In fact, consider the following verses so that this point may be driven home much clearer.

And he will place the sheep on his right, but the goats on the left.[47]

Whoever is not with me is against me, and whoever does not gather with me scatters.[48]

---

[45] Not even Hitler dared to invade Switzerland due to its neutrality.

[46] The main thing we have in common is we live in the same created universe and are made in the image of God.

[47] Matthew 25:33.

[48] Matthew 12:30.

He put another parable before them, saying, "The kingdom of heaven may be compared to a man who sowed good seed in his field, but while his men were sleeping, his enemy came and sowed weeds among the wheat and went away.[49]"

No one can serve two masters, for either he will hate the one and love the other, or he will be devoted to the one and despise the other. You cannot serve God and money.[50]

Enter by the narrow gate. For the gate is wide and the way is easy that leads to destruction, and those who enter by it are many. For the gate is narrow and the way is hard that leads to life, and those who find it are few.[51]

There are more passages than these that could be offered, but the point is simple. You are either a sheep or a goat. You are either one who is with Christ and gathers or you are against Him and scatter. You are either wheat or a weed/tare. You either are on the narrow road or the wide road. You either serve Christ as Master or you do not. Other contrasting passages can be used to show you are either elect or reprobate,[52] that you build on the rock or the sand,[53] that you have the mind of Christ or a mind of darkness,[54] that you are friend of God and enemy of the world or an enemy of God and friend of the world,[55] or that you worship the Creator or the creature.[56] The point is that there is no third option. The Scriptures again and again affirm that there are only two options: you are either saved or damned. Both are in opposite camps, and there is no neutrality. There is no being wheat and a tare, saved and damned, elect and reprobate, etc. No one sits on the fence. The nice, unbelieving grandma that has nothing against Christianity is not in a neutral third class but instead is against Christ and worships the creature. The Bible sees no neutrality between believer and unbeliever. We are as different as night and day.

Not surprisingly, it is not only some believers that appeal to neutrality. Many unbelievers do the same. They often act as though they are merely dealing with objective facts and have nothing intrinsically against religion but are forced to live

---

[49] Matthew 13:24-25.
[50] Matthew 6:24.
[51] Matthew 7:13-14.
[52] Romans 9:21-23
[53] Matthew 7:24-27.
[54] 1 Corinthians 2:16; Ephesians 4:18.
[55] James 4:4-8.
[56] Romans 1:25.

free from religion based on the "evidence." The United States of America pushes this idea in all aspects of public life. In public education, religion is kept out of schools all in the name of objective neutrality. In politics, a person is frowned upon if his political opinions are derived from his religious commitments. Sometimes evangelists are forced at the hands of police to leave public sidewalks since the cement is publicly owned and therefore must be neutral.

I hope you see the absurdity and hypocrisy in this. There is nothing neutral about this attitude. It already presupposes that it is impossible to be objective while considering religious answers as solutions. It also presupposes that truth is to be found (and can be found) apart from religious belief. It is anything but neutral when schools teach macroevolution and yet refuse the same right to creationism. It is presupposed that Christian creationism could not possibly offer the truth on this matter. There is no objectivity in their rules. The reason there is no objectivity is because there is no such thing as intellectual neutrality. Instead, the idea of neutrality is a concept inherent in fallen humanity in order to mask the fallen agenda of rebellion against God.

Thus, neutrality is nothing but a myth. It hides the eyes from the fact that a spiritual war is going on. Unfortunately, many Christians have not discerned this, and so they appeal to neutral grounds in order to reason with unbelievers. The differing presuppositions of the believer and the unbeliever are what make neutrality impossible. As Christians, we presuppose all of those doctrinal statements that were declared pages ago. We believe that the universe was created by the absolute personality that the Bible refers to as Yahweh and that the Bible speaks with total authority. We believe that since God is personal, we are grounded in His personality and thus are personal ourselves. Designed by God as part of the creation, we are specifically wired to be able to measure, interpret, and correctly predict things in the world. In order for this to be possible, the universe must be uniform, regular, and governed under predictable natural laws. The God who created it this way is sovereign over it and has the ultimate authority to do as He pleases in the universe. It is from these presuppositions that we interpret evidence. It is from this fundamental worldview that we declare what is both impossible and possible. In contrast, the unbeliever's presuppositions, regardless of religious persuasion or non-religious persuasion, always see man as the ultimate judge of meaning in the universe. As such, they presuppose an impersonal universe that operates off of some form of deterministic chance (yes I know it is inconsistent—that's the point!) and randomness. From that perspective, they too declare what is both possible and impossible.

If the Christian confronts him with logic, evidence, science, history, or any other form of evidence, the unbeliever will not agree to the believer's conclusions. This is due to both having two totally different understandings of reality. Even if the evidence for the resurrection of Christ is airtight, it means nothing to the unbeliever who believes that it is impossible for a man to come back from the dead. He will first argue that the accounts in the New Testament are legend-literature written way after the time of Christ. After showing him through textual criticism that the resurrection account recorded in 1 Corinthians 15 actually dates within three to five years of the crucifixion of Christ,[57] he will then propose ideas like the swoon theory, the Passover Plot, or a massive hallucination of Christ's followers. When the evidence then dispels those explanations, the unbeliever will finally say, "Just because the tomb was empty and people said Christ rose does not mean it happened. Superstitious people are prone to such things, and perhaps the followers of Christ made it all up to gain wealth and power." Of course, the believer can then talk about psychology and how no one would die for a lie they invented, and the argument will go back and forth until both parties get tired and call it quits. Why? The believer failed to question the unbeliever's presupposed assumptions about reality. Even if both spoke the languages of science, history, logic, and reason, they did not truly reach each other with any ability to persuade. Thus, there is no neutrality.

Furthermore, it is inadequate to simply show the unfruitfulness of a Christian acting as though there is neutrality. Actually, there is sinfulness involved in it. In Ephesians 4:17-18, Paul the apostle tells Christians not to walk as unbelievers do in the "futility of their minds" with their "darkened understanding" and ignorance. Appealing to an unbeliever's alleged autonomy is actually encouraging them not to submit to the lordship of Christ. Even worse, it is a refusal on the part of the believer to obey 1 Peter 3:15's directive to first "sanctify Christ as Lord in your hearts." Instead, he seeks to appeal to the "lordship" of "neutral knowledge" and the unbeliever's unregenerate reasoning abilities in order to prove Christ's lordship to him on his own terms. Reasoning with an unbeliever in this manner is actually dishonoring to the sovereign lordship of God.[58] In fact, in Ephesians 4:20, after it speaks of the futility and ignorance of the unbeliever, it says, "But that is not the way you learned Christ!" We did not learn Christ in the manner of "neutral autonomous" unbelieving thought. Why then would we ever try to teach others of Christ in such a

---

[57] Gary Habermas, "Evidential Apologetics," in *Five Views On Apologetics* ed. Steven Cowan (Grand Rapids, MI.: Zondervan, 2000), 108-110.

[58] Greg L. Bahnsen, *Always Ready: Directions for Defending the Faith*, ed. Robert R. Booth (Covenant Media Press, 1996), 8.

way? Appealing to neutrality is tantamount to appealing to agnostic thought. Christians should never do such a thing. Perhaps it is fitting to conclude this point with the following two passages:

> No one can serve two masters, for either he will hate the one and love the other, or he will be devoted to the one and despise the other.[59]

> You adulterous people! Do you not know that *friendship with the world is enmity with God*? Therefore *whoever wishes to be a friend of the world makes himself an enemy of God*. Or do you suppose it is to no purpose that the Scripture says, "He yearns jealously over the spirit that he has made to dwell in us"? But he gives more grace. Therefore it says, "God opposes the proud, but gives grace to the humble." *Submit yourselves therefore to God. Resist the devil*, and he will flee from you. Draw near to God, and he will draw near to you. Cleanse your hands, you sinners, and purify your hearts, *you double-minded* (emphasis added).[60]

Please, do not fall for the lie of neutrality! Given that our enemy is born in a darkened state of willful suppression of obvious truth, we cannot reason neutrally with them. In fact, to do so would be to replicate the first sin of our parents Adam and Eve. It is to that subject that we go next to see just how foolish the idea of autonomy really is.

The Cause of the Fall and the Theology of the Fool

By suppressing the truth of his own dependence on the absolute God of Scripture, the fallen man has presupposed his independence and autonomy. This conclusion becomes clear when one traces it back to the Fall of Adam and Eve. We must look closely at what occurred in the Garden to see why a presuppositional system that presupposes God's authority is absolutely crucial. There are a number of things that should be seen in the text below:

> Now the serpent was more crafty than any other beast of the field that the LORD God had made. He said to the woman, "Did God actually say, You shall not eat of any tree in the garden?" And the woman said to the serpent, "We may eat of the fruit of the trees in the garden, but God said, You shall

---

[59] Matthew 6:24.
[60] James 4:4-8.

not eat of the fruit of the tree that is in the midst of the garden, neither shall you touch it, lest you die." But the serpent said to the woman, "You will not surely die. For God knows that when you eat of it your eyes will be opened, and you will be like God, knowing good and evil." So when the woman saw that the tree was good for food, and that it was a delight to the eyes, and that the tree was to be desired to make one wise, she took of its fruit and ate, and she also gave some to her husband who was with her, and he ate.61

The serpent, who the Bible later informs us was Satan,[62] questions God's special revelation in verse one (did God actually say?). Eve replies to him in verse three with what God revealed. Yet, in verse four, Satan directly contradicts God's special revelation by saying, "You will not surely die." Instead, he tells her that God is holding out on her, but if she eats, she will "be like God, knowing good and evil." Up until this point, Adam and Eve in their perfection only had God's revelation and they dependently submitted to God's interpretation of good and evil. He told them not to eat of that tree, otherwise they would die. Eve clearly assumed God's statement to be true as she repeated it, though with some modification ("nor touch it"), in verse three. Yet, the devil's goal was to get them to question that dependence and that is exactly what occurred.

Once the serpent contradicted God directly and told Eve that if she ate, she could determine good and evil for herself, he tempted her with independence and autonomy. Verse six shows us that she fell for it as it tells us that she looked at it, saw that it was good for food, delightful to the eyes, and desirable for independent wisdom. Eve was faced with a choice of whether to obey God or disobey Him, but the choice was even more specific than that. Whose revelation was she to listen to? God is the absolute personality who made Eve and the entire universe. He is independent and has exhaustive knowledge. If anyone knew the truth, it was God. Yet, here was a creature who contradicted the creator and seemed to reason independently since he disagreed with God. Who was she to believe? We look at the situation and see that it would make much more sense to listen to God.

Here is what you may have missed, however. The fact that this conversation even continued after verse one is proof that Eve already chose to reason independently or autonomously. Had she stuck with dependence on God, she would have immediately

---

61 Genesis 3:1-6.
62 Revelation 12:9; 20:2.

rebuked the serpent and said, "God said we would die, and only He knows all things and has the authority to declare right and wrong. He told us not to eat of it, lest we die. Away from us serpent!" Dependent reasoning would presuppose the veracity of God's statement and deem all counter statements as untrue. However, by Eve continuing the conversation, she rejected dependence on God. Instead, she began to think independently. She foolishly let the serpent continue. When he totally contradicted God and promised her the ability to discern good and evil independently of God, she then stepped back and determined for herself who she was going to listen to. She chose to reason independently of God. She rejected special revelation, came to her own conclusions as to what was true concerning general revelation, and convinced herself that eating the fruit was actually desirable.

In other words, she desired the idea of being independently able to decide good and evil. Before she took the first bite, she already cast off obedience to God, intellectually declared herself as sovereign and autonomous, and invited disaster of the worst kind into the world. The text tells us nothing of Adam here other than he was there with her and ate too. We can assume that he wanted the same thing. So they ate and learned the hard way that God's special revelation was correct. Death came into the world and spread to all people.

Cornelius Van Til brilliantly pointed out that the issue here was not just epistemology, but equally involved ontology.[63] Epistemology asks the question, "How do we know what we know?" Ontology simply asks the question, "What do we know?" Eve independently reasoned and did not ask herself how the serpent knew that God was wrong. She also did not ask herself how she knew her independent reasoning would render a correct decision. Had she asked herself the ontological question before the epistemological, then she would not have made the error. She should have first asked, "What do I know?" She knew God is the independent, absolute personality who created the universe, knows all things, and carries all authority. Afterwards, if she then asked the epistemological question, "How does the serpent know God is wrong?" she would have concluded that God cannot be wrong but instead was the ground of all truth. She would have then concluded that she knew what she knew because God told her, and His word will always be sufficient. She would have immediately proclaimed her total epistemological dependence on God and disregarded the serpent.

By not directly asking the ontological question, she indirectly answered it. She indirectly decided that God was not the ultimate standard or criterion of truth, but instead she could and should reason independently. She could never justify it

---

[63] Til, *Defense of the Faith*, 33.

epistemologically due to her finitude, but that did not matter to her. In the New Testament, Paul understood exactly what occurred at the Fall of man. In 2 Corinthians 11:3 he feared that similar things would happen to the church if its people did not rely dependently on what God revealed about Christ.

> But I am afraid that as the serpent deceived Eve by his cunning, your thoughts will be led astray from a sincere and pure devotion to Christ.

Where is this going? It is quite simple. Every time a Christian apologist invites an unbeliever to independently judge the claims of God by his own "independent faculties" of reason, his is asking the unbeliever to replicate the first sin of our parents. Just as the fruit of this led to evil and dishonored God in the Garden, so too does it do the same today. Autonomy is touted as a good thing; however, in the word's Greek origin, it is the combination of the words self and law. Autonomy is the idea that you can independently be a law to yourself, deciding what is right or wrong. The great irony of autonomy is it's the very sinful thing that Satan promised Eve. We should not want to reason independently of God; instead, we should do what Eve should have done. She should have confronted the serpent with the revelation of God as the unquestionable, ontological truth by which the situation was to be judged. She would have then dependently reasoned that only evil could come from the serpent's advice.

We need to confront the unbeliever with the ontological truth of God's special revelation as the final authority for humanity. We need to appeal to his creature-hood, his status as the image of God, and we must confront his suppression of the truth. We need to ask him to change his mind about autonomy and rest in dependence on the only Being in whom truth itself is grounded. In short, we must demand repentance. The word repent means to change your mind. The first thing unbelievers have to change their mind about is who is ultimate in the universe, God or man. Then they must determine whose will reigns supreme, the will of God or the will of man. The other forms of apologetics merely encourage the autonomy that caused the Fall and subsequently all suffering.

From this standpoint, we need to realize that all who think they reason independently and choose to not live in dependence on God are fools. I mean this as no insult, but instead the Bible identifies these people as such. In the Scripture, the definition of the fool is not a shallow-minded, intellectually devoid moron. In fact, he can be highly intelligent, educated, and sophisticated. According to Scripture, the fool is a person who rejects God as the source of wisdom and knowledge but instead relies on himself as intellectually sufficient.[64] Various statements from Proverbs tell us the fool is unteachable, despises true instruction, sees his way as right in his own eyes (autonomy), trusts his own heart, does not think of himself as mistaken, and says there is no God.[65]

Proverbs 1:7 tells us that the beginning of knowledge is the reverential fear of God. From this standpoint of dependent reasoning, we can properly have true knowledge of the world around us, interpret it correctly, and obey the absolute, independent, and personal creator. True knowledge then is presuppositional. In other words, it must be founded upon, or built upon, the solid rock of God's Word. When it is built on the sand of human independence or autonomy, then it is actually the knowledge of fools. The Bible labels such knowledge as "falsely called knowledge."

> O Timothy, guard the deposit entrusted to you. Avoid the irreverent babble and contradictions of what is *falsely called "knowledge,"* (emphasis added).[66]

If you attempt to persuade a person to become a Christian by asking him to independently and autonomously reason, then you are appealing to his foolishness. Proverbs 26:4-5 forbids this.

> Answer not a fool according to his folly, lest you be like him yourself.
> Answer a fool according to his folly, lest he be wise in his own eyes.

More will be said on this verse at a future time as it will provide the fundamental way that we should do apologetics. For now, notice in verse four that if you answer a fool (which is defined above as the autonomous thinker) according to his foolishness (autonomy), then you will be just like him. So we are forbidden to encourage his sinful allegiance to his own mythical independence. Yet, the next verse tells us to then answer him according to his foolishness so that he will not be wise in his own eyes. When we get to the application chapters, I will explain that this second verse instructs us to show him with his own presuppositions the self-defeating nature of his epistemology. So we positively defend Christianity not on the autonomous presuppositions of fools but instead on the dependent presuppositions of Scripture. We then negatively answer him (i.e., refute his view) by showing him the

---

[64] Bahnsen, *Always Ready*, 55–57.

[65] Proverbs 10:8; Proverbs 15:5; Proverbs 12:15; Proverbs 28:26; Proverbs 17:10; Proverbs 14:6; Psalm 14:1.

[66] 1 Timothy 6:20.

impossibility of coherence and knowledge if his autonomous presuppositions were actually true.

Our goal in apologetics will dictate the method. If the goal is to save the lost, but we know the lost are fools (according to the Bible), then we must answer their objections the way that the Bible specifies. It suffices to say for now that we cannot answer them on their own terms. This then rules out the other methods of apologetics. Also, apologetics should not be divorced from theology. Just as our theology dictates everything else we do, it should also lead and guide our method of apologetics.

Conclusion

In summation, Christian theology is a unit that makes up our worldview or presupposition(s) as a whole. As such, Christian theology must be understood by the apologist so that he knows what it is he is to defend. The special revelation of Scripture is our final authority and the lens by which we are to interpret all things. We reason from the Scriptures so that we reason God's thoughts after Him in a God-honoring and dependent fashion. The Scriptures tell us that the Fall affected man to such a point that neutral reasoning is impossible. Thus, instead we must confront the fallen man at the presuppositional level with the truths presented in Scripture. When we appeal to fallen sinners with their own standards of false independence, we are actually encouraging them to follow the sinful manner of Eve in the Garden, and we are reasoning with fools according to their folly. As such, we are in disobedience to God, and our attempt to defend the faith actually becomes sinful. We do not serve a God that allows a good end to justify bad means. He demands the holy sanctification and righteous conduct in both our ends and means. Only by holding this high standard can we do apologetics to the glory of God. In the next chapter we will move into Christian philosophy.

Chapter Two

Philosophy of Apologetics (Christian)

Introduction

After the man reads the detailed instruction book that came with his 400 square-foot shed, his next step is to determine whether or not he has the right tools to construct it. I suppose he could act foolishly and begin the work assuming that he has the proper equipment. However, doing so runs the risk of getting half way through the job only to leave it unfinished because he is missing an important tool. Yet, if he is wise, he will look through his garage to see if he possesses the means to build in the manner the instructions directed. If he lacked the major, necessary tools, he could go and purchase them from a hardware store or borrow them from a neighbor so that he could both start and finish the project.

Apologetics carries the same requirement. In order to build a defense of the faith, the Christian must know the theological presuppositions of the Christian worldview as well as the biblical guidelines for engaging in apologetics. Chapter one was dedicated to that end. These subjects are like the instructions for the shed. In the same way that instructions alone will not build the shed, the theology of apologetics alone cannot build the defense. Thus, the shed needs the right tools for the job, as does Christian apologetics. Knowing from the Scriptures what we are supposed to build, how we are supposed to build it, and with what tools to build it from, we now need to make sure we have the tools.

Ultimately, apologetics is a battle between belief and unbelief, and this battle truly occurs at the presuppositional level. This makes apologetics primarily a matter of philosophical reasoning but in a distinctively Christian manner. With that said, some of the tools necessary to defend the faith at the presuppostional level are the various tools of philosophy. This includes, but is not limited to, metaphysics, epistemology, ethics, transcendental reasoning, logic, evidence, a theological understanding of inconsistency in the unbeliever, and a basic knowledge of the variety of unbelieving thought (both secular and religious). These tools will be the focus of the next few chapters. With them, the Christian can begin to construct the apologetic house of an unbeatable defense.

Therefore, in this chapter we will study the subject of philosophy as it relates to apologetics. In the previous chapter, the theological considerations were laid out so that we would understand the various elements of apologetics from God's revealed standards. By doing so, we saw that the popular methods of Christian apologetics ignore what God has revealed to us about defending the faith. As Christians, our first and final authority over these matters must be the Scriptures. They are our presuppositional starting point.

The next step, then, is to look into Christian philosophy. Understanding theology, although it is primary, is not enough to effectively engage in the apologetic task. We must now understand Christianity as a philosophy. We also must understand various unbelieving philosophies. Unfortunately, some Christians mistakenly interpret Colossians 2:8 to prohibit Christians from studying philosophy.

> See to it that no one takes you captive by philosophy and empty deceit, according to human tradition, according to the elemental spirits of the world, and not according to Christ.

What such well-meaning believers fail to see is that Paul prohibits a certain kind of philosophy, not philosophy in general. The passage forbids philosophy that is "according to human tradition" and "not according to Christ." Philosophy that presupposes the truth of Scripture is not "according to human tradition" but instead is "according to Christ." In fact, if anything, this passage serves as a warning to traditional apologists who reason with unbelievers on their own presuppositions. After all, it is these human traditions that can "take you captive" through "empty deceit."

Philosophy is an essential component of apologetics because every single person does philosophy. Not everyone does it well, but everyone does philosophy nevertheless. Anyone who has theories or beliefs about where we came from, what is real, what is good and evil, or anything else like this engages in philosophy. They can try to deny it all they want, but it will make no difference. Like all other philosophies, the Christian worldview addresses the questions of reality, knowledge, and ethics. As such, Christianity must be understood as just as much of a philosophy as it is a theological system of belief.

When we see how distinct and unique Christian philosophy is against the rest of the world's beliefs, it becomes easier to spot out unbelieving inconsistencies and contradictions. This then makes it much easier to tear down their philosophical worldviews. Therefore, this chapter will focus first on the nature of presuppositional argumentation, to then be followed by a general explanation of Christian philosophy. The next chapter will deal with unbelieving philosophy.

Presuppositional Reasoning

In preparing to defend the Christian faith, the believer must understand at the outset that the conflict is a total war between two opposing worldviews. The unbeliever is not attacking small portions of the Christian worldview, but ultimately, he rejects the entire foundation of it. He rejects God's authority as ultimate and instead is loyal to some form of human independence. Since the entire battle is truly a collision of worldviews, the believer must aim at this root. The mere stringing of evidential arguments together will not effectively get the job done because each line of evidence will be evaluated by the unbeliever's assumptions. As Greg Bahnsen cogently put it, "What one presupposes as to possibility will even determine how he rates 'probability.'"[1]

With this in mind, we must understand that we are dealing with an entire philosophy of unbelief in each and every unbeliever. This is why the biggest part of the battle must be at the presuppositional and philosophical level. After all, the unbeliever's antagonism is against the entire Christian worldview. In order to effectively use facts against the unbeliever, we have to first challenge their philosophy of fact. The only place that we can challenge their philosophy of fact is at the presuppositional level.

Presuppositions are the foundational, yet typically improvable, beliefs that all people build their knowledge upon. It is at this core of assumptions that we must challenge them. When we get to the chapters on apologetic application, the "how to" of this presuppositional challenge will be better explained. For now, it suffices to say that we make the challenge by giving an internal critique of the unbelievers' system of thought, thus showing that it renders knowledge and intelligibility as impossible. We also give a humble yet bold presentation of the Christian faith but only from the starting point of Christian presuppositions.[2] In so doing, we will have effectively challenged them where they ultimately need challenging.

---

[1] Greg L. Bahnsen, *Always Ready: Directions for Defending the Faith*, ed. Robert R. Booth (Covenant Media Press, 1996), 67.

[2] Ibid., 69.

A good example of this is found in Acts 26 where Paul was making his defense before King Agrippa and Festus. Paul presupposed the truth of the Bible and its authority. He also presupposed the sovereign ability for God to do anything He pleases in the universe He created. In verse eight, he makes a presuppositional appeal to the question of possibility.

> Why is it thought incredible by any of you that God raises the dead?

Paul's audience had trouble with the idea of a man being raised from the dead. However, rather than offering a laundry list of evidence for Christ's resurrection, Paul began with a mere question. Why is it so unbelievable that God can do this thing? In other words, if the God of the Bible exists, His ability to raise a man from the dead is not a problem.

I believe that had Paul given the resurrection evidence that he offered to the Christians in 1 Corinthians 15, the interpretation of such evidence would have been disputed here due to the fact that Paul and his audience had differing assumptions as to what was possible. This is further exemplified in verses 24-25 of Acts 26 when the pagan Festus calls Paul crazy, and yet Paul insists that he is rational.

> And as he was saying these things in his defense, Festus said with a loud voice, "Paul, you are out of your mind; your great learning is driving you out of your mind." But Paul said, "I am not out of my mind, most excellent Festus, but I am speaking true and rational words."

Based on Festus's presuppositions, Paul seemed crazy since in Festus's mind, the resurrection of Christ was impossible. Yet, in Paul's mind, he was being perfectly rational since logically God could do anything so long as it did not contradict His nature. It is this same dilemma that any of us have when we confront the unbeliever. Paul gave his personal testimony of everything that happened to him and his eyewitness accounts and personal contact with the risen Christ, but Festus simply wrote him off as mad. This is why at the beginning Paul first declared what was possible before he went into any evidence and testimony.[3] This encounter is a great biblical example of the collision of the two worldviews.

---

[3] In verses 1-7, Paul offers his formal salutation, but in verse 8, he begins his apologetic defense. In that verse, he starts with presuppositions by asking what is so hard to believe about God raising the dead. Only after this, does Paul begin to use testimony and evidence as recorded in verses 9-23. At verse 24, Festus interrupts and calls Paul insane, but the apostle continues to defend himself and appeals King Agrippa's personal knowledge of the events. There is a lot to be learned from this, but one thing for sure is that Paul placed presuppositional reasoning as the first

Although the crucial nature of the relationship between presuppositions and interpretation of evidence makes total sense to the Christian presuppositionalist, it is likely that one who practices the more traditional forms of apologetics might disagree. He might instead posit that believers and unbelievers both generally interpret evidence in a similar fashion when using the tool of reason. For example, scientists may disagree on whether or not diabetes type two is preventable by a physically active lifestyle, but after conducting years of research and experimentation, they could all agree that the findings show that diabetes type two is in fact a very preventable disease. Could it not also be the same with apologetics? Could we not with reason and evidence also sway the unbeliever as long as we have enough evidence?

No we cannot, for the traditional apologist misses one key point. The reason those scientists resolved their disagreement over diabetes type two is because they already agreed with each other on the more basic presuppositional assumptions. They agreed that the senses are reliable, natural events are uniform, data reporting was accurate, the researchers were honest, and that the scientific method leads to truth.[4] With those presuppositions, they counted the same kinds of things as evidence and as a result their disagreements could be resolved.

The situation drastically changes when a supernaturalist disagrees with a naturalist. The naturalist may say that reality only consists of what can be studied by science in a lab (empiricism), and that all events that occur in the universe can be explained by natural laws. Therefore, we have no need nor do we have the right to appeal to a being outside of the universe, or even outside of man's experience. The Christian supernaturalist, in contrast, believes there is a transcendent, all-powerful Creator who can intervene in the universe and perform miracles that cannot be explained with the ordinary principles of man's natural experience.[5] Due to these two opposing worldviews, it makes no difference how well accredited a report of a miracle is. The naturalist's presuppositions will force him to either deny the miracle happened or cause him to claim it to be an event that has a perfectly natural explanation as soon as more information is discovered. Evidence in and of itself is not enough to change his naturalist approach to all things.

The reason some Christians have a problem with presuppositional reasoning is they believe that the prefix "pre" in the word "presupposition" makes it something

---

priority and evidential reasoning as secondary. Why? What is the point of presenting evidence when the unbeliever's presuppositions will cause him to ignore it and conclude something different than he ought to? First state the presupposition, then state the evidence.

[4] Bahnsen, *Always Ready*, 119.
[5] Ibid.

that a person believes temporally before they believe anything else. This is not what the prefix means. Instead, it refers to eminence as in "preeminence."[6] In other words, it takes the first priority in our thoughts. Remember, presuppositions are the foundational, yet typically improvable, beliefs that all people build their knowledge upon. In that sense, they do exist temporally prior to our other beliefs, but this fact is impossible for anyone to escape. No one reasons from a blank tablet. Everyone reasons from a worldview in order to prove his worldview. It is inescapable. Even the evidential apologist who offers the evidence for the resurrection of Christ in par excellence still is presupposing that the resurrection is possible in the first place because he presupposes that God is sovereign over the universe. So the evidence used by the evidentialist is offered from the foundation of his worldview in a way that serves to further prove his worldview. The unbeliever does this as well. The naturalist assumptions are reasoned upon again and again in order to prove those assumptions.

In a sense then, it has just been argued that everyone reasons circularly. This is frowned upon in logic, but even the logician reasons circularly when he uses logic to say circular logic is unacceptable. In other words, how does he know that logic discredits circular reasoning? Well, by logic of course! Hence, everybody reasons in a circular way, but there are two different levels of circularity: a narrow circularity and a broad circularity. The former is the type of circular reasoning that must be avoided, for it is begging the question, a logical fallacy. The latter is what everyone does, whether realized or not, due to the inability to escape presuppositional reasoning. The key point is when an apologist actually begins the argument at the presuppositional level, he is often accused of logical circularity, but if the apologist is wise, he will do well to expose the same problem in the unbeliever. In fact, this is what the apologist should want to happen. It allows him to cut to the chase.

As the unbeliever is confronted with the Christian presuppositions over against his own, he may declare that he cannot accept the Christian presuppositions. Of course, the Christian should assume the more he presents it, the more it will start to make sense to the unbeliever. After all, Romans 1:18 teaches us that every unbeliever already knows the truth but is suppressing it. Remember, our theology must guide our defense. Furthermore, when the unbeliever is confronted with the fact that his own presuppositions make all things ultimately unintelligible, the Christian worldview should start to penetrate. Undoubtedly, some unbelievers will resist until the bitter end and deny the obvious truth. However, others will abandon their futile

---

[6] John M. Frame, *Apologetics to the Glory of God: An Introduction* (Phillipsburg, NJ: P & R Publishing, 1994), 13.

thinking. The Christian must remember we are not alone in this witness, but that the Holy Spirit is the one who ultimately removes the spiritual blindness of the unbeliever as we do our part. If the Spirit so calls a man, he will come to Christ.

John Frame created a superb illustration of how and why this presuppositional reasoning is important. He speaks hypothetically of a paranoid man named Oscar who is completely trapped into his disturbed state of mind:

> Let's say that Oscar presupposes this horror, so that every bit of evidence to the contrary is twisted and made to fit the conclusions. Every kind deed, for example, becomes a nefarious plot to catch him off guard and plunge a knife into his ribs. Oscar is doing what unbelievers do, according to Romans 1:21 ff. —exchanging the truth for a lie. How can we help him? What shall we say to him? What presuppositions, what criteria, what standards would we employ? Certainly not his, for to do that would lead us to embrace his paranoia. Certainly not "neutral" criteria, for there are none. One must either accept his presupposition or reject it. Of course, the answer is that we reason with him according to the truth as we perceive it, even though that truth conflicts with his deepest presuppositions. On some occasions, he might answer, "Well, we seem to be reasoning on different assumptions, so we really cannot get anywhere." But on other occasions, our true reasoning might penetrate his defenses. For Oscar is, after all, a human being. At some level, we assume, he knows everyone is not out to kill him. At some level, he is capable of hearing and being changed.[7]

The unbeliever, like Oscar, suppresses the truth and misreads the real world. By asking questions that get to the bottom of his assumed commitments, we can show him the circularity of his reasoning. We want him to no longer be able to take his worldview for granted. Now he will actually have to defend his presuppositions, and it is at this point we can show him the impossible position he is in.[8] If the Holy Spirit adds His witness to our words, then his unbelieving defenses will be penetrated, and the unbeliever will be changed. Traditional apologists get it backward when they tell

---

[7] Ibid., 12.

[8] Some unbelievers will work extremely hard to avoid having to defend their presuppositions. They will fight until the bitter end for their right to assume their presuppositions without question. In my blog debate with a host from the television show *The Atheist Experience,* my atheist opponent Russell Glasser refused to justify his presuppositions. By pressing the issue against him, it was made clear to me that he knew he was checkmated, and so he did everything he could to avoid admitting his dilemma. The debate can be found on sovereignway.blogspot.com during the year 2012.

unbelievers not to presuppose the Bible's truth until it has first been proven to them. This is problematic because first it tells them to presuppose something that is not true (i.e., a lie), and second, to do so would be similar to trying change Oscar with his own presuppositions.

Summing up the unbeliever's presuppositions, remember that he sees man's autonomy as ultimate. In so doing, he rejects the claims that God makes over all parts of the universe. He devises methods of interpretation and theories of reality to further convince himself of his own autonomy. We cannot and should not submit to his assumptions. He is not neutral, as was pointed out in chapter one, and neither are his methods.

In Greg Bahnsen's (a renowned apologist) public lectures, he often said the following against unbelievers' demand for our neutrality: "They aren't and you shouldn't be!" Their worldview must be challenged. If we try to win them on their own assumptions, we are answering fools according to their folly, and we will be like them. In answering them in such a way, we are agreeing and consenting to their lie of autonomy.

When we attack their presuppositions, we shatter their grounds of interpretation and at the same time appeal to the image of God within them. As Van Til observed, unbelievers have biased glasses cemented to their faces by which they interpret the world around them.[9] These glasses are designed according to fallen humanity's suppression of the truth in order to conclude that the biblical God does not exist. It is for this reason that we should not "talk endlessly about facts and more facts without ever challenging the nonbeliever's philosophy of fact!"[10]

Ultimately, what the Christian apologist seeks to demonstrate is that if Christianity is not true, then nothing can be proven to be true since the Christian worldview is the necessary precondition to knowing anything at all. This must be demonstrated at the presuppositional level. When the unbelieving presuppositions are called out onto the scene, it becomes clear that these presuppositions cannot account for the knowledge that nonbelievers do possess. In other words, the unbeliever's fundamental worldview is impossible. If the unbeliever's worldview is actually impossible, then there is no worry that a future fact might be discovered that can dethrone the true worldview. The argument by presupposition accomplishes this. Therefore, there are many reasons, both biblical and practical, to defend the faith at the presuppositional level. However, the ability to do so depends on a philosophical

---

[9] Cornelius Van Til, *Defense of the Faith:* (P & R Publishing, 1980), 201.
[10] Ibid., 199.

understanding of what the Christian presuppositions actually are. To that we turn next.

Christian Philosophy

Although many folks in Christian circles might deny it, Christianity is a philosophy. It is often assumed that philosophy is something that is secular, and Christianity is a matter of faith. In reality, the word philosophy means, "love of wisdom." As Christians, we should love true wisdom, which we know begins with the fear of the Lord.[11] For a broader definition of philosophy, it refers to the study of reality, knowledge, and ethics. More precisely put, all worldviews have a metaphysical outlook (theory of reality), an epistemological foundation (theory of knowledge), and a system of ethics (theory of right and wrong). Based on this definition, Christianity is most certainly a philosophy.

The Bible offers a comprehensive view of reality, knowledge, and ethics. Furthermore, every unbelieving system of thought also is a philosophy. Atheists often claim they do not hold to a philosophy but instead merely have a belief that there is no God. However, their belief that no God exists depends on a view of reality, a theory of knowledge, and usually involves a system of ethics. The worldview that one holds is wed in its entirety to the philosophy of that worldview. Thus, defending the Christian faith at the presuppositional level demands a detailed understanding of both Christian and non-Christian philosophy. In this chapter, we will focus on Christian philosophy.

Since Christianity is also a philosophy, it offers a viewpoint on everything. This means every Christian should have a distinct view on science, history, art, literature, business, economics, psychology, sociology, education, and every other subject that we can have a viewpoint on. Our understanding of reality, knowledge, and ethics will inform our opinions about all of these things. With this understanding of Christianity as a philosophy, we must accept that it competes with other philosophies: Platonism, Aristotelianism, empiricism, rationalism, skepticism, materialism, monism, pluralism, process thought, secular humanism, Marxism, New Age thought, as well as other religions like Judaism, Islam, Hinduism, and Buddhism.[12]

When it is all said and done, and every system of philosophy is looked at closely, it becomes evident that Christianity is the only one that stands against the natural inclination of the fallen mind. As we discuss the distinctive traits of Christian

---

[11] Psalm 111:10.

[12] Frame, *Apologetics to the Glory of God*, 32.

philosophy, it will become clear that Christianity truly stands against everything else. Perhaps this is why New Age movements, ecumenicalism, and tolerance and diversity movements tend to include all groups accept for biblical Christianity. The Christian view of metaphysics, epistemology, and ethics is simply too unacceptable for fallen man.

With that said, we can begin by looking at Christian metaphysics. What exactly is metaphysics? In a simple view, metaphysics is the study of existence. In other words, it asks, "What is it to exist?" and "What sort of things do exist?" It attempts to classify the things that exist (make distinctions) and to notice similarities. On a deeper level, metaphysics seeks the ultimate causes or explanations for the things that do exist. Perhaps it is best seen as an attempt to understand the entire scheme of reality (all existing things).[13]

In Christian metaphysics, there are four key things to know: 1) absolute personality of God; 2) the distinction between the creator and His creation; 3) the sovereignty of God; 4) the Trinity.[14] First, beginning with God as an absolute personality, let us focus on what is meant by absolute. By absolute, it is meant that God, as the creator of all things in the universe, is the ground of all other reality. He has no need of any other being[15] since He is self-existent, and as such He has life in Himself.[16] He was not created, nothing brought Him into existence, but instead God always existed.[17] In fact, non-existence is impossible for God. As such, He cannot be destroyed.[18] He is timeless,[19] knowing and being present in all time and space with equal perfection.[20] The Bible further tells us that not only has God created all things and is before all things, but that he is currently holding all things together.[21] This is accomplished by the Word of His power.[22] Since He is absolute, He gives all meaning to all created things by His own exhaustive interpretation of them.[23] It is He who gives common nature to some things and differing nature to others. God categorizes all things. In fact, similarity and difference exist due to the way God

---

[13] Bahnsen, *Always Ready*, 179.

[14] Frame, *Apologetics to the Glory of God*, 34.

[15] Acts 17:25.

[16] John 5:26.

[17] Psalm 90:2; Psalm 93:2.

[18] Deuteronomy 32:40; Timothy 6:16.

[19] Psalm 90:4.

[20] Isaiah 44:7-8.

[21] Colossians 1:17.

[22] Hebrews 1:3

[23] Genesis 1 shows God produced all creation, named aspects of His creation, and declares character of it as good.

designed each thing that He designed, which ultimately is everything in creation. God Himself is the one who sets the limits of possible reality by His own will and decree.[24]

God is not just absolute, but He is a personality (an absolute personality). The Bible informs us that God is "Spirit,"[25] and "spirit" in the Scriptures is applied to personal beings. Also, God speaks and uses first-person pronouns[26] when He speaks, thus demonstrating ego or personhood. In the Greek, the word "Spirit" is grammatically neuter-gendered, yet the New Testament constantly violates the Greek grammar by attaching masculine pronouns[27] to the neuter word. This means the Bible goes out of its way to declare God is a person.

God as an absolute personality answers for us a great question that faces mankind. Given the fact that the universe contains persons as well as impersonal structures, which is fundamental? In other words, we see people like you and me and know persons exist, and yet we see that impersonal things like matter, motion, time, space, and physical laws exist as well. So is the impersonal grounded in the personal, or is the personal grounded in the impersonal? Only biblical revelation declares that the impersonal is grounded in the personal, while all other worldviews claim the opposite.[28] Naturalists claim that persons are the product of a combination of matter, motion, time, and chance. Thus, to them the impersonal is ultimate. If we said my car exists because persons built it, certain naturalists would say that persons built it because atoms moved about in their brain in certain ways causing them to build it.

If the naturalist is correct in assuming an impersonal foundation, then there is no consciousness or wisdom behind anything in the universe, and logic and reason are accidental byproducts of chance. If that is the case, why trust reason and logic if they are accidents of irrational happenings?[29] Rationalism would actually have resulted from irrational sources! Furthermore, moral virtues like friendship, love, charity, and justice actually would be meaningless since there ultimately are no consequences since the universe is governed by blind and random chance.

However, if the Christian metaphysical explanation is true, then the impersonal came from the personal God, who made the universe with order, intent, and purpose.

---

[24] Isaiah 43:10; Isaiah 44:6.

[25] John 4:24.

[26] Acts 13:2.

[27] John 16:13.

[28] When I say that only biblical revelation grounds the impersonal in the personal, I am also including worldviews that are biblical counterfeits such as Islam. It is the Bible's influence on these counterfeits that cause them to agree with us that the impersonal is grounded in the personal.

[29] Frame, *Apologetics to the Glory of God*, 35.

The universe would have a rational order that can be understood by rational minds. Moral virtues would make sense in the universe since they are personal characteristics held by personal beings, who themselves came from the absolute personal being. Random chance does not explain with satisfaction at all the characteristics of personality found in humans.

It is not only the naturalists but almost every major religion of the world also holds to the impersonal as the ultimate ground of existence. The reason for this is simple. All of these religions are either pantheistic (the universe is god) or polytheistic (there are many gods, but they are not absolute personalities). Pantheistic religions do not see god as an absolute personality; rather, they see it as an impersonal force that is absolute. The polytheistic gods are persons, but since they are non-absolute they themselves are governed by the impersonal absolute of Fate, or Mana, etc. Since these religions do not advocate belief in an absolute personality (they always separate the two qualities), they all ultimately hold to an impersonal absolute. In the same way that the Greek gods were ultimately grounded in Fate, the Hindu gods are grounded in the impersonal Brahma. Most forms of Buddhism and Animism suffer in the same way. Thus, if divine personalities exist, but they are not absolute, then something absolute must exist that constrains them. In each case, it is an impersonal absolute that constrains them and therefore is their ground.

Thus, in all major world religions (except for biblical counterfeits), some impersonal, deterministic moving force is the ground of all being. Likewise, in naturalist thought the impersonal deterministic force is simply called random chance. It is a very telling point that all worldviews except for the biblical worldview see the impersonal as the ground of the personal. If this question was the type in which no certain answer existed, should we not expect that about fifty percent would favor a personal ground while the other fifty percent would favor an impersonal? Instead, what we see is that everyone whose worldview is not based on the Bible favors an impersonal ground. Perhaps this serves as more proof that fallen man suppresses the truth of God. Perhaps believing in an impersonal foundation of reality makes this suppression easier.

In the end, it makes little sense why men prefer to believe in an impersonal ultimate. Secular scientists often assume (they have no proof) that impersonal things like matter, motion, time, and chance can explain all personal things. There is nothing we observe in reality that truly supports this. We often observe that humans (personal beings) create impersonal things to do our bidding (i.e., tools and technology). John Frame uses the illustration of a farmer to make this point. Tractors are created by humans in a factory and are used by farmers to plow a field in order to create a farm. Thus, we have seen a farmer produce a plowed field, but we have never seen a plowed field produce a farmer. Likewise, we have never seen a tractor produce a human workforce.[30] So why is it so hard for naturalists to accept that impersonal matter, space, and time were created with a purpose by an absolute personality? Once again, the simplest answer is the suppression of the truth by darkened and fallen hearts.

In summation of God being an absolute personality, God is the self-existing necessary being in which all other things are grounded. He has created both personal and impersonal things and is the ground of both. This makes the most sense out of what is observed in common, human experience, but humanity in rebellion against God rejects that the ultimate ground of reality is an absolute personality. Instead they separate the two concepts and make the ultimate ground out to be impersonal. They do this because personal beings cannot be held accountable to an impersonal force. When is the last time a concrete wall in Los Angeles stood in judgment over a gang-banger who tagged it? Accountability is something that only applies to persons. As such, the fallen man thinks he can escape the judgment to come if no absolute personality exists. Thus, the biblical God is not rejected due to any evidence or a lack thereof, but instead the deception required to suppress the truth of divine judgment necessitates a rejection of the biblical God. Most human beings do not even realize that this suppression is going on in their heart of hearts, and continue to live in self-deceit.

Next we turn to the second aspect of Christian metaphysics and that is the distinction between the creator and the creation. According to the Bible, God is both transcendent and immanent. His transcendence refers to the fact that He is completely different, separate, and independent from the created universe. In fact, God is radically different, for He is the creator, and we are the creatures. As such, God is absolute, but we are not. Instead we are derivative, and He is original. He is the ground of all other being. Even our personality is different from God's in the sense that His personhood does not depend upon impersonal or personal creation but is independent of it. Our personhood depends on impersonal matter since we were made from the dust of the ground and are sustained by oxygen, gravity, and so on. Our personhood also depends on other persons since we were born from personal parents and ultimately were created by an absolute, personal God. So our existence is dependent on many factors outside of ourselves.

Yet, the Bible also tells us that God is immanent, meaning that He exists everywhere within the creation and is totally involved with it by sustaining,

---

[30] Ibid., 39.

controlling, and interpreting all things that He has created. Omnipotence necessitates immanence since God's power is felt and exists everywhere. God's personhood also sheds light on His immanence. Because God is personal, He interacts with His creation, especially given the fact that He created other persons when He created the angels and Adam and Eve. In fact, He made humans in His image, which, despite the great differences between us, also makes us like Him in many respects. As the ultimate person, God often seeks to have fellowship with His people. He spoke with Adam in the Garden, and even after the Fall, He visited mankind, made covenants,[31] adopted families, and ultimately redeemed a people for Himself. He even localized His presence in the Tabernacle, Temple, and in the person of Jesus Christ, while at the same time still remained omnipresent. God, as He has described Himself in special revelation, clearly is different than anything in creation. He is distinct from it.

The creator and creature distinction is of the utmost importance, and it is the failure to recognize and submit to this truth that results in all forms of unbelief. Naturalists refuse to have an ultimate that is transcendent of the universe, and so they posit that the universe is the ultimate, thus making no distinction between the creator and the creation. Instead, the creation is its own creator. Hinduism ultimately does the same thing, but it gives a spiritual name and dimension to the impersonal ultimate; however, in the end, the creator and the creation are one and the same thing (Atman-Brahma). Both of these worldviews miss the transcendence of God. If God is wholly different from creation, and we ourselves are part of the creation, then we can never become God and lose our creature-hood, and God could never become us in a way that causes Him to lose His deity.[32]

Due the creator-creature distinction, God being the ultimate sovereign personality has the authority to declare what is true and what is false. All non-believing worldviews deny this. As a sample, atheists outright deny it, pantheists believe the world is God, secular humanists see the human mind as the ultimate standard (as does Kantian philosophy and existentialism), natural scientists see the universe as its own creator, and Eastern religions and New Age thought demand that people look within to realize that they are God.

Liberal theologians also reject the creator-creature distinction by insisting that God is so transcendent that it is impossible to know anything about Him, and therefore, man is responsible to determine standards for himself. In the end, this is of

---

[31] A covenant is a very personalized form of a contract. The fact that God makes covenants shows that He is a person.

[32] In the incarnation of Jesus Christ, God did not cease to be God, but instead kept all of the attributes of God and also added the attributes of humanity to Himself.

no practical difference than atheism, or existentialism, since as a worldview it forces the liberal theologian to live as if there is no God at all. Of course, another class of liberal theologians rejects God's transcendence and overemphasizes His immanence equating God with the historical process. Hegelianism, secular theology, and liberation theology are all guilty of this viewpoint. When a person holds to transcendence to such an extreme that they say God is unknowable, they actually deny His immanence.[33] However, if a person holds to immanence to such a degree that God is equated with any aspect of the creation itself, then they deny His transcendence. The Bible unequivocally attributes both natures to God. Denial of either attribute to God is simply the fallen man suppressing the truth in an attempt to escape responsibility to God. If God is transcendent without being immanent, then we cannot know Him in order to be responsible to Him. If God is immanent without being transcendent, then He is on our level and does not have the right to speak with authority to us. By denying one or the other, the result is still the same: an independent, autonomous man who is not responsible to a Holy God. Thus, philosophically speaking, all non-Christian thought is a denial of the creator-creature distinction.

Christian philosophy (and specifically metaphysics) requires a two-level concept of reality, whereas non-believing thought holds to a one-level concept of reality. On a two-level concept, the creator is in a category all by Himself, fully absolute, independent, and personal. Then all of creation (matter, time, motion, physical laws, human logic, reason, people, angels, etc.) is in its own category, and it is non-absolute, totally dependent or contingent, and derivative. The creator then communicates to the creation through revelation. Van Til diagrammed this view of reality in such a way to where he drew a large circle at the top of the board and a small circle below it. The circle on the top represented God, and the circle beneath signified creation. Then lines were vertically drawn to represent communication between the two circles.[34] All non-Christian thought, in contrast, was then represented by one circle, where man was either raised to God's level or God was lowered to man's level. Since the Christian metaphysical philosophy stands in complete opposition to the unbelieving thoughts on metaphysics, we must make no philosophical compromise with them.

The next metaphysical truth that encompasses the Christian worldview is the doctrine of the sovereignty of God. It is a logical and required truth if the first two metaphysical beliefs about God are true. If God is an absolute personality who is

---

[33] Frame, *Apologetics to the Glory of God*, 42–43.
[34] Ibid., 43.

distinct and independent from creation, yet involved in the day-to-day happenings in creation, then God must at the same time be sovereign. It is perhaps easier to understand the sovereignty of God as the total lordship of God over all of creation. To possess a total lordship requires control, authority, and presence. In other words, God directs all things toward His purpose and goal.

Many Scriptures teach this truth. Since God created the universe according to His will and purpose, He has all authority in His universe, which makes miracles and so forth possible. Furthermore, it directly rules out the autonomy and independence of man. Since God's plans determine what things exist, man does not get to authoritatively define anything apart from God. This holds true for metaphysics, epistemology, and ethics. God gets to declare what is true about reality, about knowledge, and about right and wrong. To make judgments in any of these areas, we must consult God's special revelation to us; otherwise, when we contradict God's interpretation of the world, we are promoting false knowledge. By the way, since God is sovereign over all things, He is also sovereign over the decisions that arise out of our will. The Bible in all of its teaching is thoroughly Calvinistic.[35] God as the sovereign Lord over the universe has the sovereign right to bring to pass whatsoever He wills. Fallen humanity will typically reject this, and all unbiblical worldviews reflect the will of man to suppress this truth.

The final philosophical and metaphysical truth concerning God according to the Christian worldview is the Trinity. Often, people believe the Trinity is a theological doctrine only, but in actuality it is also a philosophical necessity if there is a God who is an absolute independent personality. It is on this point that both Judaism and Islam philosophically fall short.[36] It would first help to have a working philosophical definition of the Trinity. There is only one God, but there are three persons who are this one God: The Father, Son, and Holy Spirit. Somehow they are three and somehow they are one. It is not tri-theism (three gods) or Modalism (one God who takes three forms), but instead it is one God existing in three persons who are all equally and simultaneously God. All three have all of the divine attributes, are called

---

[35] As a counter to our Arminian brothers using straw-man arguments, let it be stated clearly right here that Calvinism (or the views of Jesus, Paul, John, Moses, David, etc.) is a position of compatibilism. In other words, the Bible teaches that God is sovereign in all aspects of our salvation, but it also teaches that man does in fact have a will and is therefore morally responsible to God. The Reformed view of soteriology, anthropology, and hamartiology is the only system that accurately and biblically demonstrates how this compatibilism works together.

[36] These two faiths are being viewed here as biblical in the sense that the Bible heavily influences their worldview. As such, they hold to the two-level concept of reality. Their problem is an incorrect view of God in His fullness, due to a lack of special revelation (Judaism) or falsely added revelation (Islam). Due to such errors, both religions are apostate.

Lord, and are distinct from creation. We do not know precisely how God is three and one, but the Christian Scriptures affirm it frequently.[37] At this point, it might be argued that the basis of believing in the Trinity is from biblical revelation alone. It is true that the Bible as God's revealed and authoritative, personal interpretation of Himself is where we primarily learn of it, but it is also a necessary belief since God is an absolute personality.

Before looking closer at the philosophical necessity of the Trinity, it is also important to recognize that it is completely unique to Christianity. Other religions might have triads (such as Vishnu, Shiva, and Brahma in Hinduism), but they are not trinities. They instead are three gods. In fact, when people argue for pagan parallels to the Trinity, a closer examination always yields the conclusion that they are far more different than similar, and in all cases, the pagan "parallels" constitute three separate gods or forces.

In fact, it is even through disagreement on the issue of the Trinity that Christian heretical groups such as Jehovah's Witnesses and Mormons spring up.[38] Thus, the Trinity above all other doctrines sets Christianity apart from the religions that are at least influenced by the Bible, but not in submission to it. It also sets Christianity apart from all other worldviews just as much as the other Christian metaphysical positions do.

In elaborating upon the philosophical necessity of the Trinity, I am very much in debt to John Frame's treatment of the subject. In discussing the Trinity, he first addresses the concept of unitarianism, or that God is only one person. The question at hand is, "One what?" Or if God is a unified being, we must ask, "A unity of what?" These two questions totally undermine the unitarian concept of God. A blank oneness makes absolutely no sense. Furthermore, how can God be a person if unitarianism is true? Personhood requires a personal relationship, but a unitarian God had no one to relate with until he created the universe. So how could He be an absolute personality that is independent? Instead, His personhood would be dependent on creation, which would render God as not independent. Instead, God, in order to also be personal, would have to be related to creation rather than be independent and sovereign over it.

---

[37] Deuteronomy 6:4 and Isaiah 44:6 = One God; John 20:17 = the Father is God; John 1:1-3,14 = the Son is God; Genesis 1:2 and Acts 5:3-4 = the Holy Spirit is God; Matthew 3:16-17 and Acts 7:55-56 = all three working simultaneously in one scene.

[38] Some Mormons will deceitfully claim to believe in the Trinity, but their conception of the Trinity is nothing like the biblical definition given above. Instead, they posit a "Trinity in purpose," but in reality hold to multiple gods. The biblical Trinity is a Trinity in "being" as well as "purpose" (i.e. ontological and teleological).

Understanding that this is a major problem, the ancient unitarians such as the Gnostics and Neo-Platonists decided that God must be a unity of those things that are separated in creation. In fact, they viewed all existence as a great chain of being with God ontologically on the top and everything else was thought of as downward emanations of the divine. So technically, this one God is the universe and the universe is God (which then becomes a form of pantheism). The creator-creature distinction becomes a matter of degree rather than of being.

Philosophically, all forms of unitarianism lead to this trap. The only way to escape it is to declare that God is an absolute impersonal being from which we all come. This leaves only pantheism, only now it is impersonal like the Hindu Atman-Brahma, whereas the Gnostics held to a personal pantheism. Jehovah Witnesses, like the Arians before them, also must come to terms with the implication of a non-triune God. If God is only a unity without also being a plurality at the same time, then no matter what philosophical hoops a person tries to jump through, they still are stuck with a divinity whose personality is dependent upon creation. This destroys the creator-creature distinction, which then destroys the sovereignty of God since He is dependent upon creation and ultimately allows man to boast since God depends on man to some degree.

As heavy as that may have seemed, the Trinity solves the philosophical problem. When answering the question, "One of what?" the answer immediately becomes one unity of the Father, Son, and Holy Spirit. Over and over again, the Bible emphasizes the oneness of God, but in many of those cases it also emphasizes His plurality. Many New Testament references place the Father, Son, and Holy Spirit together. In fact, Paul stresses the unity of the church by stressing the unity of God, yet he does so by mentioning all three members of the Trinity in 1 Corinthians 12:4-6 as the archetype for our unity in the church.

> Now there are varieties of gifts, but the same Spirit; and there are varieties of service, but the same Lord; and there are varieties of activities, but it is the same God who empowers them all in everyone.

In verse 4, the varieties of gifts come from the Spirit, in verse 5 the varieties of service come from Christ,[39] and in verse 6 the variety of activities come from God (the Father). Even in the Old Testament, God speaks in the plural,[40] uses a plural title

---

[39] The word Lord is the Greek title *Kurios*, which is most often applied to Christ in the New Testament epistles.

[40] Genesis 1:26-27–"Let us make man in OUR image." (emphasis mine)

connected to singular verbs,[41] and displays Himself as the Father, Son, and Holy Spirit on many occasions.[42]

The philosophical importance of these facts is that as a Trinity, God can be described as a personal being without being made relative to creation. When 1 John 4:8 declares that God is love, we need to ask, "Love of what?" If the answer is love of the world, then the divine attribute of love depends on the existence of the world, once again removing the independence of God and the creator-creature distinction. Furthermore, an attribute by definition is something that God must possess to in fact be God. If love could not exist until the creation existed, then God also could not have existed as God until He first created the creation! The position becomes logically self-defeating. Yet, if God is one, and yet three persons, then God can share love in an absolute sense being an absolute person and still be absolutely independent of creation. John 17:24 clearly teaches that the Father and Son loved each other in eternity past, thereby demonstrating from Scripture that God's attribute of love is independent of the creation. Thus, the Trinity actually is necessary in order to keep every single one of God's communicable attributes intact!

The Trinity also solves the one and many problem that philosophers of all sorts face. If God Himself exists in a One-and-Many form, then it is possible for His creation to do so as well. Philosophers have struggled with this one and many dilemma leading many to assume one of two extremes. Secular philosophers historically have either denied the existence of plurality in the world claiming all is one (monism) and plurality is just an illusion, or they have denied the existence of unity claiming that the world is disunited and unity is an illusion. On the latter (pluralism), all things in existence are completely independent of all other things in existence and have no relationship to anything else. The fact that matter and the laws of nature seem to work together in unity is either an accident of chance or completely an illusion. With the former (monism), everything is part of the same oneness, and

---

[41] E.g., Elohim is actually plural due to the plural suffix of "im," but the grammar is purposely violated in the Hebrew when a singular verb is attached to it. For example, in Genesis 1:1. it reads "*Bereshit bara Elohim et hashamayim ve'et ha'arets.*" Although Elohim is plural, "bara," which means "to create" appears in the singular form. So to transliterate this accurately would actually read, "In the beginning, Gods (he) created the heavens and the earth." This happens so frequently in the Old Testament that translators often translate Elohim into "God" in English, making it singular since that is the ultimate meaning in the contexts where the one God is clearly in view. Thus, this plurality in the very Hebrew word for God suggests a unity of a plurality.

[42] The Angel of Lord speaks as God and is worshiped as God throughout the Old Testament and appears in human form. Many conservative theologians agree that these are Christophanies or God the Son in pre-incarnate form. After the incarnation, the Angel of the Lord never appears in Scripture again. The Holy Spirit is mentioned numerous times in the Old Testament as filling men of God with gifts and power. The Father is most often in view when the word "God" is used.

even though we might feel we are different from other people and things, we are made of matter, which consists of atoms mixed together. So plurality is truly the illusion in this case.

Under the Christian, metaphysical worldview God is only one God and is a perfect unity, but is also a unity of a plurality (three persons). Since God is a unity of plurality, it is not difficult to see creation in a similar light. We are all made from the dust of the ground making us one with creation (unity), but we are different ontologically from plants, animals, rocks, and other humans (plurality). There is no absolute unity devoid of plurality, and there is no absolute plurality devoid of unity.[43] Only the Christian worldview accounts for this, and even though many secular philosophers and pagan religions reject a universe of both one and many, nearly all people live their day-to-day lives as though it were true.

Both the monists and the pluralists treat humans as though they have dignity and recognize each person's individuality, while at the same time hold each of us responsible to the whole. Individuality assumes plurality, whereas responsibility to others assumes unity. If we are all an absolute unity, why recognize any of us as individuals? Yet, any monist philosopher will be quick to condemn me if I plagiarized his work, which is his tacit admission that I am distinct from him, which favors pluralism. On the other hand, the pluralist assumes everything is radically independent of all other things, yet if I robbed his house he would demand I be held responsible, which assumes I have an obligation of respect to all other people. This denies radical independence and tacitly admits interdependence, which favors unity. Thus, these groundless secular positions prove themselves untenable due to their inconsistency.

Thus, summing up the Trinity, the Christian worldview is the only one that accounts for the one and many problem of creation. Also, it is the only philosophical possibility if God is to be an absolute independent personality, from which all other things are derivative. In fact, the other distinctive points of Christian metaphysics are impossible if God is not a unity of plurality. God's triune nature is necessary for God's absolute personality, the creator-creature distinction, and the sovereignty of God. Denying the Trinity denies God's absolute personality since this attribute would depend on relation to creation. The same applies to God's attribute of love. If God depends on creation, then the absolute distinction disappears between the creator and creature, and if God is not independent over creation, how can He be sovereign over it? After all, He would depend fully upon it. Within unbelieving philosophy and religion, it is common to deny all of these distinctive Christian views

---

[43] Frame, *Apologetics to the Glory of God*, 49.

anyway, but they are still left with their extremes of monism and pluralism. For Jews and Muslims, the philosophical necessity of the Trinity should force them to come to terms with the inadequacy and self-defeating nature of their unitarian conceptions of the one God.

Thus, Christian metaphysics clearly stands over and against all unbelieving counterparts. Christianity clearly teaches that God is an independent absolute personality that is completely distinct from the creation and is totally sovereign over it since He is above it, and He exists in the form of the Trinity. These four points make Christian metaphysics stand alone in perfect uniqueness. All other systems of thought deny and battle against the Christian metaphysical position to such a point that it truly demonstrates the unity of fallen man in suppressing the truth. The study of metaphysics makes this truth stand out in an undeniable way.

Metaphysics is perhaps the broadest of the fields of philosophy since it incorporates the study of so many subjects. Yet, there are two remaining fields of philosophy that need our attention: epistemology and ethics.

Epistemology is a very valuable field of study because it often gets to the bottom of our basic intellectual commitments. Ultimately we are forced to ask how we know what we know. If a person declares that knowledge only comes through reasoning, then we have the right to ask him how he knows this. Ultimately, human beings by themselves really cannot know anything with certainty due to their own finitude. As much as they might try to claim that they can, the fact is there is always more to learn as new facts continue to come to light from both the quantum level and the macro level. Reason itself cannot in any shape or form prove that knowledge only comes through reasoning. On the other hand, some people recognize our epistemological limitations and claim that it is impossible to have true knowledge since we cannot know anything exhaustively. Yet, apparently such people know for sure that we cannot know anything for sure, which is a self-defeating contradiction.

Christian epistemology solves the aforementioned dilemmas. Apparently, human beings do learn things and do have true knowledge that predicts outcomes. Yet, this occurs simultaneously with the fact that we cannot exhaustively know anything due to our finitude. Those who claim to know things with certainty cannot account for being able to have certain knowledge due to their finitude, and those who claim we can know nothing exhaustively cannot account for the fact that they know exhaustively that we cannot know anything exhaustively! In other words, as human beings, we are forced to be certain and uncertain at the same time, and although we can explain and observe this, we cannot account for it on our own knowledge alone.

How do we know things? How can we know things? The more a person thinks about it, the more it should frustrate him.

Christian epistemology philosophically accounts for this since the biblical God exhaustively knows everything due to His omniscience and therefore has authority over all knowledge. Knowing all things perfectly, He interprets things as they really are. So God can and does speak with certainty. Whatever He says, we can know for certain that it is certainly true. Because God is the source of all knowledge, this is why the fear of the Lord is the beginning of knowledge.[44] The Christian has a dependent certainty and dependent uncertainty simultaneously.[45] Our certainty is dependent on our knowledge that God knows everything, and thus what He reveals is certain. Yet, we also have a dependent uncertainty by recognizing our finitude and understanding that God has not chosen to reveal all things to us.[46]

The harmony of these two truths accounts for why we as humans have the ability to know things with certainty even though we do not possess exhaustive knowledge. Those who reject the authority of God over knowledge can never claim to know anything with certainty, whether they rely on reason or sense experience because new discoveries always dethrone old theories. Furthermore, they cannot account for what they do know unless the biblical worldview is true.[47] The only way they can reject God's authority over knowledge is to assume their own authority over it, but their finitude makes their claim groundless. Their reasoning, therefore, amounts to nothing more than blind men grasping for something to hold onto while they are falling infinitely downward since there is no ground for them to stand on. More will be said on this point in chapter four as it is dedicated specifically to epistemology.

The final area of Christian philosophy that we will discuss is ethics. Like its metaphysical and epistemological claims, Christianity also possesses a distinct system of ethics. In the same way that our personality and knowledge is grounded in God, so too are our ethics. In other words, we are not independently persons, but instead our personhood is dependent on God as the absolute ground of personality. Our knowledge also is not independent, nor ultimate, but instead it is grounded in God's independent and infinite knowledge. Just as we are dependent on God with these two aspects of our common experience, we also are dependent regarding our ethics. We do not independently know good from evil or right from wrong. God

---

[44] Proverbs 1:7

[45] Jr. Richard L. Pratt, *Every Thought Captive: A Study Manual for the Defense of Christian Truth* (P & R Press, 1979), 57.

[46] Deuteronomy 29:29.

[47] This will be fleshed out in chapters four and five and demonstrated in all chapters that follow.

being the independent and absolute personality that is distinct from creation also is the supreme standard of right and wrong and good and evil. It is not that God arbitrarily deems some things good and others evil, but instead all good things are defined as such according to God's perfect nature. Unbelievers often advance the fallacy that if good and evil are not independent of God, but are dependent on His decree, then God could arbitrarily call rape good, and it would be so. They fail to realize that God's decree of good and evil is not arbitrary at all but dependent fully on His nature. Lying is evil because by God's perfect nature, He cannot lie.[48] It is contrary to His moral nature and is therefore morally evil. Since God is the ground of all created existence, He also is the ground of goodness.

As part of their suppression of the truth, unbelievers also deny God's right to declare good and evil in an authoritative manner. Romans 1:32 says that fallen man knows God's ethical decrees, but he ignores them and encourages others to do so as well. In order to escape accountability to God, unbelievers claim that humans independently determine good or evil, which requires them to appeal to a number of theories to justify this.

Fallen man attempts to define good and evil in terms of pragmatism, idealistic duty, or relativism.[49] Whatever view unbelievers take, they deny that good and evil are dependent upon God's interpretation. Under pragmatism, man autonomously determines what is good by its usefulness. With duty-based ethics, man sees good and evil as perfect ideals that exist independently of man and God thus binding both. As such, man independently discovers these truths and has no need to trust God's revelation. Furthermore, since God Himself is dependent on this independent sense of duty, He is not the ultimate judge, but is Himself judged by this standard. It may be from this standpoint that fallen man tries to judge God's actions in the Bible as questionable. Relativism is the most pervasive form of ethics in the West today. Each person gets to choose for himself what is right and wrong, and there is no standard that binds anyone. Whatever the case, these types of systems of ethics are what emerge when man assumes autonomy over ethics.

Thus, as in all other fields of philosophy, the main difference between believing and unbelieving ethical thought comes down to dependence versus independence. The Christian knows that God created man in His image, and that man was originally created good. Even though the Fall damaged the divine image within us, in our heart of hearts (conscience) we know certain things are good and certain things are evil.

---

[48] Hebrews 6:18.

[49] Although there are many variations of these three categories, unbelieving ethical views typically fit neatly into these three.

Our will, however, seeks rebellion against God and rejects His authority to declare right and wrong. With our damaged image, we need more than ever to heed His interpretation of ethical standards; however, as a race we prefer autonomy in order to deny the reality of the judgment to come.

Even before the Fall, Adam and Eve's moral will was never meant to function by itself; rather, it was designed to operate dependently on what God revealed. God gave them positive decrees as well as one clear prohibition. Thus, even perfect humanity needed dependence on God in order to uphold His ethical standards. Yet, as we noticed in the last chapter, it was their very refusal to depend on God concerning the issue of ethics that led to the Fall in the first place. Since then, God has revealed, through special revelation (the Bible), His perfect, moral standards that all men will be judged in accordance with. Apparently, the conscience (like all other aspects of general revelation) is only enough to reveal to us our wickedness and the coming doom. Through special revelation, God is specifically telling mankind in human words what we ought to do. It is absolute, authoritative, and binding on all humans. It requires a day of judgment in order for God to be just. For this reason, fallen man rejects God's sovereign right in ethics and deceives himself with groundless theories of ethics.

Conclusion

Christianity is a worldview and philosophy that stands over and against all of the competing philosophies of the world. It offers a comprehensive view of metaphysics, epistemology, and ethics that is internally consistent (without contradiction), logically flawless, and perfectly accountable for everything that we see in the real world. Unbelieving philosophy, regardless of its many varieties, cannot account for what we see and know from the real world.

In the next chapter, the various philosophies and worldviews of unbelievers will be discussed and evaluated. At that point, both the Christian and unbelieving worldviews will be out on the table for you to clearly see. Once the Christian sees both types of worldviews clearly out on the table, he should begin to see why arguing from a presuppositional standpoint makes so much sense. Unbelieving presuppositions are internally inconsistent and logically flawed. Unbelieving worldviews are unable to account for reality, and thus they make a perfect target of apologetic attack.

Chapter Three

Philosophy of Apologetics (Unbelieving)

Introduction

In the last chapter, we studied the need for presuppositional argumentation, followed by a probing look into the distinctive traits of Christian philosophy: mainly Christian metaphysics, epistemology, and ethics. The Christian philosophy, which exists through dependent agreement with Christian theology, is the worldview and presupposition by which we interpret all things. It is logically consistent, makes perfect sense out of the real world, and is the necessary precondition of all knowledge.

Contrary to Christian philosophy stands the philosophy of the world. Unbelievers have a variety of viewpoints and beliefs that ultimately deny the key points of Christian metaphysics. Epistemologically speaking, all forms of unbelief assume (either intentionally or unintentionally) the autonomy and independent authority of man over knowledge, which then leads to a multitude of differing metaphysical schemes. Christians should expect this since we know that man is finite and cannot possess exhaustive knowledge of anything. Therefore, man in his ignorance will arrive at hundreds and thousands of different conclusions concerning the nature of reality (metaphysics) as long as man assumes his own authority over knowledge (epistemology). Incomplete knowledge by necessity would lead to such a diversity of opinion.

Ultimately, this demonstrates the fundamental difference between the fallen and regenerated man. The Christian places metaphysics above epistemology, whereas the unbeliever places epistemology over metaphysics. In other words, Christians derive their theory of knowledge from their view about reality, and unbelievers derive their theories of reality based on their view of knowledge. In the chapter on theology, it was noted that Eve's primary mistake was placing epistemology before ontology.

She should have contemplated first, "What she knew," and not have asked, "How does one know?" Had she first asked what she knew about reality, she would have realized that God is sovereign, and her knowledge must be dependent upon His exhaustive knowledge. Such thinking should have caused her not to eat the forbidden fruit. Instead, she wondered how she could know whom to believe between the serpent and God, independently deciding for herself what to think, resulting in the most severe of errors.

Since unbelievers assume their own authority over knowledge, it is from there that they determine the nature of reality. Their determinations always run against the biblical view of reality. Once again, the primary difference in philosophy between believer and unbeliever is dependence versus independence. Dependence on God leads to consistent and true knowledge and a consistent view of reality that makes learning and discovery possible. Independence from God leads to millions of inconsistencies on various views of reality, and it renders the idea of true knowledge and standards as impossible.

In this chapter, we are going to specifically look at unbelieving philosophy and will only really cover the subject of metaphysics. We already know the unbelievers' stance on epistemology, which determines their varied views of both metaphysics and ethics. Such is obvious. Our task as apologists is to bring them to the root of their thinking, namely, the presuppositions that they take for granted. In order to do this, we must understand the various options of metaphysics that the fallen mind has created. When we understand their views of reality, we will be able to break them apart due to their inconsistencies and ultimately bring them back to the issue of epistemology, which will be covered in more detail in the next chapter. Once this is accomplished, we can move on to the chapters that focus on application of apologetics.

Categorizing Worldly Philosophy

It is important that the Christian understand the different types of worldviews as well as the different schools of worldly philosophy. It is from this standpoint that we are able to defend our worldview against theirs, thus demonstrating to them the impossibility of their position. When the various philosophical positions of unbelievers are examined, it becomes rather easy to classify all opposing worldviews into one of four categories. I am grateful to Greg Bahnsen for his audio lessons on unbelieving philosophy where he neatly provided the four categories that follow.[1]

---

[1] Greg Bahnsen, "Types of Worldviews," *Defending the Christian Worldview Against All Opposition, Series One* (Powder Springs, Georgia: American Vision, 2006), compact disc audio

The four categories are spiritual monism, dualism, materialistic atomism, and pragmatism. Within each of these categories are subdivisions. By understanding the four categories and the most noteworthy subdivisions within them, the Christian will be able to immediately classify all types of opposition he might encounter in apologetic endeavors, and thereby know exactly where to start when challenging any given unbeliever's presuppositions.

The first of the categories to cover is that of spiritual monism. This worldview asserts that reality is made up of only one kind of thing. In other words, all is one. Furthermore, the one kind of thing of which everything is must be spiritual in character, rather than physical. Under these types of philosophies, the physical world is believed to be something of an illusion. It is in this illusory world that we see distinctions between each other, humans and animals, tables and trees, and so on. Despite the way the world seems, nothing is truly distinct in true reality, but instead, all is one, and all is spiritual. Another way this could be stated is that all is mental or of the nature of idea rather than that of hard reality.

Perhaps the best-known example of spiritual monism is Hinduism. Hinduism teaches that contrary to appearances, everything is one, and that one entity is a spiritual force or existence known as Atman-Brahma. There is no true distinction between you and this book, or the grass and the trees. Instead, all is one, and all is god. Hinduism, therefore, is a pantheistic worldview, meaning that it views god as the universe and the universe as god. Within this framework, god is not material but spiritual. If all is god, but god is spiritual, then all must be spiritual. If that is the case, then the physical world must be one giant illusion. Even the millions of Hindu deities are considered to be illusions.

In this illusory world, we are on the wheel of life (samsarra) and must perform our prescribed duty (dharma) in order to obtain good karma. If we fail to achieve our duty, then we obtain bad karma. If at the end of life we have more bad karma than good, then we are reincarnated into a lower form of humanity or even a lower form of life in general. If we have more good karma, then we are reincarnated to a higher station. Eventually, we can move up through various reincarnations to the final point in which the illusion for us will end, and we will enter into Nirvana like drops of water falling into the shoreless ocean of being. In such a case, the individual who achieved this will no longer be distinct even in illusion and will no longer be reincarnated, but instead, will be in a state of Nirvana, which literally means

---

lectures. I am in debt to Dr. Bahnsen for his organization of unbelieving philosophy into these categories. With my background in the social sciences, I am well informed on each of the mentioned varieties of unbelief, but Dr. Bahnsen's categorization of it is powerfully useful.

extinction (or extinguished). In this case, extinction is the opposite of distinction. So rather than being distinct within the illusory world, you are one with god and no longer exist with any distinction. Bear in mind, if this worldview is true, you already are one with god. The only difference is that in Nirvana, you lose your illusory distinction from it.[2] Hinduism is merely the leading example of spiritual monism, but the Christian apologist needs to understand that anyone who claims all is one is a monist. We can deal with each form of this similarly.

The next major category of worldly philosophy is that of dualism. In dualism there are two types of reality: mind and matter or spirit and body. Some things are material in nature, and some realities are spiritual or mental. In other words, there is the world of ideals and the world of matter. Among the classical dualists, there are two subdivisions: Idealism and Stoicism.

Idealism is the notion that there is a physical world, but it is organized by ideas or types that lie outside of the physical world. Plato is perhaps the best known and the most articulate dualist to ever write on the subject. He believed that in the world of ideas, there exist perfect representations of everything we see in the physical world. All humans are altered reflections of the idea of humanity that exists in the world of ideas. Idealists understand that ideas themselves are not physical.

For example, we all know what a dog is. We have seen dogs, we have pet them, and many of us care for them. However, the idealist believes the idea of a dog exists outside of the physical world itself. If every single dog was killed, and they became an extinct species, we would still know what a dog is and have a concept or idea of a dog in our minds. You can kill dogs, but you cannot kill the idea of "dogness."[3] Just as there are no dinosaurs today, we all have the idea of dinosaurs in our minds. Likewise, we are all human beings, but we ourselves are not the idea of human beings but are the human beings themselves. Furthermore, since we have imperfections, none of us are the model or type from which humanness is derived. Another example is we all know what a perfect triangle is and have the idea in our heads, but no perfect triangle exists in the real world, and it is impossible for us to construct one. Because we cannot find the perfect triangle in the real world or a perfect human, but the concept exists intuitively inside of our minds, there must be an ideal triangle and an ideal human outside of this world.[4]

---

[2] I refer to Brahman as "it" because the Hindu understanding of this single entity is that of an impersonal, spiritual force. It would be inappropriate to ascribe personal pronouns to an impersonal entity.

[3] Greg Bahnsen, "Types of Worldviews," *Defending the Christian Worldview Against All Opposition, Series One.*

[4] Ibid.

Since all physical things by their nature are imperfect, changing, and decaying, the ideal of these physical things must be non-physical. Hence there is a mental-idea-spiritual world above the physical world by which the physical world is organized. How do we know about these ideas? We intuit them, or we come into the world with them a priori. Since these ideas are ultimately mental or spiritual, we as humans must be both spiritual and physical since we are able to perceive such spiritual ideas in a way that is distinct from the material world. I can hold the idea of a dog without actually being with a physical dog, and therefore, I am performing a spiritual or mental operation. Ultimately then, the physical things of this world are the physical representations of the spiritual or mental ideas.

The other major subdivision of dualism is stoicism, and it too holds to a physical and mental/spiritual reality. Yet, it is distinct from idealism. Stoics were moralists who argued that you cannot help the circumstances of this life, and therefore, you should go with the flow. They believed that there was a law or reason that flowed throughout the physical world, and this law or reason was the spiritual or mental reality in their brand of dualism. It is best to simply ride the wave of this flow to the shore that it is taking you to, rather than fighting it. Stoics believed that the only way a person could be happy, is if they gave up their desires that were contrary to the flow of life.

A good example of this is if you are on your way to a movie that you have wanted to see very much, but you get stuck in traffic, then you should give up the desire to get to the movie on time. If the desire changes, the frustration goes away. Thanks to this way of thinking, Stoics were good soldiers for Rome since they were obedient and submissive and were not concerned about their rights. Obviously the Stoic was more practical and less philosophical than the idealist. The key difference that distinguishes the two is that the idealist sees the idea-based reality as outside of this world; whereas, the Stoic sees it as a law flowing through the world. Both believe in dualistic reality, but Stoicism is more concerned about using such dualistic belief to navigate through life by submitting to the spiritual law at work in the world.

Although many forms of thought are dualistic today (i.e., world religions), it is unlikely that as Christians, any of us will be forced to debate with a Stoic or a full-blown Platonic idealist. Some people mix and match various ideas of dualism, and so it is important to understand the general premise that there is a spiritual and physical world. It is from this standpoint that we can demonstrate the presuppositional weakness of their systems. Such will be discussed in chapter nine.

The third category of philosophy is materialistic atomism. This particular worldview has two broad subdivisions that are then broken down into even more subdivisions. The basic premise of materialistic atomism is there are an innumerable number of bits of reality, but they are made of matter alone. Thus, reality is only made of things that are physical, and the physical is broken up into smaller bits of matter. Although this view is as ancient as the previous views, it clearly is the most prevalent position of scientists and universities today. In this worldview, there is no mind only brain tissue, consisting of bits of matter performing explainable physical actions.

Materialistic atomism often falls prey to questions like, "What is love?" Some would say it is a way to describe a material process of the brain; however, many scientists do not take this route. The special way they treat their spouse,[5] or the way people throw themselves on grenades to save others is hard to explain for the materialistic atomist. Most materialists will either say there is no such thing as love, or they will back off their materialism and give some sort of answer that falls under dualism. This example demonstrates the inherit weakness in this view, since all materialists live in a way totally contrary to their stated belief.

As stated two paragraphs ago, there are major and minor subdivisions of materialistic atomism. The first main subdivision is that of determinism, and within this subdivision, there are two more subdivisions. Determinism is the idea that everything and every event that takes place are theoretically predictable if you knew all of the antecedent causes. If you could take into account all causes and put them in a super computer that can process far beyond anything we have now, then theoretically you could predict all outcomes. This would hold true for human behavior as well. There is no randomness in the universe, but instead, everything is based on antecedent causes. Within the camp of determinism, there are two types of subdivisions: Behaviorism and Marxism.

Behaviorism is a psychological school of thought that says you act as you were conditioned to act. All human behavior, therefore, is the predictable behavior of antecedent conditioning. A person might think they have a free will and make choices, but this is nothing more than a series of antecedent causes leading him to do something. You never had a choice, and the outcome was 100% determined by antecedent causes. Thus, if it was possible to pinpoint all such causes, then in theory, it should be possible to show a person that he did not truly act freely.

Marxism focuses on historical and economic forces rather than psychological ones. It is the idea that historic and economic forces determine the outcome of a society. All motivations are economic according to Karl Marx, and the dialectical process in history makes the ultimate historically determined future predictable.

---

[5] Ibid.

Thus, Marxism is more aggregate in focus emphasizing the whole group, whereas Behaviorism focuses on the individual.

The second, main division of materialistic atomism is Hedonism. Hedonism is a form of materialism that believes in free will, whereas determinism obviously does not. Under Hedonism, there are three smaller subdivisions: egoism, utilitarianism, and existentialism. Hedonistic worldviews, in general, argue that we live for one thing or another, and each of the three schools argue specifically for what they think we should live for.

Egoists say we should exercise our free will for our own benefit. Thus, whatever gets you ahead in life is the course of action you should take. In other words, humans utilize their free will to advance their own cause. Keep in mind that this does not prohibit the egoist from helping other people out. However, the only reason the egoist believes one person will help another is because it advances his own cause since one day he might need help himself. A political example of egoism is Libertarianism.

Contrary to egoism is utilitarianism. According to this viewpoint, a person should do what is in the interest of the greatest number of people. The best example we see in our culture of this today is socialism. Socialists argue that the state should own the factors of production (land, labor, and capital) and govern most (if not all) aspects of life in order that it may take everyone's interests into account. It must be noted, however, that not all utilitarian thinkers are socialists. Some believe in a welfare state instead. Since views like socialism are utilitarian, which is based on the presuppositions of materialistic atomism, it is not compatible with Christianity. Christians with socialist viewpoints are not consistent with their Christian presuppositions.

Separate from egoism and utilitarianism is the third hedonistic view, which is existentialism. Existentialism stresses the freedom of man so much, that its tenants believe that nothing governs what a person will be. Properly stated, all persons come into the world as an *existent*, but as they develop, they decide what they will become by free will alone. Nothing determines a person's essence from outside, according to this view. An existentialist would claim that God does not determine what you will be; furthermore, neither does the state, your parents, your social status, your biology, or anything else for that matter. You choose entirely what you will become. Thus, first you come into existence apart from your will, but once your existence begins, it is completely up to you as to what your essence will be. A popular recent example of this is the *Matrix* movies.[6]

It would be beneficial to take a moment to point something out about everything stated thus far concerning worldly philosophy. All three broad categories are distinct based on the way they answer the question of, "What is reality?" Is it one, but spiritual; two, but both spiritual and material; or is it one again, but comprised of many little bits of the one kind of thing (matter)? Thus, these various categories are ultimately different views of metaphysics. Setting up the three categories as they have been set up here allows us to understand that any type of view that we come across will fit somewhere into one of the three. There are no other general views of reality. Reality is either one or many. It is either spiritual or material, or both. However, there is a fourth view that we have to cover. The fourth view does not have a new answer to the question of the nature of reality, but instead the epistemology of it makes it unique. Thus, this fourth view gets its own category.[7]

The fourth general category is that of pragmatism. Pragmatists watch all of these other schools of thought argue back and forth about the nature of reality, and they in turn then ask, "Who cares?" They do not try to answer the question of reality because they believe these old arguments are worthless. Ultimately, so says the pragmatist, all that matters is whether or not a person is successful, and these old philosophical debates solve nothing. Instead of arguing about theoretical issues, people should instead seek to simply solve things. It does not matter what the nature of reality is as long as we are adapting to our environment and advancing the species by making evolution move forward.[8] Thus, truth does not correspond to reality or the world, but instead, truth is synonymous with success. Something is right, moral, or true if it leads to success.

Bahnsen liked to demonstrate the difference between the older schools of philosophy and pragmatism with an illustration of an elephant in a barge a little ways off the shore. The question is how do you get the elephant off the barge onto the

---

[6] In the first movie, the main character was told he was the chosen one to defeat the machines. In the second movie, the matrix architect told him that he is not really a chosen savior, but instead, is a reboot mechanism for the matrix computer program. This truth disillusions him at first, but then in the third movie he defies all previous expectations others have placed on him and creates a truce between humans and machines. His line of existential victory comes when he answers agent Smith's question of, "Why?" with, "Because I choose to." The philosophy of existentialism permeates the entire series.

[7] Greg Bahnsen, "Types of Worldviews," *Defending the Christian Worldview Against All Opposition, Series One.*

[8] This statement itself betrays that many pragmatists do in fact hold to a view of reality, whether they admit it or not.

shore. The continental European philosopher would begin by asking, "Ah yes, but is the elephant real?" He would then move on from there. The British philosopher, being more empirical in orientation would ask, "How much does the elephant weigh?" He would then move forward from there. The American philosopher would be the pragmatist and would only ask, "How much would you pay me to move the elephant?"[9] This example gets to the heart of pragmatism. He does not care whether the elephant is real or how much it weighs, but if he gets paid, he will find a way to make it work. He only cares about making things work.

A subdivision of pragmatism is skepticism. Skepticism does not go so far as to say truth equals success. Instead, skeptics will say no one knows anything for sure, and so there is no attainable truth. They are still pragmatists in the sense that they really do not care too much about the philosophical debates. Instead, they deny that anybody possesses the truth. They doubt all arguments due to the limited nature of man's attainable knowledge. Often they become cynical. Since nobody knows anything for sure, nobody knows what objective values exist or what the true nature of reality is. If this is the case, the cynical skeptic declares that our only concern should be to get by in this world. Yet, rather than succeeding for the advancement of the species as regular pragmatists would promote, the skeptic succeeds only for a selfish and self-serving reason.

In ancient Greece, these people were called the Sophists, and they often served as debate coaches. They were skeptics who said there was no absolute truth and no way to know if such truth existed. Therefore, they offered to teach people how to get what they wanted in life by learning how to debate in the local assemblies. They were trained to debate any given position on any given day, and they had no moral problem with this since they did not believe in any position in the first place. Some have likened them to modern lawyers who argue a case simply based on who pay them. In a particular lawsuit, a lawyer argues for one side, but if the other side had hired him first, then he would be sitting on the other side of the room arguing the exact opposite position—thus, the skeptics were/are the opportunistic pragmatists. As a disclaimer, let me say not all lawyers, however, are that amoral.

This concludes a quick survey of the categories of worldly philosophy. However, a few comments are in order concerning this subject. What has been covered is enough to get the Christian by in knowing where any given opponent is coming from regarding his presuppositions. Although an entry-level philosophy course in college would cover all of this information, the subject can and does go a great deal deeper in

---

[9] Greg Bahnsen, "Types of Worldviews," *Defending the Christian Worldview Against All Opposition, Series One.*

succeeding philosophy classes. This entry-level information is enough for the Christian apologist simply because every point of view a Christian comes across will in one form or another fall into these categories and their subdivisions. Everyone is a philosopher because everyone has a theory of reality, knowledge, and ethics. However, not everyone does philosophy well. Many unbelievers will be very inconsistent and mix and match bits and pieces from the various categories, even if doing so renders them as inconsistent. Knowing the categories will help you classify the worldview you are about discredit, and it also helps to point out the inconsistencies of people when they mix the pieces of these together. Furthermore, this information is even useful when dealing with other religions. Other religions are not true since they are not based on God's special revelation, and so they too are manmade philosophies. They have the same pitfalls and fall into some of the same categories.[10]

The apologist would do well to have the following outline memorized so that when they come across these various philosophies, they will know how to classify them:

Spiritual Monism
  1. Hinduism

Dualism
  2. Idealism
  3. Stoicism

Materialistic Atomism
  1. Determinism
        a. Behaviorism
        b. Marxism
  2. Hedonism
        a. Egoism
        b. Utilitarianism
        c. Existentialism

Pragmatism
  1. Skepticism

---

[10] World religions will be dealt with in chapters ten and eleven.

One important truth is that all who do philosophy, if they are to do it well, must do the following: they must come to reliable presuppositions that undergird everything else in their study, and they must be able to unify knowledge into a worldview where every part of man's experience has an appropriate place and is interpreted. When we critique their view, we want to find what Bahnsen refers to as the two key intellectual sins of arbitrariness and inconsistency.[11] Arbitrariness is not allowed in philosophical discourse since it amounts to being irrational since it offers no logical reason for holding a position. Arbitrariness exists when there is no argument for a particular position. Fancy vocabulary does not amount to an argument, and thus the Christian must be keen to listen to the argument itself to spot out whether or not it is arbitrary. When the unbeliever declares something, we should ask, "How do you know that?" We keep following up with such questions until we drive him down to his assumed and unproven presuppositions. Often by doing so, we can demonstrate his position to be arbitrary once we show it to lack justifiable evidence. Equally prohibited is inconsistency. In philosophical discourse, no one is allowed to contradict himself. True contradictions (P and not-P) allow for a person to believe any irrational thing he wants, which then brings us right back to arbitrariness. By looking for arbitrariness and inconsistency, we can actually pick apart every worldview that was explained above.

Due to the fact that the current prevailing theory of the secular and university system is that of materialistic atomism, it would be beneficial to discuss a few more philosophical details of its viewpoint. By its very nature, materialistic atomism is atheistic since all that exists is matter. For this reason, materialistic atheists deny that metaphysics itself is even a valid field to study. Since the prefix "meta" means "above," metaphysics itself often studies supersensible reality.[12] In other words, the study of metaphysics is a claim to study issues that transcend physical nature or matter and are therefore not measurable by sense experience. For example, when idealists say the ultimate form of reality is in a non-tangible world of ideas, they are explaining and categorizing the things we see on earth from things that are unseen and non-sensuous. Thus, to support such metaphysical claims, one will utilize non-physical things such as logic, reason, and intuition. The materialistic atomist takes great offense to metaphysics due to the fact that he believes truth is only to be discovered from empirical experience perceived through the senses. Therefore, he

---

[11] Greg L. Bahnsen, *Always Ready: Directions for Defending the Faith*, ed. Robert R. Booth (Covenant Media Press, 1996), 141.

[12] Ibid., 181.

often reject metaphysics altogether as a legitimate field of study and deny that it can lead to the discovery of truth.

Materialist atomists' opposition to metaphysics is even worse when it comes to Christianity. Christian views about the existence and character of God, the origin and nature of the world, and the nature and destiny of man are an affront to them.[13] From the materialists' presuppositional standpoint on how truth is attained, the Christian view seems preposterous since its doctrine does not stem from direct sense experience but instead comes from divine revelation. Ultimately, the claims of Christianity concerning the existence of God cannot be placed under the authority of man to experiment upon. Since the heart of the issue is fallen man not wanting to accept God's authority, this is unacceptable to the materialistic atomist. The venom with which the secular atheists oppose metaphysical considerations suggests that their hostility is far more than academic. As previously stated, the Bible explains that the situation actually is an issue of the heart.

Contrary to their beliefs, nonbelievers cannot truly claim to have no metaphysical commitments. Greg Bahnsen correctly observed that, "The very denial of the possibility of knowledge transcending experience is in itself a metaphysical judgment."[14] It is a statement about the nature of reality that depends ultimately on knowledge that is beyond the senses. For example, when atheists say all truth comes only through observation, we must ask if they have observed that all truth comes only through observation. That is something that is not observable but instead is assumed as a presupposition by which atheists interpret all other things. Their assumption requires belief beyond their sense experience. Thus the unbeliever rests upon a metaphysical position to say that there can be no metaphysical position known to be true. This is that second intellectual sin of inconsistency. Much more can be said during the applicatory chapters, but it suffices for now to understand the general philosophical mindset of unbelievers. For the time being, the next step is to understand more specifically the nature of unbelieving thought, to which we now turn.

The Nature of Unbelieving Thought

Underneath the four broad categories of philosophy, and beneath all of the various subcategories, all unbelieving thought can actually be classified more ultimately into just two categories: atheism and idolatry. Doing so requires that the apologist rely heavily upon Christian theology, yet much philosophical analysis is necessary as

---

[13] Ibid., 182.
[14] Ibid., 183.

well. Of course, just because all unbelieving thought can be narrowed down to two large categories, it does not negate the fact that we should know and understand the broader categories.[15]

Theologically speaking, we must recall from Romans 1:21 that fallen man knows the truth of Yahweh's existence but suppresses it. Unknowingly, this suppressed knowledge guides him in daily life as he assumes there to be benefit in working for a living or assumes validity when criticizing corrupt politicians or hypocritical Christians.[16] Yet, his thinking is overwhelmingly representative of unbelieving presuppositions. He lives and thinks as though the absolute, personal, independent, sovereign, and triune God does not exist. There are only two ways that the unbeliever can think and live this way, and they are through atheism and idolatry. Let us first talk about atheism.

Atheism can be theoretical or practical, or both.[17] The theoretical atheist outright denies the existence of God, whereas the practical atheist just lives as though there is no God. Based on the definition of practical atheism, agnostics truly are atheists just in disguise. After all, if they truly did not know whether or not God existed, would they not show up to church every other week and try to live in obedience to Scripture half of the time in order to shore up their bets? Yet, just about every agnostic most of us have ever met never goes to church and live their lives as though no God exists. Their words do not comport with their actions but instead are a mere attempt to take some misconstrued highroad of humility. Like agnosticism, deism and forms of theism that claim God is unknowable tend to produce the same result, namely, people who live as though no God exists. Often these groups cling to God's transcendence at the expense of His immanence in an attempt to justify their belief that God is unknowable. They too are atheists-in-action when it comes down to the wire.

One large consequence of atheism is a loss of standards since the existence of an absolute personality that is independent and sovereign is necessary for authoritative

---

[15] Some may liken it to a Dispensational understanding of Scripture. Beneath the dispensations and God's dealings with Jews, Gentiles, and the Church, we see more clearly that ultimately there are only two types of people–those in Adam and those in Christ. The most important thing to know is the Adam and Christ division, yet it is still helpful nevertheless to study the dispensations found throughout Scripture to see how the two types of people react to the given revelation in their particular dispensations. Likewise, the broad categories of unbelieving philosophy show us "how" those trapped in unbelief utilize atheism and idolatry to justify their beliefs.

[16] John M. Frame, *Apologetics to the Glory of God: An Introduction* (P & R Publishing, 1994), 193.

[17] Ibid., 194.

standards to exist in the first place. As a result, atheists tend to be relativists, which actually is part of what entices many to become atheists to begin with. Remember, the key purpose of all unbelieving thought is to escape accountability and responsibility to God, thus avoiding the judgment to come. Atheists, like all unbelievers, do not want to be responsible to God, and thus they flee from Him like Adam did in the Garden after he sinned. Yet, there are atheists who deny relativism and claim to hold to objective reality, even though they have no basis for making such judgments. If a Christian presuppositionalist pushed epistemology with such atheists, he could easily reveal to the atheist the impossibility of objective truth in an atheistic worldview. Thus consistent atheism requires the extreme of relativism, which itself is self-defeating. After all, would not a declaration that there is no absolute truth be in of itself an absolute truth? Furthermore, the atheist who holds to relativism is never consistent with it. After all, he acts as though reason and logic are trustworthy (absolute) and would seek justice if robbed (a moral absolute). Thus, the unbeliever committed to atheism in either its theoretical or practical form is left in a state of absolute certainty (rationalism) and absolute uncertainty (irrationalism) simultaneously and cannot account for it.[18]

The other major mode of unbelief is idolatry. Idolatry is when a person gives his allegiance to something other than the biblical God. Often people assume idolatry requires the worship of statues or images, but it is far more than that. It is true that idolatry can take on the form of worship of primitive gods such as Zeus, Baal, Ra, Molech, etc., but it also could be the worship of an abstract idea such as Plato's world of ideas or the existentialist's devotion to the concept of free will. Even the belief in a monotheistic deity such as Islam's Allah is still idolatry even if no images are made of him. Many rationalists place their ultimate allegiance and loyalty in human reason, and New Age spiritualists place their loyalty in their pantheism. Both are examples of spiritual idolatry. Finally, any person who rejects the Word of God and places his own opinion as higher has made himself the idol, which ultimately is true of all unbelievers. The apostle Paul in Colossians 3:5 teaches clearly that idolatry is beyond the worship of mere images but instead involves all rebellion against God. Idolatry is when people serve the creature instead of the Creator, as Romans 1:24-25 so powerfully states.

---

[18] Jr. Richard L. Pratt, *Every Thought Captive: A Study Manual for the Defense of Christian Truth* (P & R Press, 1979), 47-48.

> Put to death therefore what is earthly in you: sexual immorality, impurity, passion, evil desire, and covetousness, which is idolatry.[19]

> Therefore God gave them up in the lusts of their hearts to impurity, to the dishonoring of their bodies among themselves, because they exchanged the truth about God for a lie and worshiped and served the creature rather than the Creator, who is blessed forever! Amen.[20]

Atheism and idolatry are the only alternatives to Christianity for unbelievers. The only way to reject Christianity is to deny the existence of gods altogether or to substitute the true God with something else. There is no third option. John Frame, however, observed that these two alternatives actually form a single alternative. The atheist must allow for some absolute, even if it is his own reasoning abilities, which is itself idolatry. Yet the idolater depends on autonomous thinking and the rejection of God's special revelation, which is the reverting back to atheistic assumptions. Like atheism, idolatry can be theoretical (Marxism, reason, evolution, pantheism etc.) or practical (money, pleasure, non-Christian religion, or self).[21] Furthermore, idolatry is similar to atheism in that its main goal is to escape responsibility to the true God by giving man the authority to define god for himself. Idolatry tends to be less relativistic than atheism and accounts for the dogmatic certainty that accompanies unbelief. Frame again captures this perfectly when he writes:

> Many other ideas today are often presented today as undoubted fact, even though they do not have any serious justification. For example: corporal punishment is wrong; abortion is right; the state has the competence and obligation to provide education and welfare; all races, genders, religions, and sexual preference groups are equal in every way, and the greatest sin is that of disparaging one of these groups (except for Anglo-Saxon Protestant males).[22]

What this all goes to show is that atheism needs idolatry since it is impossible to live consistently without some constant and absolute meaning in life. Yet idolatry needs atheism since it uses so-called autonomous independence to reject the true God in favor of something manmade so that man ultimately would have authority over the idol. Most unbelievers combine these two positions in a very inconsistent

---

[19] Colossians 3:5.
[20] Romans 1:24-25.
[21] Frame, *Apologetics to the Glory of God*, 196.
[22] Ibid., 197.

manner, and this is why ultimately these two alternatives truly are only one mixed alternative. For example, when political liberalists cries for relativism and an "anything goes" approach to life, they lean on atheism, but when they adamantly opposed traditional values and dogmatically hold to abortion rights, socialism, and special rights for minorities, they are clinging to idolatry.

They are attempting to be both rational and irrational at the exact same time, even though they do not realize that this is what they are doing. It is the same situation when educators forbid "politically incorrect" speech, while insisting that all viewpoints deserve equal respect. When the universities claim they are the bastion for free thinking and the open exchange of ideas, but then forbid intelligent design advocates from dialoguing with evolutionists, they too are holding to atheism and idolatry at the same time. Ultimately, the combination of atheism and idolatry is the unbeliever's way of suppressing the truth of God that is within them, and yet being able to navigate through the world with set standards. When the Christian apologist begins to critique unbelieving thought, unbelievers will move thoughtlessly back and forth between these two positions making it difficult to pin them down. For example, when you press their relativism to its conclusion, they will then appeal to reason (their idol) to support the items that they feel are absolutely true. When you then push them with reason into a self-defeating position, they will effortlessly move right back into their atheistic relativism. It will take patience and skill to reveal this to them, and ultimately it will take the work of the Holy Spirit.

How Fallen Man Gets Some Things Right

Now that the major categories of unbelief have been discussed, it is time to answer a question that is bound to come up. When we begin to actually defend the faith against these various unbelieving worldviews, we will rest highly on the transcendental argument for the existence of the biblical God, which states that if Christianity is not true, then it is impossible to know anything at all. In other words, without the Christian presuppositions being true, then nothing can be true, science is not possible, and knowledge itself would be unintelligible. It is not the purpose to elucidate this argument now (that will come later), but now is a good time to deal with what nearly every thinking unbeliever would say regarding this principle. They would be quick to say that they do have knowledge, and they do perform science, and that they discover predictable truths all of the time. Yet, they perform these functions while rejecting the Christian worldview. Truly, it can be shown that if any of the worldviews mentioned in this chapter were true, then none of these common functions performed by unbelievers would be even remotely possible. So the question asked is, "How do we account for the unbeliever having knowledge and performing science correctly?"

A simple answer can come by way of analogy. Before scientists knew about gravity, they still operated under the effects of gravity and predicted the speed of falling objects based on the acceleration due to gravity. Thus, believing that gravity exists, or even understanding the nature of gravity, is not necessary to discover scientific truths about how fast objects fall. Gravity is real whether someone admits it or not. It has the same power over the primitive in the middle of the jungle as it does over the modern scientist who knows a plethora about it. Both the primitive man and the modern man know not to jump off of a cliff onto sharp rocks below. Likewise, whether or not modern scientists admit that the biblical God exists, they are still in His world nevertheless; a world completely governed by His sovereign control over all of creation and nature in general. By God's common grace, and the image of God within them, they too have been designed to understand the uniformity of nature and to conduct experiments within it.

As a result, both believers and unbelievers assert that two plus two equals four. Classical apologists, evidentialists, and cumulative case apologists mistakenly interpret this fact to mean there is neutrality between the unbeliever and believer with regard to factual knowledge. Such a notion was refuted in previous chapters. So then how do we understand this? Even though unbelievers reject God's revelation of Himself, they do not and cannot reject it consistently since His image is embedded within them.[23] This image allows man to reason and perceive things in the world, and through God's common grace of keeping nature uniform, man's reasoning abilities can accurately predict outcomes, thereby leading to knowledge. If fallen man operated off of his presupposition of independence, then knowledge would be impossible. Uniformity of nature, regularity of physical law, and predictable outcomes are inconsistent in an accidental universe governed by chance. Furthermore, man's interpretation of the world could not be trusted if man were the final judge because man's finitude prohibits exhaustive knowledge of anything. Yet, we do know things, we can predict things, and we actually can to come to consensus on issues like 2 + 2 = 4. Therefore, in their acquisition of knowledge, they assume the very things that the Christian worldview presupposes: uniformity, regularity, purpose, dignity, reliability of the senses, etc.

Thus, the atheist knows things. The atheist does science. That is not the issue. Neither atheists nor any unbeliever can account for the fact that they know things and

---

[23] Jr. Richard L. Pratt, *Every Thought Captive: A Study Manual for the Defense of Christian Truth*, 32.

do science. Their presuppositions render knowledge and science as impossible. Thus, they as Van Til observed, are like a child slapping their father's face while sitting on his lap. The child's ability to slap the father is dependent on the father holding the child up on the lap. Likewise, the unbeliever's rejection of God in science is dependent on God's common grace allowing for intelligibility at all.

Furthermore, when Christians and unbelievers make statements that are in agreement, the agreement is only at the surface level. For example, when both the Christian and the unbeliever assert that the world is round, there is agreement on the surface but great disagreement underneath the surface. The two would disagree on what is meant by world. The Christian would say the world is the creation of the God of Scripture and the unbeliever would say the world is the result of a long process of evolution. The Christian and non-Christian could both say that man is a dignified being but underneath the surface they disagree on what is man. The Christian would argue that man is a being comprised of a body, mind, and spirit who exists in the image of God with dominion over the earth, but the atheist would say man is merely a highly evolved animal with a large brain capable of dignified behavior. Examples could be drawn for hours, but the point has been made. Even where unbelievers get things right, they are only right on the surface, but they are almost always wrong on the fundamental aspects that go far below the surface. So in one sense unbelievers do science and discover surface truths, but they ultimately never do it right because they miss the teleological (purpose oriented) and ontological (truth oriented) roots to their discoveries. They may understand what causes rain through the evaporation cycle, but they miss the point that rain reveals to us the mercy of God and how God expects us to treat our enemies with kindness (Matthew 5:45).[24]

Thus, through the uniformity of nature and the image of God in all men, unbelievers can take advantage of general revelation (the created order itself) to learn and discover true things about the world. But they cannot, without a radical change in their presuppositions and a dependence on God's special revelation, account for their knowledge or ever arrive at the meaning behind the things that they discover. All things are to give glory to God, but they will always miss that point. When the believer realizes the magnitude of the universe, the order in which the galaxies are clustered, and the specific details associated with our own solar system, he proclaims the greatness of God. When the unbeliever realizes the same things about the universe, he proclaims how unlikely our existence is in the world of chance and is thankful the dice rolled the way they did. Due to the nature of unbelieving thought,

---

[24] Ibid., 41.

the Christian must challenge the most fundamental presuppositions of the atheistic idolater.

Conclusion

In conclusion, the mess of unbelieving philosophy is the result of fallen epistemology. From the impossible position of man having authority over knowledge, unbelievers devise many different opinions concerning the nature of reality. Fortunately for the Christian, this variety of possible positions gets trapped easily in our net of categorization. For the sake of dialogue it is good to know the specifics of their philosophies. Yet, known to the Christian, however, is the truth that the unbeliever is trapped in atheistic idolatry. As we dialogue with a hedonistic socialist we can use his understanding of the world to begin to defeat his position, all the while realizing his dodging techniques result from his staggering between idolatry and atheism. This is something he would never admit, but we realize what is really going on in his mind due to our knowledge of the Bible, God's special revelation. We simply have to keep pushing until the Holy Spirit changes the heart, or our defense of the faith shuts their mouth. Either way, we will have done our task.

Chapter Four

Epistemology and the Transcendental Argument

Introduction

The shed is nearly built! The instructions were thoroughly read and understood, and the proper tools were acquired to begin and finish the construction. So, what comes next? Well, a shed is no good if it does not have a door allowing entry and exit. The door must be the right size in order to allow for tools, lawnmowers, and anything else that goes in a shed to be placed in there. Thus, the builder must now think carefully about the purpose and goal of the shed and what kinds of things he envisions as being stored there. This will lead him to choosing the right door for the shed, which will then lead to the shed being useful according to its purpose.

For the subject of apologetics, epistemology is the door. Epistemology, or the study of knowledge, is the bridge that connects all of the content discussed in previous chapters with the actual practice of engaging in apologetic dialogue with unbelievers. Understanding how the believer justifies knowledge over against the unbeliever's own theories of knowledge is the necessary ingredient to challenge them at the presuppositional or worldview level. Thus, only with the door of epistemology can we apply what has been discussed so far.

Amazingly, epistemological reasoning allows for the Christian to construct a particular type of argument that some have called irrefutable. This argument is known as the Transcendental Argument for the Existence of God, or TAG, and it properly demonstrates the futility of unbelieving thought. Therefore, the goal of this chapter is to show the door of Christian apologetics by elaborating upon epistemology and the transcendental argument. Once this is accomplished, we will be able to move into the chapters focused on application.

Christian Epistemology

Christian epistemology was previously discussed in chapter two. In that discussion, it was pointed out that due to God's sovereignty and exhaustive knowledge of everything that exists, He is the only one with certain epistemology. In our dependence upon His revelation to us, we as Christians can have a certainty of things, even if on our own authority such certainty would be impossible. Therefore, it is on God's authority that we will know things for certain. Yet, we also know that our finitude limits what we can know, and therefore we are uncertain as well. Thus, the Christian has a dependent certainty and a dependent uncertainty that is coherent and makes sense of the world. The unbeliever, in contrast, relies upon his own finite authority and as a result he ultimately can know nothing for sure, placing him in total uncertainty. Yet, if he claims then that nothing can be known for certain, it would require him to know for certain that nothing can be known for certain. Thus, his position also is one of certainty and uncertainty, but he cannot account for his ability to understand either of the two. Apparently as humans we do know things for certain, and we can predict outcomes, yet we also are uncertain due to our natural limitations. Unbelieving epistemology cannot make any sense out of this, but Christian epistemology makes perfect sense out of it.

With that basic review, we now can move into a more detailed look at epistemology. Ultimately, we know that the unbeliever cannot account for what he knows. Knowing this, we must always and repeatedly ask unbelievers, "How do you know?" This will push them to justify their arguments epistemologically rather than allowing them to take their presuppositions for granted. It will reveal to them that they too are biased and live much of their life by faith. It will show them that their arguments do not meet their own standards.

Some of these points have been made previously, but it is beneficial to hear them again. If an atheist claimed all truth is learned by sense experience, then we simply need to ask him if he personally observed with his personal senses that all truth is learned by sense experience. His finite nature makes his ability to meet that demand impossible, yet that is the very requirement necessary to confirm his statement. Thus, by asking him "how do you know all truth is learned by sense experience," we in effect show him that his statement is impossible. If we did not ask the epistemological question, then he would simply take his view for granted and try to force the Christian to reason from the same assumptions during apologetic dialogue.

Additionally, if an atheist claimed that it is foolish to believe things on faith, you can show him his own faith by a series of epistemological questions. For example, to believe in macroevolution would require that he believe in something that cannot be observed or tested in a lab, and that ultimately he is claiming certain things happened in a time and place in which no human witness existed, and therefore, he believes this on the authority of modern biology textbooks alone. That is the very type of faith the unbeliever criticizes, and yet we expose it in his own beliefs with epistemological questions.

Examples could continue, but for now it would be prudent to look a little closer at the nature of knowledge. The more we understand about the concept of "knowing," the clearer it becomes as to why unbelieving philosophy is epistemologically helpless. Their epistemological assumptions render them incapable of meeting the required standards necessary to claim they actually "know" something.

Since epistemology is the study of knowledge, or how we know what we know, it would help to have an understanding of what constitutes true knowledge. There are three necessary ingredients for true knowledge: knowing, belief, and truth. Concerning "knowing," there are three different ways that it is used in language. First, "knowing" can refer to knowing truths such as facts, claims, and propositions.[1] An example would be that I know nuclear bombs were dropped on Japan at the end of the World War II. Second, "knowing" can refer to a person having an ability to do something. "Jim knows how to build a fence," is an example of this. Finally, "knowing" can also refer to intimate knowledge of persons in such a way that we can say, "I have known her for many years." All three of these usages of "know" are found in the Bible as well as in our normal use of language apart from the Bible. For our purposes here we will focus on the first form, which speaks of knowing in the intellectual sense. It speaks of knowing propositions.

Often unnoticed, knowledge is a subcategory of belief since knowing something also means to believe it. Due to this, we also need to understand the nature of belief and its relation to knowing. Beliefs can be held with differing levels of confidence in them such as suspicions, opinions, and convictions.[2] Thus, a simple definition of belief is that it constitutes a positive attitude toward a proposition. When the atheist claims to know that there is no God and that macroevolution is true, he also "believes" what he is saying. The Christian can show that the atheist does not really know such a thing at all, but instead he merely has a positive attitude toward the proposition of non-belief. Therefore, knowing and believing propositions are not enough to establish true knowledge. If knowledge only concerned the act of knowing and believing propositions, then we would be stuck with relativism. However, to truly "know" something, there must be a third ingredient, that is, truth.

---

[1] Greg L. Bahnsen and Bahnsen, *Van Til's Apologetic* (P & R Publishing, 1998), 158.
[2] Ibid., 160.

If two people believe propositions that contradict one another, both of them cannot truly "know" what they are asserting.[3] If one person claims Abraham Lincoln was murdered in 1865 and a second person says that he was not, the second person does not have correct knowledge about Abraham Lincoln's death. Therefore, we can say quite clearly that even though the second person knew and believed a proposition, he did not possess knowledge because the proposition he was positive toward turned out to be untrue. You can only legitimately "know" a proposition if it is true. Truth, therefore, cannot refer to relative opinions, but instead it speaks of conformity to the facts of reality.[4] A person who claims that absolute truth does not exist cannot legitimately deny that an atomic bomb was dropped on Hiroshima on August 6, 1945. Even if he denied it as the truth, it does not change the fact that the proposition is true in that it conforms to the facts of reality.

It is at this point, however, where unbelieving philosophy hits a dead end. There are different theories of truth, which all sound good on the surface—correspondence, coherence, pragmatic,[5] and semantic theories—yet they are all circular in their reasoning. The correspondence theory tries to explain the nature of truth, the coherence and pragmatic theories try to explain the evidence for the presence of truth, and the semantic theory attempts to explain the logical structure of the sentences that describe any given truth.[6] As already stated, each view is circular, even though they do adequately express different aspects of the concept of truth. Each view presupposes the very thing it attempts to explain or prove. This will always be the pitfall of all human attempts at having an autonomous understanding of concepts.

The Christian, in contrast, understands that truth is whatever conforms to the mind of God. Facts are facts because they are predetermined by the mind of God, and therefore they are reliable thus justifying for the Christian the correspondence theory. Due to the faithfulness of God, His Word (which reflects His mind) is not contradictory, and God cannot contradict Himself. Consequently, propositions that correspond to God's mind will be coherent with each other thereby justifying the coherence theory. Finally, submitting to God's wisdom is the most pragmatic way to live in God's universe as the book of Proverbs clearly teaches, thus justifying the pragmatic theory of truth.

---

[3] This is the coherence theory of truth—truth is unable to contradict.

[4] This is the correspondence theory of truth—truth conforms to reality.

[5] The pragmatic theory of truth says that true statements are confirmed by practical results.

[6] Bahnsen and Bahnsen, *Van Til's Apologetic*, 162.

It is important that the Christian not overlook this point concerning knowledge and truth. Many unbelievers seem to understand that there is an objective reality called truth that corresponds to the real world, does not contradict, and is ultimately practical. Yet, their worldview cannot account for it and independent human reasoning could never justify it. Instead, to hold to the correspondence view, they have to presuppose that reality is knowable, uniform, and that an immaterial concept known as truth exists. They then must presuppose that they can compare material things against the immaterial concept of truth and in so doing have the ability to declare the material things to have the immaterial quality of truth. How can the finite human mind ever justify this?

With the coherence theory, the unbeliever presupposes the concept of truth in order to define it. In other words, the statement that "true statements cannot contradict" already presupposes that they know something about truth, namely, that it does not contradict! It is circular and once again autonomous human knowledge cannot justify it. How can any human know this on his own authority? The pragmatic theory presupposes that we know ahead of time what "good" results should be expected in order for something to be true. Once again, we have the problem of circularity. On one hand, those who hold this position say we know something is true because it is practical, but on the other hand they say something is practical because it is true! They may not readily admit to the second part of the previous statement, but it is necessary since the pragmatist already predefines what is practical or successful. Furthermore, untrue beliefs have had practical results throughout history. Ancient astronomers used the geocentric model to accurately predict the movement of the stars, thus showing the model to be practical, yet it still was not true. The semantic theory presupposes truth to already be known and then uses linguistic logic to determine what sentences are true. This too is circular. How can truth be determined by sentence structure unless truth is already known apart from sentence structure?

The Christian has no problem claiming truth corresponds to reality since reality conforms to the mind of God. The Christian can also hold that truth does not contradict because God's mind does not contradict. The Christian can declare what good, practical results should accompany truth based upon God's goodness. The Christian also can use sentences to determine whether or not statements are true because the truth of God is known. In other words, the Christian has what presuppositionalists refer to as a revelational epistemology.[7] Christian philosophy restates what God has authoritatively revealed about Himself, the world, and man.

---

[7] Ibid., 165–166.

Our knowledge begins as a matter of revelation. Christians understand that the fear of the Lord is the beginning of knowledge.[8] Our theory of truth then does not presuppose truth and its knowability in any way that is independent of God. We simply presuppose the God of the Bible, and this presupposition adequately accounts for and explains the way truth works but does so in a way that is not contradictory and self-defeating. The narrow circularity of unbelieving justifications for various theories of truth is self-defeating and demonstrates a great dilemma for finite creatures attempting to authoritatively determine truth. Their views will always be self-defeating.

Therefore, to sum up the subject of knowledge, there must be knowledge of propositions, belief in them, and then the truthfulness of them. On this framework, unbelievers cannot account for the possession of any true knowledge. They may know a proposition, and believe it, but they can never independently verify its truthfulness since all of their various tests are self-defeating and narrowly circular. People may object to this because unbelievers do seem to know true things about history, science, and so forth. This fact is actually the checkmate in favor of the Christian. Unbelieving autonomy and theories of knowledge (epistemology) cannot account for anything they know, nor can it justify the things they do know. Yet, they clearly do know things because truth does correspond to reality, is coherent, pragmatic, and semantically understood. The Christian God is the necessary precondition to make the existence of truth possible.

When the unbeliever gets things right, it is because he lives in God's world and borrows from the Christian worldview, even when he does not realize it. Greg Bahnsen writes, "This is the critical epistemological question in our apologetical challenge to unbelief. Is rationality (science, logic, intention, etc.) to be accounted for in terms of the mind of man or the mind of God?"[9] If the answer lies in the mind of man, then knowledge could never be justified. After all, many men assume reality to be random, and so how could randomness account for any theory of knowledge? Since when does chaotic chance cause things to be coherent? Is pragmatism even possible in a world governed by chance, since in theory, chance should frequently lead to a change of natural law? Truly, if random chance was the ultimate reality of existence, it would be impossible for us to know anything, let alone have theories about knowledge. Since things are known, this leaves us with the alternative—God.

God is the only being in a position to be self-attesting. By definition, the God of the Bible is eternal, independent of the creation (meaning He is a necessary being

---

[8] Proverbs 1:7
[9] Bahnsen and Bahnsen, *Van Til's Apologetic*, 175.

whereas all other existents are contingent beings), and He is omniscient, omnipotent, omnipresent, and sovereign. Such a being who created the entire created order (which is everything that is not Himself) is the only one in any position to declare authoritatively what is true and what is false. Since the entire universe is contingent upon Him and His sovereignty, then the universe is what it is because that is the way God made it and interpreted it to be. The fact that there is order, uniformity, regularity, logic, physical law, objective truth, and so forth is because this is all reflected in God's mind.

There is nothing in the universe, whether galaxies or mere men, that is self-attesting. All things in the universe are contingent upon factors outside of themselves that they have no control over. Any given galaxy relies on the movement and speed of other galaxies, which depends on the mass of such galaxies and their distances from each other, which then in turn determines the physical motions of the galaxy in question. So, it is impossible to declare of the galaxy, "It just is." Its existence and nature is dependent on so many other factors, and without those other factors, the galaxy as we know it would not exist. The same can be said of man. Anyone of us depends on an innumerable amount factors outside of our control just to exist and think. Therefore, humans cannot be self-attesting.

God, however, is the only being that is not contingent, but instead is independent of everything. He is the only being that is self-attesting. He is what He is, because He simply is! As such, He has total authority to speak of Himself and reveal Himself in a way that is beyond our ability to contest. He has done so in nature by making a universe where there is uniformity, regularity, logic, laws, morality, justice, and an abundance of what is needed for us to survive. He created us with minds to perceive all of this, minds that despite their finitude seem capable of learning truth. We did not give ourselves these minds, yet unbelievers often act as though they did by using their minds to reject God, who is the very precondition of the existence of their minds.[10]

In addition to nature, God gave us His written Word, which also reflects His mind and goodness. Looking at the Bible, it bears all of the signs expected if the self-attesting God who is beyond contestation decided to give a written revelation. It is a unity of plurality (one theme but diverse human authors), is truthful (corresponds to reality and does not contradict itself), is powerful (changed more lives than any other book), demonstrates knowledge far beyond that of humans (hundreds of detailed

---

[10] In chapter six, the notion of the mind being a separate entity from the brain will be discussed.

prophecies predict the future), and identifies itself as the Word of God (over 3,000 times).

The Bible as the Word of God then is self-attesting. We cannot put it on trial anymore than we can put God on trial. Our knowledge is finite and limited, but God is infinite and unlimited. Yet, fallen man assumes his own independence and autonomy in knowledge and thinking. Therefore, even though he is groundless, he will not accept the true God because he will not accept the idea of a self-attesting God that is beyond the trial and judgment of man. Without realizing it, the fallen man declares his own mind to be self-attesting since he deems it to be worthy to judge the claims of God. We already have seen that Eve did this very thing, which is folly. The finitude of the human mind makes this impossible. Intellectually it is unfeasible.

Even the skeptic, who grants that our finitude renders us unable to know anything, still somehow "knows" that the God of the Bible does not exist and that the Bible is false! Once again, fallen man is in an epistemological dilemma that ultimately makes his wisdom and philosophy to be foolishness. A survey of worldly philosophy from the time of Plato to now shows inconsistency, arbitrariness, disagreement, and the utter helplessness of man to independently declare what the world is really like. Yet, with that track record, unbelievers still choose to think independently of God's revelation and to act like He does not exist.

As Christians, we do not have this problem. We understand that the God of the Bible is the only explanation that philosophically can account for all that we see and experience. Therefore, we reason and think dependently on Him. We recognize that our thinking is not original nor is it independent but instead it is analogical. In our revelational epistemology, the ultimate reference point for all of our judgments is the original and comprehensive system in God's self-sufficient mind. Knowledge for all men (both believer and unbeliever) is analogous to God's knowledge, not autonomous from it. Revelation from God brings coherence and meaning to all human experience and knowledge, and He created the mind of man with its interpretive abilities thereby allowing for man's attainment of knowledge in meaningful, uniform, and regular contexts.[11]

When we use logic, deductive and inductive reasoning, categorization, etc., we are imaging God's thinking about the same things, however, only at the creaturely level. This is what is meant when it is said that the relationship between our thinking and God's is analogical. It explains why these tools are reliable and explains why

---

[11] Greg Bahnsen, *Presuppositional Apologetics Stated and Defended* (American Vision, 2010), 275.

what man knows is reliable and certain, in spite of our finitude. Without this analogical understanding of knowledge, fallen man cannot account for the fact that he knows anything, which is evidenced by the epistemological weakness of every theory of knowledge ever advanced by fallen philosophers.

Greg Bahnsen offers a nice synopsis identifying the key difference between believing and unbelieving epistemology:

> The Christian submits to the self-identifying, self-authorizing, final authority of God for all he does or thinks, but the non-Christian takes for granted that this kind of authority belongs to himself. Man presumes to interpret and explain himself by his own internal principles and to give the original interpretation to the brute facts in a random universe. Indeed, every aspect of reality is subject to the reference point, prescriptive values, and autonomy of man's interpretive efforts. The Christian, by contrast, takes God to be the ultimate interpreter and God's mind to be the appropriate reference point for reasoning. The unbeliever seeks abstract and general principles about truth, about reality, and even about whatever gods there may be, while the Christian follows principles that are concrete and personal, revealed by and revelatory of God Himself. The unbeliever assumes that man and the facts of his environment can be understood intelligibly whether or not there is a God who created the universe. Both the facts and the mind of man are assumed to be self-existent and independent of any God. Finally, the unbeliever takes man to be morally innocent, even if as yet ignorant. He certainly is not, as the Christian worldview maintains he is willfully blind, morally rebellious, and spiritually lost.[12]

Ultimately, the unbeliever arbitrarily decides what is possible and impossible in this universe consigning everything to random chance (or some other impersonal ultimate) on the authority of his own mind alone. The reason the unbeliever does not see the absurdity in this is because he totally takes his self-proclaimed epistemological authority for granted. In other words, he often does not realize he is doing it since he fails to question his underlying presuppositions. The truth is obvious as Van Til points out, "The finite mind cannot thus … be made the standard of what is possible and impossible. It is the divine mind that is determinative of the possible."[13] When comparing God's knowledge and man's, God's knowledge is the standard, ours is not. His knowledge is original; ours by default must be derivative

---

[12] Bahnsen and Bahnsen, *Van Til's Apologetic*, 280.

[13] Cornelius Van Til, *Defense of the Faith:* (P & R Publishing, 1980), 39.

and analogical. Thus, there are two levels of thought, absolute and derivative, and thus two levels of interpreters. God interprets everything absolutely, and man must be the re-interpreter of God's interpretation.[14] We cannot, as Christians, give into the fallen man's dishonest presupposition that he possesses authority over knowledge. If we tried to win the unbeliever to Christ by appealing to his "independence" in reasoning, then we are arguing with a fool according to his folly and we are lying to him by approving of his method of reasoning and interpretation. This is why understanding Christian epistemology is so important in the apologetic process.

One-By-One Myth

Of course, before using epistemology to move into the Transcendental Argument for the Existence of God, we must grasp the inherent folly of what Bahnsen called the "one-by-one myth."[15] This myth is entirely prevalent in unbelieving epistemology. What Bahnsen was referring to is the notion that we arrive at our beliefs one point at a time. In other words, evolutionists claims to believe in macroevolution due to a line-by-line evaluation of evidence and reasoning, and thus by one point at a time they arrive at their conclusion. The Christian would do well to understand that this is nonsense, and he would do even better if he could demonstrate this to the evolutionist.

In reality, our beliefs are always connected to a multitude of other beliefs through linguistic meaning, logical order, evidential dependence, causal order, indexical conception, and self-conception. Bahnsen illustrates the meaning of this with an example of seeing a ladybug on a rose.[16] By saying that I see a ladybug on the rose, I am not affirming one proposition (according to the one-by-one myth), but instead I am affirming numerous propositions. For example, my statement would assume the objective meaning of English words and their intelligibility to other people. The fact that I am claiming that "I" see anything assumes that I truly do exist, which is an assumption of ego and personhood. Additionally, the statement assumes that a perceptual event has occurred and that my perception is accurate. Furthermore, it assumes the categorization of bugs, thus allowing me to distinguish between various kinds, thus making the identification of the ladybug possible.

Those are some of the obvious beliefs connected to my statement, but there are also subtle ones worth considering. First, the statement assumes my own linguistic,

---

[14] Ibid., 47.

[15] Greg L. Bahnsen, *Always Ready: Directions for Defending the Faith*, ed. Robert R. Booth (Covenant Media Press, 1996), 216–217.

[16] Ibid.

entomological, and botanical competences. It also assumes the normalcy of my brain stem and my eyes. Second, the statement assumes the veracity and objectivity of theories of light refraction, shared grammar, shared semantics, the reality of the external world, the laws of logic, and an innumerable host of other things. Thus, rather than coming to beliefs in a one-by-one fashion, we actually possess a network of presupposed beliefs that work synergistically together serving as the tribunal of our sense experience. All of those presuppositions working in cooperation with each other allow me to conclude that a ladybug is on the rose and to declare it in intelligible words.

If a conflict is detected between what we are experiencing in our senses and our network of presuppositions, then some kind of adjustment is made in one's beliefs to restore consistency. If someone disagreed with my statement and countered that there is no ladybug on the rose, I have to then take that statement from him and evaluate it by my network of beliefs. Perhaps I might conclude that he did not see the lady bug at the same time I did, or maybe I would reason that he has his bug categorization confused and does not know what a lady bug is. The point is I do not come to my resolution of the conflict in a one-by-one fashion. Instead, my network of presuppositions helps me to determine what options are consistent and what options are not.

Here is the bottom line. The reason why unbelievers look at nature and come to a contrary decision from the Bible is because their network of presupposed and unproven beliefs causes them to rule out the biblical account. They did not arrive at their conclusion in a one-by-one manner. Too often, atheists accuse Christians of rejecting macroevolution because we presuppose the Bible, yet they will then exonerate themselves acting as if they have no presuppositions, but instead arrived at their conclusion by the evidence alone. They apparently do not realize how much they actually take for granted.[17] Therefore, it is the Christian's job to point out to them the presuppositional nature of their thinking and then to use the door of epistemology to demonstrate to them the impossibility of all intelligibility, if their unbelieving presuppositions were in fact true.

It is at this point then, that we are now ready to see exactly how to do this. The tool in our pocket that demonstrates the impossibility of their worldview is none other than the Transcendental Argument for the Existence of God. To that we now turn.

---

[17] This was clear in my blog debate with atheist Russell Glasser of the television show, *The Atheist Experience*. He took all of his assumptions for granted and refused to justify them. This was special pleading of the worst kind.

Transcendental Argument for the Existence of God

Any Christian who has engaged in apologetic dialogue with unbelievers has undoubtedly argued back and forth concerning certain facts of history or science. The unbeliever, due to various philosophical or pseudo-scientific reasons, rejects the testimony of the Bible and the faith of the believer. Yet, all of this back and forth argumentation could actually mean something if the Christian would truly challenge the unbeliever where he needs to be challenged. When we argue back and forth, fact vs. fact, we are operating on the false assumption that the unbeliever simply needs more knowledge to convince him so that he can then make a free-will decision to be saved. Instead, we would do much better to challenge the unbeliever to give a solid and credible account of how he knows anything at all if his presuppositions about reality, knowledge, and ethics (his worldview) are true.[18] It is to this end that we now turn.

The Christian can cut to the chase if they utilize the Transcendental Argument for the Existence of God. A great deal goes into understanding this argument, but once it is understood, it carries more weight than any other argument known to philosophy. The goal is to critique the unbelieving system of thought by analyzing it at the transcendental level. As Christians, we are to demonstrate to the unbeliever that the person who suppresses the truth of God has become "futile in their thinking."[19] Transcendental reasoning can accomplish this. As the unbeliever attempts to use logic, science, and morality in his debate against the truth of Christianity, we can argue that logic, science, and morality can only have any meaning to begin with if Christianity is true.

Transcendental reasoning seeks to determine what conditions must be fulfilled for any particular instance of knowledge to be possible.[20] Or as Van Til put it, "A truly transcendental argument takes any fact of experience that it wishes to investigate and tries to determine what the presuppositions of such a fact must be, in order to make it what it is."[21] When this is performed, it can be demonstrated that man's reasoning about anything is unintelligible unless the truth of the Christian Scriptures is presupposed. Thus, the truth of Christianity is to be argued "from the impossibility of

---

[18] Bahnsen and Bahnsen, *Van Til's Apologetic*, 5.

[19] Romans 1:21.

[20] The TAG argument, therefore, cuts to the chase of epistemology in order to prove all unbelieving presuppositions to be groundless.

[21] Cornelius Van Til, *A Survey of Christian Epistemology*, In Defense of the Faith, vol.2 (Philadelphia: Presbyterian and Reformed Publishing Co., 1969), 10.

the contrary," in order to show unbelieving views to be *reductio ad absurdum*, or reduced to absurdity.

The transcendental argument can begin with any item of experience or belief, and from there we ask what conditions would need to be true in order for the experience or belief to make sense.[22] For example, if the unbeliever attempts to disprove the existence of God with the argument of evil, you can take that item of belief or experience and ask what preconditions are necessary for the argument to even be made in the first place. An atheistic worldview hardly offers the right preconditions to make any argument from evil. Or someone might argue that knowledge comes from sense experience alone, not the Bible, and so you would then ask what preconditions are necessary for meaningful knowledge to be gathered from the senses. Materialistic atomistic atheism fails to have the right preconditions for this as well. Thus, the transcendental argument is extremely useful since it evaluates any given argument at any given time, and it does not cause the Christian to fall into the trap of arguing back and forth about facts. It gives the Christian the direct access to demonstrate the impossibility of the unbelieving worldview, which then only leaves the Christian worldview standing.

There are many reasons this argument is to be commended. First, as Greg Bahnsen said, "It is a forceful all or nothing intellectual challenge to unbelief in all of its manifestations."[23] Second, it covers all types of arguments made by unbelievers, and it does not allow the unbeliever to interpret any experience by his own principles since doing so would destroy all meaningfulness. Third, it upholds that Christianity is the only answer to man's woes. In other words, the transcendental argument demonstrates all unbelieving presuppositions to destroy intelligibility, but it demonstrates the opposite of the Christian presuppositions. Fourth, as an argument, it is capable of handling any unbelieving objections or challenges, and gives the Christian a confident assurance that he can reject in advance any hypothesis that contradicts biblical Christianity. Fifth, since the transcendental argument deals with the necessary preconditions of intelligibility, the Christian does not have to worry about the discovery of some new fact. No new fact can undo the validity of the argument, but instead each new fact would still have to be understood in light of the necessary preconditions for intelligibility, which ultimately are only justified in the Christian worldview. Finally, it has great spiritual strength towards the purpose of conversion since it penetrates right to the heart of all unbelief by appealing to the very knowledge of God suppressed in the heart of each man. It shows the unbeliever

---

[22] Bahnsen and Bahnsen, *Van Til's Apologetic*, 502.
[23] Ibid., 502–503.

what he already knows to be true deep down; namely, that the God of the Bible is the only explanation for anything that exists.

Presuppositionalism, as an apologetic methodology, relies strongly on this type of argument for a few reasons. It forcefully proclaims that all sides have presuppositions that guide their interpretation of facts and logic. It immediately removes the lies of neutrality and unbiased observation; lies that the unbeliever almost always attempts to hide behind. In U.S. Army vernacular, it is a BLUF (Bottom Line Up Front) form of argumentation. It readily admits that the Christian begins with the presupposition of belief in the living and true God. We seek to show that the kind of God necessary as the precondition of everything that exists is not an abstract entity, but instead is the God of the Bible alone, since the Bible alone describes a God that fits the necessary preconditions. As demonstrated in chapter three, all other conceptions of God fall short; He must be an absolute personality that is distinct from creation, that is sovereign, and that is triune. Thus, with the transcendental argument, we are arguing for a God of concrete detail rather than a mere abstraction. To put it bluntly, the transcendental argument is an argument over entire worldviews[24] that is far superior to the cumulative case method of worldview comparison. The latter method seeks to argue about worldviews, but it does so according to the unbelieving worldview's assumptions. Presuppositionalism argues in favor of the Christian worldview by immediately showing all other worldviews to be impossible. As a method, it agrees perfectly with the Bible's teaching that there is no neutrality. It truly is a God-honoring and biblically based apologetic.

I would like to show how the transcendental method works by way of example. Greg Bahnsen was renowned for using this type of argument in his debates with atheists. In his debate with the atheist ACLU lawyer Edward Tabash, Bahnsen utilized the argument to criticize Tabash's usage of the argument of evil. Tabash's relatives were victims of the Holocaust, and so he used the evil of the Holocaust to argue that the biblical God could not exist. He made other arguments, emphasizing that the God of the Bible is immoral. He then tried to seal it by saying an omnipotent God allowing the Holocaust to happen is not a good God, and thus the biblical God does not exist since He is supposed to be all-good and all-powerful.

Bahnsen uses the transcendental argument on Tabash to demonstrate to him that his worldview lacks the necessary preconditions to make his argument intelligible in the first place. Thus, his whole argument presupposes a Christian worldview in order to try to disprove that very worldview. Therefore it is inconsistent and arbitrary,

---

[24] Ibid., 509.

which renders it as false. Take a look at how Bahnsen used the transcendental argument here:

He says, " If the God of the Bible actually exists, I want to sue Him for negligence for being asleep at the wheel of the universe while my grandfather and uncle were gassed to death at Awsvitch. And let me, before I deal with you as a philosopher, deal with you as a person. I think it's tragic that that happened and I don't want you to think for a minute that it's just a matter of playing debate games when we talk about this but since you've raised it I want to respond to that. You have to understand that if the God of the Bible does not exist you have lost all principle moral complaint about what Hitler did to your relatives. In a godless universe, what one animal does to another animal is ethically irrelevant. You see, there is no rational basis for moral indignation or outrage in a godless universe. There is no moral obligation. What happens in a world where it's matter and motion just happens. Period. See, we're left, on the atheist conception, we're left with Mr. Tabash's feelings and desires. We're left with his feelings, verses the feeling and desires of say, a Hitler. And neither one of them in a godless universe have any more right than the other. Indeed, as a staunch defender of liberalism and a supporter of personal freedom, Tabash really should, in terms of his atheist world view, defend Hitler's freedom to do whatever he wanted to do. In a godless world, might makes right. Hitler had the might to kill your relatives and you have no complaint with that. Of course, you really do have a complaint, you refuse to see the foundation of that. I have a complaint and you should join me in making that complaint based on the character of God. My main point here is that moral absolutes do not comport with materialistic view of the universe, the atheist view of the universe. It makes no objective sense to call Hitler evil if this is a godless universe. I mean, a certain bag of biological stuff, that is subject to the laws of laws of chemistry and physics, did certain things to other bags of biological stuff on the atheist universe. There's no moral consideration here at all.

Mr. Tabash has used what is often called in philosophy of religion the problem of evil against the Christian world view. But he has to understand that in order to use that argument from evil he must first be able to show that his own judgments about the existence of evil are meaningful. Which is precisely what his unbelieving world view cannot do. Logically speaking, the question is how the atheist can make sense of taking evil seriously, not simply as something inconvenient, not simply as something unpleasant, not simply something contrary to your desires. The moral indignation which we feel about Auschwitz and other kinds of evil in this world just doesn't comport with theories of ethics which atheists dispose. Theories which prove to be arbitrary, or subjective or relativistic in character upon analysis Usually, atheists try to argue that evil is based on human reasoning and human choices and thus in the final analysis it is relative to the individual or culture. When the atheist professes that people determine ethical values for themselves rather than having them based on the absolute, unchanging character of God who has made Himself known to all men, the atheist implicitly hold that those who commit evil are not really doing anything evil given the values that they have chosen for themselves. Given the values chosen by Hitler, who can complain? He didn't do anything evil. The atheist must secretly rely upon the Christian worldview in order to make sense of his argument against God based on Auschwitz and other things of that nature. That is to say, anti-theism, presupposes theism in order to even make its case. The problem of evil, you see, is a logical problem for the unbeliever, not the believer."[25]

Many more examples of this argument will be used in the application chapters. Bahnsen's usage of the transcendental argument is just a foretaste of how this argument can be used in any situation. We can take any issue raised by unbelievers and demonstrate that their ability to raise the issue makes no sense on their given presuppositions. With the above example, it is possible for the critic to claim that Bahnsen failed to deal with the inconsistency of a good God that is all-powerful allowing for the Holocaust. *The main point of the transcendental argument is to show that such an argument cannot be made unless the God of the Bible exists.* However, all one would really need to do is add the premise that God has a morally good reason for the evil that does exist in the world, and the syllogistic "inconsistency" actually is resolved.[26] God in His sovereignty cannot be put on trial by man, and if God says all things work for the good of those who love Him (Romans 8:28), then He has a morally good reason for the evil that exists in the world.

---

[25] "Transcript of Greg Bahnsen and Edward Tabash Debate,"
http://www.foranswer.org/Top_Ath/Bahnsen_Tabash.pdf (accessed March 26, 2014).
[26] This will be further elaborated upon in chapter eight where the problem of evil is discussed.

Whatever the case, we are not in a position to independently judge God with morality and declare Him as unjust. Job thought he was in such a position until God turned it around on him with many questions designed to teach him the limitations of his finitude and therefore his inability to grasp the reasoning of God. Ultimately, our goal is to get the unbeliever to conclude with Job the following:

> I know that you can do all things, and that no purpose of yours can be thwarted. "Who is this that hides counsel without knowledge?" Therefore I have uttered what I did not understand, things too wonderful for me, which I did not know. "Hear, and I will speak; I will question you, and you make it known to me." I had heard of you by the hearing of the ear, but now my eye sees you; therefore I despise myself, and repent in dust and ashes.[27]

Conclusion

Every Christian apologist needs to have a basic understanding of Christian epistemology for two reasons. First, it justifies for the Christian the existence of both certainty and uncertainty in his life, and it demonstrates that the Christian worldview is the necessary precondition of intelligibility. Second, it makes it clear that autonomous reasoning has a groundless epistemology that ultimately is reduced to total skepticism and absurdity due to the finite nature of the human mind.

It is this very fact that makes the transcendental argument work. The unbeliever often does not realize that he takes for granted his own autonomy, and so he reasons from there assuming that his reasoning skills, sense interpretation, induction, deduction, and so forth are reliable. Therefore, he devises philosophies that he thinks explain the world and disproves Christianity. However, when his presuppositions are pointed out to him, it becomes clear that what he takes for granted cannot be true; otherwise, knowledge would be impossible. Thus, it is not that the transcendental argument is a good magician's trick for debating, but instead it works because it points out the truth about unbelieving epistemology 100% of the time. The only epistemology that survives the argument is the Christian one, and because of this, unbelievers unknowingly borrow from our worldview to get by in this world. Thus, they know things (when they borrow from the Christian worldview), but they cannot account for how they know things. This Achilles Heel is what Christians should have been striking at from the earliest days of church history.

---

[27] Job 42:2-6.

So far, Christian theology, Christian philosophy, and Christian epistemology have been presented and tied together in order to equip the apologist with the correct foundation of thinking. Too often, people do not "think" about thinking. When the Christian truly reflects upon who God is, and who man is, then he will begin to think and reason dependently upon God and His revelation. Scripture frames our thinking since it is God's Word given to us. Our framed thinking then must be applied to philosophy, in which we put forth scriptural answers to the philosophical categories of metaphysics, epistemology, and ethics. We then take this philosophy, test it against epistemological questions, and we realize that we have the only worldview that meets the preconditions of intelligibility. Once the Christian arrives to this place of understanding, he is now ready to apply this knowledge in practical apologetic dialogue. In keeping with the anecdote of building a shed, we can say that the shed is now completely built.

However, a shed that is built would be considered useless if it was then left unused. If no tools were put in it, and if routine maintenance was nonexistent, then disuse, time, and the elements would cause the shed to fall into disrepair. Likewise, having a firm grasp on Christian theology, philosophy, and epistemology will not be much use to the one who does not continue to study it (routine maintenance), and it will certainly be useless to the person who refuses to apply it and use it in dialogue with unbelievers. This knowledge requires action. It is a common saying that orthodoxy, or right knowledge, must lead to orthopraxy, which is right actions. The rest of this book is designed to meet this end. It will carry us from knowledge into action as we move from the "what we do," to the "how we do it."

Stephen Feinstein

Section Two

Applying the Apologetic

Chapter Five

Preparation of the Heart and Mind

Introduction

In the first section of this book, the subject was building a God-honoring apologetic. We spoke of foundations, instructions, tools, and doors. The act of building a shed was a good analogy to guide us through the subject matter. Yet, now we are beyond the building of a shed. Now we are moving into something entirely different. Knowing that we are in a state of spiritual war and that we are spiritual warriors, the new analogy is going to be warfare, in specific martial arts.

Every serious student of martial arts trains multiple hours each week for the purpose of being able to successfully defend himself when attacked. Countless hours are poured into pad drills, bag work, sparring, and then combat. Only through such dedication can a person take these techniques and download them into muscle memory, thereby making them instinctual. Yet, one thing that is often missed by observers is that it is more than just physical training. There is a philosophical and mental side to the training. Each distinct martial art has its own history and philosophy that guides its techniques and informs its theory of violence. Furthermore, each uses anatomy and physics to determine rules of leverage in order to allow for physically weaker people to physically control those who are stronger. Since many practitioners compete, they also learn the distinct traits of other fighting systems so that they will know how to fight them effectively. Additionally, good practitioners also study crime data and the psychology of criminals in order to heighten their situational awareness. Add to this the massive amounts of memorization that goes into the process, and it becomes clear that martial arts is both physically and intellectually demanding.

Likewise, apologetics is demanding. Perhaps it is not physically demanding, but intellectually it can go well beyond martial arts in the amount of data to study. As the first section of this book already demonstrated, a firm grasp on systematic theology, Christian and non-Christian philosophy, and epistemology are necessary for apologetics. I must add to this that it is good and right to also gather data, logically construct arguments, and study many different fields of knowledge. The amount of work that intellectually goes into this frightens many Christians away; however, they fail to realize that studying these various bodies of knowledge and thought serves to strengthen their faith. For example, knowing that our finitude causes us to reason dependently on God assists the Christian in "renewing the mind."[1] It helps us to think God's thoughts after Him. It reminds us why we must drop our opinions that contradict Scripture. If a Christian studied everything mentioned thus far, but he was never to engage in apologetic dialogue, his Christian walk would still improve nevertheless since his mind would be renewed with Christian thinking. Of course, God does not give us the option to ignore apologetics, and so it is important to know these things in order to fulfill biblical commands given to us.

Like each distinct martial art, Christian apologetics has its own philosophy and methodology derived from Scripture. It offers its own unique strategy for apologetic combat. And like the well-rounded martial artist, the good Christian apologist will study the basic information of opposing worldviews in order to know where they fall short. With all of this said, let this all serve as an exhortation for us to roll up our sleeves, get to work training, and then put that training to use trying to win souls.

As mentioned above, there is a distinct Christian strategy for apologetic combat that must be covered in this chapter. Yet, even before learning of it, the Christian must also understand that the manner in which he debates is very important to the Lord. There is a certain attitude expected by the Lord of His people. Therefore, it is important that we first discuss the proper Christian attitude for apologetics, and then we can move to the strategy. Afterward, two helpful checklists will be offered to help apologists monitor their level of readiness, and to equip them with useful and easy-to-remember tools.

Christian Attitude

In studying the necessary Christian attitude for apologetics, perhaps it is wise to start with the classic text on apologetics, 1 Peter 3:15-16:

> But in your hearts honor Christ the Lord as holy, always being prepared to make a defense to anyone who asks you for a reason for the hope that is in you; yet do it with gentleness and respect, having a good conscience, so that, when you are slandered, those who revile your good behavior in Christ may be put to shame.

---

[1] Romans 12:2

Not only is this passage important for establishing a mandate for apologetics, but it is also important for application purposes since it speaks of our attitude and the way we come across to people. In 1 Peter 3:15, we see the mandate of "always being prepared to make a defense," but in verse 16 we are commanded to do so with "gentleness and respect." Peter thus makes the point that our approach can be the deciding factor in persuasion when we defend the faith. Richard Pratt Jr. made a cogent point when he wrote, "Sometimes an approach speaks louder than the actual words. There are numerous non-Christians who were not persuaded by the arguments but by the attitudes of the apologist speaking to them."[2] There are a number of passages from Scripture that echo this sentiment, and so it would be beneficial to look at a few of them.

> Walk in *wisdom toward outsiders*, making the best use of the time. *Let your speech always be gracious, seasoned with salt*, so that you *may know how you ought to answer each person*.[3]

> Remind them to be submissive to rulers and authorities, to be obedient, to be ready for every good work, *to speak evil of no one*, to avoid quarreling, *to be gentle*, and *to show perfect courtesy toward all people*.[4]

> Have nothing to do with foolish, ignorant controversies; you know that they breed quarrels. And the Lord's servant must not be quarrelsome but *kind to everyone*, able to teach, patiently enduring evil, *correcting his opponents with gentleness*. God may perhaps grant them repentance leading to a knowledge of the truth, and they may come to their senses and escape from the snare of the devil, after being captured by him to do his will.[5]

There is much to be learned from these passages. Ultimately, we are called to approach apologetics with a combination of gentleness and firmness. Too often Christians lean to one or the other, but do not balance the two together. Peter clearly commanded that we be gentle, and Paul in 2 Timothy 2:25 wrote that we are to instruct/correct our opponents with gentleness. Correcting implies firmness. There are some Christians that take the injunction of gentleness to such an extreme that they speak in a way that makes them sound uncertain, since certainty might offend

---

[2] Jr. Richard L. Pratt, *Every Thought Captive: A Study Manual for the Defense of Christian Truth* (P & R Press, 1979), 65.
[3] Colossians 4:5-6 (emphasis mine).
[4] Titus 3:1-2 (emphasis mine).
[5] 2Timothy 2:23-26 (emphasis mine).

the nonbeliever. They act as though gentleness means that one must not speak with certainty since it might come off as arrogant. They may say things such as, "It is possible that I am wrong." Their hope is that their "humility" and gentleness will win the unbeliever over, perhaps through feelings of guilt. Such Christians need to understand that gentleness cannot compromise the reliability of the Word of God. Otherwise, the apologist is trying to please men rather than God.[6] The Bible would never command us to behave in a way that calls doubt upon it. Biblical gentleness must be accompanied by firmness.

However, there is exhortation for those who fall on the opposite side as well. Some Christians are too firm. They go after the non-Christian with all guns blazing, or as mighty crusaders swinging their sword without mercy in an attempt to chase a person into the kingdom.[7] These Christians must be reminded of the command of gentleness. Thus, both are needed. We do the non-Christian a great disservice if we are not firm, yet we also push such people away if we are arrogant, insulting, and overbearing in conversation. Imagine caring for a person who is recovering from a stroke. If he had a stroke, but refused to see a doctor, you would have to be firm with him, otherwise he would just blow you off. Yet, if you were too firm, he would avoid speaking with you at all costs, which also would do no good. Instead, you must firmly tell him that he needs to see a doctor, offer the reasons and consequences, but at the same time in gentleness show him that you truly care about him and want to see his life spared. If a blind man were walking toward a cliff, you would need to firmly call out to him, but if you were too firm in trying to turn him around, you might actually push him off the cliff. Yet, if you spoke too softly and with great uncertainty in your voice, the blind man would continue to walk until he fell off the cliff. Thus, it is truly imperative that the Christian match the gentleness and firmness together and become masterful at it. Otherwise, his attempts at winning the lost will prove to be in vain.

The result of combining these principles of firmness and gentleness is the advancement of a respectful challenge to the unbeliever. As noted in this book's introduction, when Peter writes in 1 Peter 3:16 that we must answer with "respect," the Greek actually implies "reverence." Some take this to the point to where they act like we cannot challenge the unbeliever, but in doing so they miss the point of verse 15, which commands us to always be ready to make a defense. Often, the Christian assumes the non-Christian is far more intellectual, and sometimes this is the case. Yet, he is not arguing from his authority or intelligence, but instead he is arguing

---

[6] 1 Thessalonians 2:4
[7] Pratt, *Every Thought Captive*, 66.

from the authority of the Word of God—an authority infinitely greater than the opponent and himself. Furthermore, the Christian is to trust that the Holy Spirit is at work in him empowering his witness. Truly, Christians, in general, need to stop fooling themselves into thinking that apologetic discourse is only for the intellectually savvy. Paul refutes this notion in 1 Corinthians 1:26-29:

> For consider your calling, brothers: not many of you were wise according to worldly standards, not many were powerful, not many were of noble birth. *But God chose what is foolish in the world to shame the wise; God chose what is weak in the world to shame the strong*; God chose what is low and despised in the world, even things that are not, to bring to nothing things that are, *so that no human being might boast in the presence of God* (emphasis added).

Ultimately, God gets more glory when He uses weak vessels to shame the wise. We are totally up to the task since we possess God's Word, the indwelling of the Holy Spirit, and a mind renewed by Scripture that reasons dependently upon God. We have the ability and the tools to shut the mouth of any unbeliever. This is true simply because we wield divine weapons given to us by God. Paul says nearly this exact thing in 2 Corinthians 10:3-5.

> For though we walk in the flesh, we are not waging war according to the flesh. For the weapons of our warfare are not of the flesh but have divine power to destroy strongholds. We destroy arguments and every lofty opinion raised against the knowledge of God, and take every thought captive to obey Christ...

Therefore, we are in a position to challenge even the greatest of men. We simply need to make sure that we do so with respect or reverence. Our goal should be to demonstrate to the unbeliever that he has no reason to have confidence or pride in his abilities. After all, our opponent is a mere man trapped by the limitations of finitude, regardless of how educated he is. Yet, the Christian must resist the temptation to take this information and use it to treat the unbeliever as a "nobody," trapped in folly, deserving to be talked down to. Even when unbelieving academics talk in such a way to us, we must not return fire in the like manner. The mere demonstration of their lack of true autonomy should shake them enough. Some Christians may believe that if the unbeliever is venomous, then the Christian is right to respond in kind, but Titus 3:2 corrects against this by commanding that we, "speak evil of no one."

With our attitude right, we also must ensure that our apologetic discourse is specific to our hearer. Sometimes Christians will ignore the unbeliever's questions and try to direct the argument as they see fit, but this shows a lack of respect for the unbeliever, and it leaves him with an excuse to ignore the Christian argument since his own argument was ignored. At the same time, we do not have to answer every question the unbeliever asks, since 2 Timothy 2:23 commands us to avoid foolish and ignorant disputes. In other words, if the unbeliever is simply trying to waste your time with foolish questions, you should direct the dialogue in a more fruitful direction. However, if the unbeliever has what he believes is a legitimate argument that is damning to the Christian case, then we must demonstrate to the unbeliever his error. Our conversation must have the goal of God granting the unbeliever repentance. As a result we need to direct the conversation back to the point, which is submission to the Lordship of Jesus Christ. This is why it is important to be ready in season and out of season, knowing how to answer all people, regardless of their objection or objecting circumstances.

Presuppositional apologetics works against any and all objections, which makes fulfilling this possible. In each situation, the Christian must offer a defense that is comprised of the five following elements: 1) it is based on Scripture; 2) it is presented with total certainty; 3) it maintains the creator-creature distinction; 4) it takes into account the effects of sin and regeneration; 5) it appeals to the image of God in each person.[8]

When learning to do apologetics, believers often wonder when and how they are going to get in intellectual battles with unbelievers. The answer is actually quite simple. Since 1 Peter 3:15 says we must always be ready to give a defense for the hope that we have, it means we must engage in apologetics every time the faith is challenged. There are two key situations in which it is very likely to happen. The first is if the Christian rightly engages in evangelism. Unbelievers will advance challenges during gospel presentations, and the Christian is obligated to defend the faith. The second situation is when the believer is in a casual conversation with the unbeliever and controversial issues come up. Christians, if they sanctify Christ as Lord in their heart, will reveal that they think the way they do via their commitment to Christ. For example, if the issue of capital punishment came up, the Christian would say he believes it is a just practice since God commanded it in the Bible. The unbeliever at that point may begin to question the accuracy of the Bible, and hence the apologetic encounter begins. As long as a Christian consistently wears Christ on his sleeve, as he should, there will be plenty of circumstances to defend the faith.

---

[8] Ibid., 69–71.

And when those circumstances come to you, be sure to have the right attitude and respect for your opponent.

Christian Strategy

At this point, the Christian apologist is now ready to begin to make cogent and powerful, intellectual defenses against those who oppose the Lord Jesus Christ. Assuming that an argument has now begun with an unbeliever of any persuasion of unbelief, remember how not argue with them:

Answer not a fool according to his folly, lest you be like him yourself.[9]

As already explained, do not try to persuade him on his own terms. Do not for even one second allow him to use the myth of neutrality and to determine the meaning of evidence based on his false notions of human autonomy. We have already seen that doing so is ineffectual; even worse, it is sinful. It is a reenactment of the sin of Eve. The solution is to answer him according to the truth. We are to confront him with the Christian worldview, not just as the truth but also as the very precondition of all intelligibility. Our argument is that if Christianity is not true, then nothing can be known to be true at all. This is accomplished by inviting the unbeliever, for argument sake, to see things through our worldview. Do not take for granted that the unbeliever understands the Christian worldview, for often they know very little about it. From that perspective, we can show him how we see things, but more importantly, how we can justify belief in science, logic, history, morality, experience, etc. Some presuppositionalists call this the Argument from Truth. Our main goal in "arguing from truth" is to show the unbeliever that we are justified in what we believe.

Yet, the apologist's task is two-fold. Not only do we not answer them according to their foolishness, but we also must answer them according to their foolishness:

Answer a fool according to his folly, lest he be wise in his own eyes.[10]

Although it seems like a bit of a contradiction, look at the two endings. In verse 4, you are not to answer them according to their folly because you do not want to "be like him yourself." In other words, you do not want to be in a hopeless, sinful, and futile situation of epistemological bankruptcy. But in verse 5, we do not want him to "become wise in his own eyes." Thus, the caution in verse 4 is for us not to think and

---

[9] Proverbs 26:4.
[10] Proverbs 26:5

reason like unbelievers; rather, the exhortation in verse 5 is for us to show them how futile their worldview really is.

In this way, we answer them according to their folly. We assume their worldview for argument sake. And from that standpoint, we show them how futile it is in that it cannot account for intelligibility at all. This will prevent them from walking away wise in their own eyes. Therefore, verse 5 calls for us to perform an internal critique of their worldview in order to demonstrate its inability to account for knowledge. This part of the apologetic is called the Argument from Folly. When the two-fold approach is done, we will have demonstrated that our worldview meets the preconditions of intelligibility, but their worldview does not and cannot.

There is no prescribed order as to how you would perform the two-fold method. In other words, you are not obligated to first answer them according to the Christian worldview (argument from truth) and then only afterward answer them according to their foolishness (argument from folly). Instead, you can begin by dismantling their worldview and then afterward demonstrating the truth of Christianity. It is possible to move back and forth between the two steps as the argument takes different directions. The important thing to remember is that both steps must be done, but it is up to the individual apologist in any given situation to determine the order.

Thus, it is quite the simple strategy for the Christian apologist. It is not a ten-step cosmological argument as some classical apologists would use, nor is it a historical case of evidential reasoning. It is not a cumulative case of all fields of knowledge, and it certainly is not a mere epistemological exercise to prove Christians are rational. Instead, it is an all-or-nothing challenge to the unbeliever's entire system of thought. In just two simple steps it is accomplished. The argument from truth accounts for all human experience by showing the Christian worldview to be the necessary precondition of such experience, and the argument from folly demonstrates that the unbeliever's worldview actually makes all human experience impossible. Both steps involve using the transcendental argument to prove the point being made, and both steps allow for the use of evidence afterward to demonstrate that the Christian's faith is not arbitrary—the unbeliever's is. More will be said on this in upcoming chapters. For now, it would be best to provide an easy method by which to conduct worldview comparisons. To that we turn next.

PIA Technique & Consequences

Unfortunately, fear grips many Christians as they are frightened of the possible apologetic encounter with the intelligent unbeliever. They cower because they are not sure how to cast down the lofty opinions exalted against the knowledge of God.

In other words, they are unsure as to how they will perform the internal critique of the unbeliever's worldview. They wonder how to apply the transcendental argument against each of the many varieties of worldviews. Thanks to the apologists who have gone on before us, it is rather easy to defeat unbelieving thought.[11]

There is a pretty simple checklist to have in mind when evaluating any unbelieving worldview. Look for arbitrariness, inconsistency, and the failure to provide the preconditions of intelligibility. Jason Lisle, a Christian apologist and scientist, refers to it as the AIP test, thus making it easy to remember.[12] The "A" is for arbitrariness, which is when a person believes something with no justifiable reason. The "I" is for inconsistency, which is when a person believes contradicting propositions. If they even have one clear irrefutable contradiction, then their worldview cannot be true. The "P" is for the preconditions of intelligibility, as we look to see if the unbeliever's worldview can account for the things that are necessary to make sense out of anything; namely, the laws of logic, uniformity of nature, and moral absolutes.

Rather than designating the internal critique as the AIP test, I would rather designate it as the PIA technique for two reasons. First, in keeping with the martial arts motif, in Jeet Kune Do,[13] the most fundamental engaging attack is called the PIA, which stands for progressive indirect attack.[14] Given that apologetics ultimately is a category of spiritual warfare, it makes sense to think of our defense in terms of spiritual combat as we cast down the unbelievers' lofty opinions raised against the knowledge of Christ. By using PIA, it reminds me that my internal critique of the unbelievers' worldview is an attack against their way of thinking. My second reason for preferring PIA over AIP, is that in many cases the first thing the presuppositional apologist does is ask for the preconditions of intelligibility within the unbeliever's

---

[11] Personally, I am greatly indebted to the late Dr. Greg Bahnsen. He superbly tied together his teaching on philosophy, epistemology, and worldviews and religions to provide for us easy-to-use tools by which to perform the internal critique with TAG. Those who are untrained in philosophy can use what he taught to confound unbelievers who are trained in philosophy. Much of what is written in the remaining chapters is based on Dr. Bahnsen's teachings.

[12] Jason Lisle, *Ultimate Proof of Creation* (New Leaf Publishing Group/Master Books, 2009), 84–87.

[13] Jeet Kune Do means, "Way of the Intercepting Fist," and it refers to the martial arts philosophy created by martial arts legend, Bruce Lee.

[14] For those interested, the progressive, indirect attack is one of the key ways to bridge the distance between you and your opponent. This is done by throwing a diversionary attack to capture the opponent's attention. As they deflect or respond to the diversionary attack, the true attack breaks through their defenses allowing you to follow with a combination of attacks to end the fight quickly.

worldview.[15] It is through this part of the critique that unbelieving arbitrariness and inconsistency manifests itself. Thus, PIA, in my opinion, better represents the order in which we do each part of the critique.[16] As various unbelieving worldviews are critiqued in upcoming chapters, the reader will see PIA in action.

Beyond the PIA technique, you also can look at the consequences of the particular worldview to see pragmatically what bad things it wrought into this world. Thus, the PIA technique and an analysis of consequences allows for a straightforward evaluation of any given worldview. When you apply this simple technique, every non-Christian worldview in existence unquestionably fails. Only the Christian worldview can ace the technique, for it is precondition of everything, including the PIA itself.

While engaging in apologetics, either in practice or in study, there are two common scenarios that will allow the Christian to use the PIA technique. The easiest way is to let your opponent explain his worldview to you, and as you listen to every word, you will quickly notice the contradictions, arbitrariness, and failure to meet the preconditions of intelligibility. Another way is to study many worldviews ahead of time, that way when you get into an argument, you already know where the particular worldview has failed the technique and then you can easily point it out. Both ways are very effective. One of the greatest strengths of presuppositional apologetics is that you are not required to have an in-depth knowledge of an opposing worldview, though it is nice to have such knowledge if possible. With presuppositionalism, you can always be ready to refute any unbelieving view by performing this internal critique. All that a Christian needs to do is to carefully listen to the opponent's argument and then point out the faults.

Within the PIA, it is possible to further expand the P (preconditions), the I (inconsistency), and the A (arbitrariness) with more subcategories. This allows for an even more precise internal critique. When looking for the preconditions of intelligibility, there can be many subcategories, but the big three are as follows: 1) uniformity of nature; 2) laws of logic; 3) moral absolutes. These three will be further elaborated upon in the next chapter as they are used in a refutation against atheism.

---

[15] The exception to this is with competing religious claims. I find it easier to immediately look for arbitrariness and inconsistency when dealing with false religions. Afterward, I then look at the preconditions of intelligibility.

[16] Of course, there is freedom in presuppositionalism to critique the unbeliever's worldview in any order you want. I believe many people will find it easier to begin with "P." My comments are in no way meant to detract from Jason Lisle's AIP test. The man is brilliant, and I actually got the idea from him to create a memorable acronym. PIA goes well with my motif and the order in which I perform the internal critique.

In terms of inconsistency, there are also four easy variants to look for: 1) logical fallacies; 2) behavioral inconsistency; 3) presuppositional tensions; 4) reductio ad absurdum.[17] A decent understanding of logic will help the apologist spot out logical fallacies, or logically incoherent arguments. Often, unbelievers violate one or more of the many known logical fallacies when they argue against the Christian position and in favor of their own. Being able to name the fallacy and then to give an example of it to show the absurdity of their argument can be an effective tool against the unbeliever. Behavioral inconsistencies are best understood as not practicing what you preach. If an evolutionist professor teaches his class that humans are merely glorified goop, and our thoughts are nothing more than random chemical reactions in the brain, and that there is no meaning or purpose to any of us, then it makes no sense for him to hug and kiss his kids and tell his wife he loves her. His practice is different than his preaching, since he clearly sees his family as more than reformed pre-biotic soup.

Presuppositional tensions occur when people have conflicting presuppositions. A good example is the naturalist who claims all things that exist are material, but then uses the immaterial laws of logic to make arguments to justify his view. Finally, reductio ad absurdum can be used to show the unbeliever that when his position is taken to its logical consequences, it is nothing less than absurdity. For example, if a naturalist claims we are just animals, then you can claim that since animals seem free to do whatever they desire, you are free to shoot the man and steal his wallet. Nothing stops a lion from ripping a weaker animal to shreds, thus what is to stop us from doing the same to each other? This argument demonstrates that his worldview is absurd and cannot be lived out.

When looking for arbitrariness, there are four types that you may notice: 1) mere opinion; 2) relativism; 3) prejudicial conjecture; 4) unargued philosophical bias.[18] When people think something is true simply because they believe it to be true, it is nothing but a mere opinion and is irrelevant regarding the truth. The facts of the world do not change just because a person has a contrary opinion to the facts. It is important to listen very carefully to your opponent because it is possible for a mere opinion to sound very scientific. Take the following statement as an example: "There is no way that dinosaurs walked the earth at the same time as man." The statement sounds as though it is a fact, but it really is a mere opinion since the real-time evidence to prove it is lacking. Thus it is a person's mere opinion. And even if it

---

[17] Greg L. Bahnsen, *Always Ready: Directions for Defending the Faith*, ed. Robert R. Booth (Covenant Media Press, 1996), 133–148.

[18] Lisle, *Ultimate Proof of Creation*, 87–89.

happens to be the opinion of the majority of the people, it does not change the fact that it is only an opinion rather than the truth. The majority has been wrong in its opinions many times in the past (e.g., the earth being flat). In fact, looking to the majority opinion as support of one's position is actually the logical fallacy of *argumentum ad populum*.

The second type of arbitrariness is relativism, the idea that truth is not absolute but is made up by each individual. It is arbitrary because it is logically indefensible, as has been shown in previous chapters, and because unbelievers attempt to use it to deny clear truth without any justification. Prejudicial conjecture, the third type of arbitrariness, is when a person assumes his reasoning to be based on facts, when in reality he is reasoning from nothing more than a personal opinion. A famous example is when a person claims that the Bible would have suffered corruption due to the telephone effect, and therefore, we cannot trust its accuracy. Such a statement may sound intellectual, but in reality it is arbitrary since it is not justified by any facts. Any rational person who has studied the textual transmission of the Bible would most likely never make that claim due to the manuscript evidence available.

Finally, we are left with unargued philosophical bias. This is an unstated bias a person has, and it is presumed to be true rather than proven, and the one who holds the bias expects others to presume it too. If someone tells a Christian that he cannot use the Bible as a historical source to prove a point, he is unjustified in this, especially since archeologists use it quite often to find where to dig. The person in this case has an arbitrary bias by which he creates an unfair rule. Watch closely for these four types of arbitrariness and be quick to point them out to your opponent in an apologetic encounter.

In summary of the PIA technique, the following breakdown should be useful to assist the Christian in remembering it. If necessary, review this part of this chapter as many times as you need to in order to commit this to memory. In the upcoming chapters, you will see each of these in use as various unbelieving worldviews are evaluated.

Preconditions
    1.   Uniformity of Nature
    2.   Laws of Logic
    3.   Moral Absolutes
Inconsistencies
    1.   Logical Fallacies
    2.   Behavioral Inconsistencies

    3.   Presuppositional Tensions
    4.   Reductio Ad Absurdum

Arbitrariness
    1.   Mere Opinion
    2.   Relativism
    3.   Prejudicial Conjecture
    4.   Unargued Philosophical Bias

The Role of Evidence

The final issue to cover prior to evaluating any given worldview is the place that evidence plays in the Christian apologetic. Evidence is a good tool for the Christian apologist when used correctly and righteously, but at the same time, it is counterproductive when used as a "neutral" means of appeal to the unbeliever. With that said, the Christian apologist should use evidence to show the consistency of the Christian worldview. It often strikes the unbeliever with surprise when a Christian counters him with positive evidences for Christianity and negative evidences against non-Christian worldviews. Furthermore, this strengthens the faith of believers when they realize their faith is reasonable.

We should also use evidence to demonstrate that evidence itself can be interpreted multiple ways, thus showing that evidence does not speak for itself, but instead a person's presuppositions are what make sense of the evidence in the first place. Claiming that evidence proves a worldview is actually the fallacy of reification.[19] This fallacy occurs when personal characteristics are attributed to a non-personal abstract entity. Thus, to say, "The evidence speaks for itself," is to be guilty of this fallacy since evidence is not personal and cannot speak or prove anything. Instead, humans, as personal beings, do speak and prove things, and evidence plays into that, but the human must speak for the evidence. Since all humans interpret evidence according to their presuppositions, evidence is never unaided by biased interpretation. This is why it is far more important to debate at the presuppositional level than the evidential level.

Another way to use evidence is to show the inconsistency and arbitrariness of the non-Christian worldview. Evidence is useful in pointing out prejudicial conjecture, unargued philosophical bias, and inconsistency in the argument of the unbeliever. Probability arguments can also be used for this end, since it is inconsistent for atheists to believe life sprang from non-living matter when the probability of that

---

[19] Ibid, 110-111.

occurring is impossibly low, but then they fail to bring umbrellas to work when there is only a 10% chance of rain. Finally, the Christian can use evidence as a lead-in to the transcendental argument. For example, the Christian offers evidence and then quickly argues that the Christian worldview is the precondition of intelligible evidence in the first place. As long as evidence is used for these purposes, its use does not dishonor God.

Now you have the required information to actually engage the unbeliever in an apologetic dialogue. You have been taught much concerning Christian theology, philosophy, and epistemology. You also have been instructed about having a proper attitude and using the Proverbs 26:4-5 strategy of apologetic debate. Finally, you have been given the PIA technique to use as a tool to evaluate unbelieving worldviews along with being reminded to look for the consequences of any given worldview. Before we move into applying this to specific worldviews of unbelief, it would be beneficial to have two checklists (one mental and the other practical) to monitor your readiness.

Mental and Practical Checklists

With the above discussions of attitude and strategy now complete, we can create a mental checklist, followed by a practical checklist, to assist in apologetic encounters. In many respects, these checklists are a reminder of the main principles covered in all the previous chapters, only now they are being bridged to the actual practice of apologetics. They are broken into two parts. The first part is comprised of all that the Christian apologist must know mentally in order to guide his argumentation. The second part consists of the step-by-step procedural guidelines that should be followed while engaging in apologetic dialogue. The two checklists below may need to be reviewed while rereading the previous chapters to ensure maximal understanding.

Mental Checklist

- Jesus Christ must be sanctified as Lord in our hearts at all times, and we must never surrender this by entertaining the idea that we can defend Him from any other standpoint.

- We are obligated to offer a defense whenever Christ is challenged (1 Peter 3:15; Phil 1:7), but it must be in gentle firmness.

- We are defending Christian theism as an entire unit, not in a piece-by-piece fashion. The apologist must be familiar with all doctrines (systematic theology).

- God's revelation is everywhere—there is nothing that does not point to Him—and we have two forms of His revelation: general revelation in nature and special revelation in the Bible. God's revelation is self-attesting.

- Believers and unbelievers are fundamentally different due to regeneration and spiritual death. Total depravity leads to the intellectual suppression of God's truth in the unbeliever.

- There is no neutrality between believer and unbeliever. Do not fall into this unbelieving trap for even a moment.

- False belief in human autonomy caused the Fall with Eve.

- Reasoning must begin at the presuppositional level to expose the unbeliever's biased commitments and to destroy the myth of neutrality.

- Christianity is a distinct philosophy that stands against all worldly philosophies. Christian theology and philosophy as a unit is our fundamental presupposition and commitment in our reasoning.

- Worldly philosophy begins with human autonomy thus leading to a variety of positions, but ultimately, all unbelieving thought is a mix of atheism and idolatry.

- Worldly philosophy is incapable of discovering truth, yet unbelievers can discover and know true things with certainty because they borrow from the Christian worldview.

- Worldly epistemology cannot account for knowledge at all, but Christian epistemology accounts for knowledge.

- Unbelievers commit the two intellectual sins of arbitrariness and inconsistency. Believers must perform an internal critique of the unbelieving worldview to demonstrate this.

- The transcendental argument for the existence of God demonstrates in all circumstances the impossibility of the unbelieving presuppositions.

Practical Checklist

- When an unbelieving argument is advanced, readily admit your presuppositional commitment to Christ in a firm but gentle way.

- Use the argument from folly to demonstrate to them that they cannot even legitimately make an argument against God without already presupposing Him. This is transcendental argumentation (*reductio ad absurdum*).

- Use the argument from folly to demonstrate that unbelievers cannot account for anything they know: uniformity of nature, regularity, reliability of the senses, etc. This is an internal critique of their worldview.

- Use the argument from truth to demonstrate that the Christian worldview provides the necessary preconditions for knowledge, truth, science, morality, etc.

- Use the argument from truth to demonstrate that only the Christian God is philosophically consistent and is the only God that conceptually is not logically self-defeating (i.e., absolute personality, creator-creature distinction, sovereignty of God, and the Trinity).

- Make strong use of epistemology to demonstrate the arbitrariness and inconsistency in any position the unbeliever claims to believe. Show him that he too believes most things on faith—an unstable faith.

- Make strong use of epistemology to demonstrate the futility in human autonomy.

- Know as much as you can about various systems of unbelief so that your internal critique of it comes easy. This means you have to do homework. If you are unfamiliar with one's worldview, listen to him long enough to find points to critique.

- Explain to the unbeliever that he already knows the biblical God exists, but he is suppressing his knowledge. It is God's image within the unbeliever that makes human understanding possible. Appeal to his conscience.

- Command repentance and faith.[20]

- Pray before and after for your heart and attitude to be right and for the Holy Spirit to grant regeneration and faith to the unbeliever.

These two checklists are somewhat lengthy, but apologetics need not be too complicated. The mental checklist, which is the longer of the two, should actually require minimal effort on the part of the mature Christian to master. If the Christian already is sanctifying Christ as Lord in his heart, then the Christian is thinking

---

[20] Acts 17:30-31.

dependently upon God and His special revelation anyway. If the Christian is focused on understanding biblical doctrine, and attends a church that teaches the doctrines of grace,[21] then the Christian will already understand the depravity of the unbeliever and the effects of regeneration upon the believer. The rest of the checklist is simply a few more details that help to understand these truths with a little more clarity. Honestly, it would take an insignificant amount of time to permanently commit such truths to memory if a person already consistently studies the Bible and understands correct doctrine.

The practical checklist will take a little more time. First, it will take much practice to learn how to use epistemological probing to expose the unbeliever's arbitrariness and inconsistency. Second, it might require deep pondering to learn how to use the transcendental argument for all possible circumstances. Third, the Christian might have to pick up a few entry-level philosophy books to become acquainted with the field of study and the history that surrounds it. Fourth, the Christian will undoubtedly have to practice in using logical argumentation to lead the unbeliever to proper conclusions. Fifth, each Christian must discover for himself how to advance the argument from truth in a way that demonstrates the preconditions of intelligibility.

Sixth, the Christian will need to become acquainted with the positive evidences for Christianity from the fields of science, history, archeology, and textual criticism. If anything, knowledge in these fields comes in handy to demonstrate that as Christians we too respect evidence, but we also can use such knowledge to demonstrate to the unbeliever his prejudicial conjectures. For example, knowledge of New Testament manuscripts comes in handy when an unbeliever argues that we cannot trust the copies of the New Testament that we have today. The instant we begin naming off the thousands of manuscripts and the 98.33% agreement between them, we can then accuse the unbeliever of arbitrariness and show him he has no right to assume manuscript corruption when he has not even looked at the evidence.

---

[21] The traditional acronym of TULIP is one way to express the doctrines of grace. T = Total Depravity of man, meaning that all parts of mankind (i.e. heart, mind, body, and soul) are affected by the Fall; U = Unconditional Election, signifying that God chose in eternity past those who He would save by grace; L = Limited Atonement, referring to the fact that Christ's death on the cross was a particular redemption for a particular people; I = Irresistible Grace, teaching that once the Holy Spirit regenerates a person, Jesus Christ becomes irresistible to them, and they will come in faith; P = Perseverance of the Saints, which means that true Christians will never fall away into sin permanently, but instead will make it to the end by the preserving and sanctifying power of the Holy Spirit. The sub-biblical views of the Arminians and Wesleyans dishonor God, overlook the direct teaching of Scripture, and in my opinion offer no true defense of the Christian faith against the unbeliever. The problem is even worse with the semi-pelegian views of the Roman Catholic Church. A correct view of salvation (soteriology) is extremely important for God-honoring apologetics.

Thus, evidence is not used to win the argument but to expose to unbelievers their own arbitrariness, which ultimately exposes their blind faith commitments.

Seventh, the apologist will need to take much time studying unbelieving views (evolution, idealism, Marxism, etc.) and the evidence that refutes them. This serves the same purpose as studying positive Christian evidence. It too allows the Christian to expose arbitrariness and blind faith in the unbeliever. Finally, the Christian must pray for boldness to assert Christian certainty without remorse or guilt.

Undoubtedly, the practical side of apologetics takes a decent amount of work. However, all Christians are called to defend the faith, which clearly means all Christians are to be apologists. It takes no more work to master presuppositionalism than it would to master classical, evidential, or cumulative case apologetic methodologies. Even with those flawed systems, it takes many hours to memorize the facts, evidence, and logical syllogisms used to promote Christianity and just as many hours to study worldly viewpoints to try to refute them. The difference with presuppositionalism is when all of the tools are in place, the Christian is equipped to be truly victorious and will honor God in each circumstance by not denying any of God's attributes.

Furthermore, presuppositionalism is greatly concerned with thinking God's thoughts after Him all of the time, which actually assists greatly in the Christian's sanctification and godly living, thus leading to a renewed mind.[22] It is the only methodology of apologetics that is not disconnected from Christian theology and doctrine. The other systems operate primarily off of general revelation and do not take into consideration what the Bible says about "everything." [23] Finally, presuppositionalism cuts directly at the root of unbelief and makes a more effective and direct form of argumentation. In a sense, it reduces a great deal of wasted time.

The Christians who do not take the time to learn how to defend the faith will have to answer to Christ at the Bema Seat of judgment.[24] They will be called on to justify the numerous hours spent putting together puzzles, writing research papers for school, learning to be a master at a blue collar trade, and yet not seeing Jesus Christ as precious enough to work equally hard to defend. Consider Matthew 10:37-38 when it comes to placing other things before our Lord Jesus Christ:

---

[22] Romans 12:2.

[23] I say this while acknowledging that evidentialists do appeal to the Bible when making a case for the resurrection of Jesus Christ. My point is that presuppositionalists see what the Bible says about everything (truth, reasoning, apologetics, etc.). Our apologetic is entirely directed by true Christian theology, whereas the other systems of apologetics operate off of primarily general revelation and only consider Christian theology secondarily.

[24] 2 Corinthians 5:10.

Whoever loves father or mother more than me is not worthy of me, and whoever loves son or daughter more than me is not worthy of me. And whoever does not take his cross and follow me is not worthy of me.

Conclusion

Truly, it can be very intimidating after studying Christian theology, philosophy, and epistemology to then realize that it must be used to the glory of God. These fields of study are broad, covering leagues of ground, and it could be difficult mentally organizing the information to be useful at any unexpected time. Yet, with tools such as the PIA technique and the biblical strategy set forth in Proverbs 26:4-5, the difficulty diminishes greatly. Using the argument from truth reminds the Christian of the principles set forth in theology, philosophy, and epistemology, and the argument from folly allows for the transcendental argument to show every unbiblical worldview as hopeless. Presuppositional apologetics not only provides the necessary and orthodox knowledge necessary to defend the faith in a biblical manner, but it also provides a simple bridge to move our biblical thoughts into biblical actions. The only thing it cannot do for the Christian is provide him the boldness to obey God's commands. Prayer and the Holy Spirit will provide this but only when the Christian walks by faith and engages unbelievers in evangelistic dialogue. The Lord will give the boldness necessary to obey His commands.

Chapter Six

Defeating Atheism

Introduction

Christians often are intimidated when a person claims to be an atheist. Perhaps it is assumed that he has studied fields of science and has really good arguments in favor of his atheism. Or maybe, since atheism is an extreme claim that expresses certainty against the existence of God, the Christian is intimidated by that "certainty." The truth be told, atheism has no credibility at all from a philosophical standpoint. It cannot account for the preconditions of intelligibility, nor can it escape woeful arbitrariness and inconsistency. Even worse, the consequence of atheism upon the world has led to an inordinate body count due to mass murder. Thus, atheism fails against the PIA technique discussed in the previous chapter, and it also bears horrific consequences. Truly, atheism's greatest weakness is its aforementioned inability to account for the preconditions of intelligibility.

Dr. Van Til made the simple argument that unless Christianity is true, nothing can be proven at all.[1] This flies right over the head of atheists and is instantly dismissed because they do not think about what the preconditions of intelligibility are. In other words, what presuppositions would have to be true for atheism to be true? And if such were true, could we even know it? If they actually asked and answered this question, they would realize they have major problems. The Christian worldview, in contrast, is the transcendental precondition of intelligibility. It is what must be the case for anything in human experience to be intelligible. On a basic level, then, if an atheist said to you that there is no God, no afterlife, no soul, and so on, but instead, there is only matter, the Christian can respond that if such were the case, he (the atheist) could not know it was the case, and ultimately, he could not prove anything at all.

---

[1] Cornelius Van Til, *Defense of the Faith:* (P & R Publishing, 3d ed., 1967), 266–267.

Whenever a Christian encounters an atheist and dialogues with him over the truth of Christian theism, the Christian merely needs to demonstrate the futility of atheism with the PIA technique. I believe that starting with the "P" (preconditions of intelligibility) is an effective strategy against atheism, since through it, we can also demonstrate the "I" and the "A." As this chapter progresses, atheism will be evaluated against each of the major preconditions of intelligibility, and in the process, it will be shown as arbitrary and inconsistent. Afterward, a brief statement concerning the consequences of atheism will be added as one more reason why atheism is absurd.

One important point to note is that the PIA technique plays a crucial role in both parts of the apologetic process, namely, in the argument from truth and folly. That is, the Christian worldview prevails against the PIA, but the atheistic worldview does not. Whether or not a person uses the argument from truth first rather than the argument from folly largely depends upon his personality. In a similar manner, every martial artist is different. Some immediately unleash a barrage of offensive attacks and others patiently wait and defend until they see an opening. It depends upon the fighter's attributes and personality. Likewise, some apologists would prefer to immediately show that Christianity makes sense out of human experience before they show that the opposite holds true for atheism.

Personally, I like to begin with the argument from folly to demonstrate to unbelievers the hopelessness of their worldview. Only after I have succeeded at that do I then show them that Christian theism solves the problem of transcendental reasoning. Are there exceptions to how I engage in apologetics? Of course! Sometimes my starting point depends upon the particular attack of the nonbeliever. The beauty of presuppositional apologetics is that the apologist has great flexibility in how and when certain arguments are presented.

With that said, the basic breakdown of this chapter is rather simple. Atheism shall first be evaluated through the lens of "P" from the PIA technique. In this particular discussion, there will be four aspects of the preconditions of intelligibility that atheism will be tested against and in them, atheism's inconsistency and arbitrariness will be plainly seen. Afterwards, the consequences of atheism will be briefly discussed, followed by helpful guidelines on how to use the information of this chapter to construct both the argument from truth and folly.

Preconditions of Intelligibility

The simple truth is that there are at least four necessary preconditions for human beings to possess knowledge in the first place: 1) Inductive Inference; 2) Deductive

Inference; 3) Reliability of the Brain; 4) Moral Absolutes.[2] In the last chapter, they were listed as the uniformity of nature, laws of logic, and moral absolutes, with the reliability of the brain being one of the many unmentioned subcategories of "P" in the PIA technique. Knowledge, certainty of knowledge, and true meaning to our experience depend on all four of these. Since it is these very four preconditions that atheism cannot philosophically account for, each of these four need to be understood by the Christian so that he can perform the internal critique of the atheist's worldview to reduce it to absurdity.

Uniformity of Nature

Inductive inference can also be referred to as the uniformity of nature or the problem of causality. All types of science rest upon this necessary precondition. Inductive inference takes something that we experienced in the past and then projects it into the future.[3] For example, a young man signs up in a kickboxing school, and on his first day he gets punched in the nose. His eyes water and tingle simultaneously, and he also gets a little dizzy. On day two he covers his face better so that he will not get hit in the nose. Why? He has the expectation that the pain he felt on day one would be repeated at any time in the future if he were to be punched in the nose again. In other words, the way things were in the past in terms of causal relationships will also be present in the future. All science depends upon this being true. If we could not project into the future what we have learned from the past, then scientific experiments would be a waste of time. If you learned everything you could about physics on Friday from twenty-four straight hours of experiments, but then none of the laws of physics were the same on Saturday, you would have wasted your time.

During a lecture, Greg Bahnsen illustrated the importance of this with a simple, yet strong, example.[4] He asked his class what would happen if he dropped a marker from his hand. The answer was obvious, but he made it difficult by forbidding the audience from generalizing the outcome based on past personal experiences with similar objects dropped. Since they have never seen that particular marker dropped, they cannot depend upon past knowledge. Instead, as good philosophers, they would have to say they do not know what will happen since it would be their first time experiencing such with this particular marker. So he went on to drop the marker, and it fell to the ground. He then told them that he is going to do another experiment by

---

[2] Greg Bahnsen, "Types of Worldviews," *Defending the Christian Worldview Against All Opposition, Series One.*
[3] Ibid.
[4] Ibid.

dropping the marker again. Knowing what happened twenty seconds earlier under the same atmospheric and barometric conditions, what would the audience predict now? Most would assume the marker would fall to the ground again, but is that assumption justified? If the issue is pushed and it is pointed out that the second experiment is still future, and we have not experienced the future, then we still cannot know what will happen. There is no guarantee that the future will respond in the same way as the past. If this example were stated to the atheist, he would object and claim that since the experiment is performed under the same conditions, you can expect the same result. Good. By an atheist making that point, he has just now assumed (not proved) that under the same conditions one event will lead to the same effect as before. They just assumed the uniformity of nature or inductive inference. We want them to assume this.

A good philosopher could argue that the marker might float upward this time since no one knows what will happen, unless it is certainly true that the past is the key to predictability in the future. The question is, "Can the atheist on his worldview assume this to be true?" The Christian can justifiably go to the science lab since he knows there is a sovereign, personal God who governs this universe, controls it, and has made it regular so that we could learn about it through projecting past experience into the future, and therefore, have dominion over the world. The Christian knows we can govern certain chemical reactions, build automobiles and airplanes, and launch rockets into space because the Christian worldview can make sense out of projecting from the past what will work in the future. But why would the atheist go to the science lab? In a random, chance universe, why expect regularity or uniformity? In an uncertain, material cosmos, why anticipate predication is possible since ultimately the dice can roll the other way at any time? This is a destructive criticism against atheism. The science it claims to believe in would not even be possible if its worldview were true. Atheists have no right to rely on inductive inference or to expect causality, and therefore they have no basis for doing science. Biology, Physics, Astronomy, Psychology, Mathematics, and even Grammar are all destroyed without inductive inference. The Christian worldview makes complete sense out of inductive inference.

Of course, the atheist most likely will not give up that easily and will try to recover from the problem of induction by claiming the future "probably" will be like the past. Thus, the marker probably will hit the ground because it did so in the past, and the basis for believing this will happen is because it has always happened that way in the past. Although most Christians would be tempted to stop and let the argument go at this point, it is important to continue on. The atheist is pulling a trick with that argument, for he is smuggling right back into the argument the very thing he is trying to prove. When he says the future will probably be like the past, he is assuming past information. Why is this a problem for the atheist? If he does not assume the future will be like the past, then all probabilities from the past are just wasted information, since they can tell us nothing about future, unless the uniformity of nature is true. It does not matter how many times something occurred in the past if nature is not uniform.[5] Since nature is uniform, we can project past experience into the future, and once again, we as Christians can account for a universe with the uniformity of nature. Can the atheist? No. Any and every argument the atheist can give will ultimately have to "assume" the uniformity of nature is true, just as the above example demonstrates. Thus, he assumes the principle to prove the principle, which in logic is called the fallacy of begging the question.[6] He is borrowing from the Christian worldview to perform operational science.

Simply put, the uniformity of nature means that the laws of nature do not arbitrarily change in time and space.[7] The Bible informs us in Genesis 8:22 that there

---

[5] There is even another problem with this. Appealing to the past still depends upon the uniformity of nature, since appealing to the past depends upon one's memory. The accessing of memory depends upon chemical reactions and processes in the brain. If those reactions changed constantly because nature was not uniform, then our memory would be useless and untrustworthy. Even if all of nature were uniform, but the chemical processes in our brains were not, we could not trust what our memory is telling us occurred in the past. And if the chemical reactions in our brains were uniform but nature itself was not, then our memory would still be no good to us since there would be no predictable pattern in the past for us to learn from. No matter what, the atheist is trapped by the fact that the uniformity of nature must be presupposed in all things, and yet, the concept of a uniform nature is inconsistent with the atheist's worldview that presupposes ultimate reality to be nothing more than randomness and chance.

[6] Creationist Jason Lisle from Answers in Genesis used a good example of this fallacy to show that if it were applied to other things, it would simply be absurd. For example, I could say I am immortal and therefore I will never die. How do I know? I never died in the past. Everyone instantly recognizes this as absurd because we know some things change with time. Even though all of us who are alive have never died before, we all expect that to change. Why not expect the laws of nature to change? The Christian does not expect them to change because God has promised uniformity of nature in Scripture—Genesis 8:22. The unbeliever, however, is forced to say nature is uniform because of the uniformity of nature, which is begging the question.

[7] Jason Lisle, *Ultimate Proof of Creation* (New Leaf Publishing Group/Master Books, 2009), 65. Be careful not to confuse uniformity of nature with the theory of uniformitarianism—the belief that rates and conditions do not change. This was the entire basis for 18th and 19th century geologists to assume an old earth since assumed that the rates and conditions of earth now are identical to the past. There is plenty of evidence that rates and conditions have changed. The decaying magnetic field of the earth is one example of such a change. Also, if what the Bible describes of pre-flood conditions were true, the rates and conditions would be far different than they are now. Atheists have no justification for holding to uniformitarianism since they have no way to know what the rates and conditions were like prior to human records of such rates and

is a degree of orderliness in nature, and we can expect such to continue on into the future:

> While the earth remains, seedtime and harvest, cold and heat, summer and winter, day and night, shall not cease."[8]

The Lord God promised the uniformity of nature, namely, that we can expect the laws of nature to remain the same as long as the earth remains. Science depends on this since it studies predictability. As God's image bearers on earth, we are hardwired by the Lord to know that nature is uniform so that we could have dominion. If we did not know the uniformity of nature in our heart of hearts, our lives would be chaotic since we would lack the predictability we are used to. Why expect gravity to work two seconds from now and so on? Instead we presuppose that gravity will work as it always has, and as Christians, we have no dilemma with it since God created the world and sustains it in a uniform way.[9] We also have no problem with miracles because it is nothing more than God going above and beyond the laws of nature that He Himself is sustaining. The fact that the naturalistic atheists know of the uniformity of nature in their heart of hearts should trouble them if they followed their presuppositions and worldview to its natural and logical conclusions.

From a purely scientific standpoint, we cannot know the future since we have not experienced it. But due to the wiring of our brain, we can know the past with some degree of certainty, as well as the present (but we know neither exhaustively). Knowing the past and the present depends upon the reliability of our senses, which is another manifestation of the uniformity of nature. It is peculiar that humans not knowing the future still presume it will be like the past. Christians understand with a dependent certainty that God is beyond all time, knows the future, is sovereign over all history,[10] and has revealed some of His knowledge to us in His Word. Therefore, it makes sense for us to presume the future will be like the past.

It is possible that the atheist will object that the Christian worldview is not needed since everyone presupposes or knows of the uniformity of nature without it. Do not be fooled by that argument. In fact, it is the fallacy of irrelevant thesis.[11] The fact that

---

conditions. This is another case of them assuming what they are trying to prove or begging the question.

[8] In context, the Lord YHWH made this statement soon after the flood. I do think this is significant in relation to the last footnote, since we have good reason to assume conditions are different after the flood.

[9] Colossians 1:15-17; Hebrews 1:3.

[10] Isaiah 46:10.

[11] Lisle, *Ultimate Proof of Creation*, 124.

everyone knows of the uniformity of nature is irrelevant to the question of "why" is there uniformity and "how" do humans know about it. So once again, the question to the atheist is how can he know the future will be like the past? At this point, we know he cannot appeal to the past since that is begging the question.

The fallacies of begging the question and irrelevant thesis do not allow the atheist an escape. Yet, the atheist Gordon Stein during a debate with Greg Bahnsen asserted that the inherent properties of matter cause it to behave in a uniform way. This does not to prove to be much of an answer since we do not know what the inherent properties of matter are. Really, such an argument is tantamount to saying, "That is just the way it is." At this point, the atheist is being absolutely arbitrary. Perhaps giving him an equally arbitrary argument will show him how unsatisfactory he sounds. After all, how would the atheist like it if the Christian said, "Creation is true and that is just the way it is," or "The inherent properties of creation cause matter to behave in a uniform way."[12] What this teaches us is sometimes arbitrariness sounds like an argument simply because the atheist uses scientific vocabulary to cover up the arbitrary nature of his response.

Due to the fact that the unbeliever in all operations (thinking, speaking, moving, experimenting, etc.) depends upon the uniformity of nature, he is standing upon creationism to argue against it. It is similar to a person arguing that air does not exist, all the while he is breathing in air in order to make his argument. Atheism truly is foolish.

When the atheist ridicules the Christian for having faith in Jesus and the teachings of the Bible, the Christian needs to remember that such a faith grants him the ability to do many things. He can do science because God created the universe and allows it to operate in a regular way, and He created humans with minds that can understand the world around them. Humans can build bridges, cure diseases, go to the moon, and many other things. Although the Bible does not directly tell people how to make a rocket, it does reveal to us that the world is regular and that man has the ability to learn and control many aspects of the real world. From that basis, we can build rockets through inductive inference.

Atheists have no reason to go to the science lab on the basis of their worldview. Of course, atheists do operational science frequently and often are among the most competent scientists in the world. However, this is not a problem. As Bahnsen said in his lectures, this merely demonstrates that most atheists are not really good atheists.[13] They may say one thing with their mouths, but they believe an entirely different

---

[12] Ben Wilt, *Ultimate Apologetics* (Answers in Genesis, 2009).
[13] Greg Bahnsen, "Types of Worldviews," *Series One.*

thing in their hearts. In other words, they say there is no God, and the universe is random, but in their heart of hearts they believe in regularity and uniformity. They are not worried that a safe experiment that has been performed safely in the past will all of a sudden explode in their face. Based on their worldview, they should be very worried since there is no way to know what would happen in a random, chance-based future. Therefore, the problem of induction undermines materialistic atheism. They cannot function as atheists without it, but the truth of it actually contradicts their worldview, thus demonstrating their worldview to be guilty of inconsistency.[14] Thus, atheism's failure to stand the evaluation of "P" also shows it as failing "I" in the PIA technique.

Laws of the Logic

The next big problem for the atheistic worldview is the problem of deduction, or deductive inference. These terms simply refer to the laws of logic. Human beings deduce conclusions with the laws of logic, and these conclusions are considered to be genuine knowledge. Deduction is when a person takes a group of information, applies certain laws of thought and relationships to that information, and then draws a conclusion. As an example, what conclusion would be drawn from the following information? 1) All men are less than twenty feet tall, and 2) Stephen Feinstein is a man. The conclusion is 3) Stephen Feinstein is less than twenty feet tall. The above process is deduction.

Logic allows for connections to be made between "classes."[15] In this example, the classes were the class of men, the class of height, and the single-member class, Stephen Feinstein. The relationship between these particular classes could be symbolically communicated as follows: all P is Q; D is P; therefore D is Q.[16] Without the laws of logic, humans would never be able to truly advance knowledge because all we would have to rely upon are one-time experiences all isolated from each other. We would only know momentary experience since we would not be able

---

[14] In this case, atheism demonstrates the following three types of inconsistency: 1) behavioral inconsistency, 2) presuppositional tensions, and 3) *reductio ad absurdum*. Atheists display behavioral inconsistency and presuppositional tensions by living with the assumption of predictable order in a supposedly random universe. Consistent behavior would include fearfulness that the world is unpredictable and science is impossible. They demonstrate *reductio ad absurdum* because if their worldview were true, then the way we live now would be impossible since there would be no inductive inference.

[15] This is called categorical logic.

[16] That is, all men are less than twenty feet tall (all P is Q), Stephen Feinstein is a man (D is P); therefore, Stephen Feinstein is less than twenty feet tall (D is Q).

to relate classes or propositions to each other. Since the laws of logic exist, we can learn a lot about things that we have not directly experienced. There are billions of people on earth that you or I have never met, yet without seeing them, we can know they are all less than twenty feet tall. The conclusion follows from the premises, and as long as the premises are true, then the conclusion is valid. If it were discovered that there exists a man over twenty feet tall, it would not disprove logic, but instead, it would merely prove false the premise of all men being less than twenty feet tall.

Another important example of deductive inference is "if P, then Q."[17] In other words, if P was our premise, the conclusion would be Q. If the premise is true and we know "if P, then Q," then whenever we have P, we also have Q. Every argument in this form is a valid argument. There are no exceptions. Related to this are the arguments of modus podens and modus tollens. Modus Podens says, "If P, then Q. P. Therefore, Q." Modus Tollens says, "If P, then Q. Not P, Therefore not Q."[18] What is the difference? The former is an argument that affirms, and the latter is an argument that denies. Putting this principle in words, we can use the following examples. Modus Podens: If an Army soldier was a commissioned officer (P), he does not live in the barracks with enlisted soldiers (Q). It is the case that Soldier John Doe is a commissioned officer (P); therefore, John Doe does not live in the barracks with enlisted soldiers (Q). Modus Tollens: If an Army soldier was a commissioned officer (P), he does not live in the barracks with enlisted soldiers (Q). It is not the case that Soldier John Doe is a commissioned officer (not P); therefore, John Doe may live in the barracks with enlisted soldiers (not Q).

The two illustrations of logic (categorical and propositional) given thus far were designed to demonstrate in a simple way that logic works by relating classes to each other as well as propositions. Humans cannot do academic work nor can they understand anything without logic. Much, if not most, of what any given individual knows was not learned by direct experience but instead by deduction.

How does this relate to a critique of materialistic atheism? It is rather simple. The laws of logic are destructive to the view of materialism. When the atheist claims all of reality is physical in nature, a simple refutation is to ask him if "classes" or "categories" are material things. For example, is the class or category of humanity physical? If so, where is that class or category in physical time and space? The question is not whether or not human beings are physical things, since the answer to that is obvious. The question is whether or not the "concept" of humanity is a physical thing. A person cannot touch a concept because it is not physical. The

---

[17] This form is called propositional logic.

[18] Lisle, *Ultimate Proof of Creation*, 131–132.

concept of humanity cannot be kicked, burned, tackled, frozen, cuddled, smelled, etc. The same can be said of the class of height. Specific heights measured in time and space are indeed physical, but the concept of height is not physical. No class or category or concept is physical. Yet, with these non-material concepts, and non-material thoughts and mental laws (logic), humans can relate classes and categories together that allow us to have knowledge of the world that is not based on empirical observation or experience. Thus, there can be no doubt that these non-physical concepts are real since they influence our ability to dominate the physical world.

Even something like simple mathematical reasoning proves this point. If a materialist writes 3+3=6 on a whiteboard and uses it to show that humans can know deductive relationships, the Christian can legitimately ask whether or not the "3" on the board really and truly is "3." If the unbeliever answers yes, the believer simply can erase both threes off of the board and claim that the concept of three, or "threeness," was eliminated from the universe. At this point, the atheist must reconsider whether or not the "3" written on the board is really and truly three. Of course it is not! It is nothing more than the numeral three, which is only a physical representation of the immaterial concept of three. If someone said he was going to pull three out of the closet, we would have to ask, "Three of what?" because he cannot pull the concept of three out of the closet. Looking back at the earlier example of categorical logic, the atheist cannot pull the concept of humanity, or of height, out of the closet either. Here is the point. Atheists who claim that all reality is physical speak and think in a way on a daily basis that betrays their claim. They talk about numbers and concepts, which are immaterial, yet they claim all reality is material. They cannot live according to their stated worldview.

Moving back to the laws of logic, they also are immaterial. You cannot have the laws of logic served on a plate at the restaurant. Thus, the atheist needs to be questioned on his inconsistency. If he is going to insist that all things in existence must be physical or material, then his view also requires him to deny the existence of logic, classes, and concepts since they are not made out of physical matter. Ultimately, then, there can be no numbers, concept of humanity, class of height, and laws of logic. Without these things there can be no deduction, and without deduction, there can be no reasoning since reasoning itself is deductive. Add to this the fact that they already have no grounds for inductive inference, they are now twice killed intellectually. As a worldview, atheism is groundless.[19]

---

[19] This point concerning logic is very damning to the atheists that claim to be dedicated to reason. If their worldview were true, then reason would not exist. Thus, they truly are not dedicated to reason, since the Christian worldview is the necessary precondition of reason.

The Problem of Mind[20]

Related to the laws of logic is the problem of mind. Can a materialistic atheist believe anyone has a mind? Sometimes this question confuses people since current practice in English language often confuses the mind with the brain. When people equate the two concepts, they are not being philosophically precise since there is a difference between the mind and brain. A person can say his brain is six feet off the ground and lodged in-between his ears, but this cannot be said of the mind. What a person thinks in his mind is more than what occurs in his brain. This is not to say that there is no relationship between the mind and brain. However, what the mind does cannot in totality be reduced down to what happens in the brain. The reason this can be asserted is that if a scientist opened up the skull and operated on the brain with the most sophisticated equipment, he could not describe what the person was thinking just minutes prior. If the person was thinking about their favorite childhood television show, the scientist has no way to know that. Synapses and dendrites have nothing to do with the conceptual content being transmitted over the synaptic arcs. It is the same with fiber optic wiring. The wire that transmits the information is not identical to the information itself. On this basis, it is impossible to reduce the mind to nothing more than the gray matter in the skull.

If the atheist insists that the mind is nothing more than the brain, then he is also insisting that humans do not have any thinking process that is part of one's free investigation and choosing. Instead all thinking is nothing more than electro-chemical responses taking place in the matter of our brain. With this being his viewpoint, it is easy to refute his position. If all thinking is simply electro-chemical reactions within the brain, then humans have no control over what they think. Some atheists will agree with this. For example, Behaviorists claim that any given human thought is simply the result of antecedent physical causes. Such a view plays very well into the Christian refutation. If it is true that there is no mind, and all individual thoughts are reduced to electrical and chemical responses in the brain, then all of the atheist's thoughts are not of his own choosing, and thus he could not prove his thoughts to be true because both the atheist and the Christian cannot control or change the electrical and chemical responses in the brain.

In other words, the atheist's claim to materialism is just an uncontrolled electrical chemical reaction in his brain, and the Christian's claim to the biblical worldview is equally just an uncontrolled electrical chemical reaction in his brain. Therefore, if what the atheist believes is true, he has no reason for believing it to be true because

---

[20] Greg Bahnsen, "Types of Worldviews," *Series One.*

he did not arrive at it by true proof or reason, but by material responses in the brain that could have swung the other way. No one could help what he thinks, says, or does because there is no mind or freedom of thought, and therefore there is no real reasoning behind choosing between different options. Instead, the brain simply fired out the things people have said and did.[21] The criminal justice system, notions of fairness, right and wrong, and the debating of contrary positions are all useless and need to vanish. Such is the consequence of the atheist view if it reduces the mind down to the brain.

Thus, if atheism is true, there is no reason to believe it is true because if it is, we have no mind to prove it, just random reactions from the brain that make us believe a variety of positions. If the mind is only a brain, then there is no reason for the atheist to try to convince others since the brain is going to make us believe what we believe anyway. Debate becomes pointless since there are no laws of logic, no laws of science, and no minds from which to reason and debate. In fact, Bahnsen argued that any atheist that shows up to a debate already lost, since it takes the laws of logic to debate and evaluate arguments, and these laws undermine the materialist's position. His showing up to debate means he assumes the laws of logic, yet these laws assume immaterial reality, which disproves the atheistic position. Materialism cannot be defended then by mental argumentation. Since the atheistic view of materialism destroys both logic and the mind, knowledge becomes impossible. Therefore, the atheist position, which supposedly depends on knowledge, has been reduced to absurdity. It cannot account for the knowledge, science, and logic that all humans use and possess on a daily basis.

Of course, many atheists will not fall into the trap as easily as the Behaviorists. They will claim that humans via macroevolution have control over the electro-chemical processes of the brain, and therefore, they can use reason and perform science. Hopefully by now, the readers see that this offers atheists no true escape. First, they are assuming the reliability of the brain, which means they are assuming the uniformity of nature. On their own worldview, they cannot assume this without committing a self-refuting contradiction. Furthermore, their claim to reason depends on the laws of logic since reason itself is not material. They need the Christian worldview to believe in a uniform nature and immaterial reality beyond the material world! Yet, both of these must be present in order for the brain to be reliable. However, the existence of logic proves that the "brain" is computing information that is itself immaterial, thus undermining the position that the mind is the brain. Given

---

[21] Many in our culture have run with the, "My brain made me do it," mentality. A really good book on this subject is *Blame it on the Brain* written by Ed Welch.

that we use immaterial logic to determine truth about material relationships, it stands to reason that the mind itself is immaterial like logic, but uses the material brain like wiring to transmit the immaterial information throughout the physical system of our bodies.

What about the situations where people get brain injuries? Clearly their reasoning and thinking get affected. Is this not evidence that the mind is identical to the brain? No, not really. If a person pays for a high-speed fiber-optic Internet connection and then attempts to send a research paper attached to e-mail to the professor, the e-mail depends on the fiber-optic wiring working properly. Neither the e-mail nor the attached document are the same thing as the fiber-optic wire, but the wire is used to transmit the e-mail to the internet server, which then transfers it through other wires into the recipient's computer. What happens if the fiber-optic wire gets cut? The research paper never leaves the writer's computer. Likewise, if the brain gets severely injured, the immaterial thoughts carried through the medium of the brain will be severely restricted. This is yet one more example of the Christian worldview making sense of common human experience by meeting the preconditions of intelligibility. Yet, the atheistic worldview cannot even get far enough to talk about brain/mind relations since it cannot even get past the problems of induction and deduction. Add to that the problem of the mind and atheism's dilemma grows even further. Yet, add even to that the problem of moral absolutes, and things just keep getting worse.

Moral Absolutes

There is yet another major problem for the atheistic worldview, and that is the problem of moral absolutes. Why should one person be decent to another, and forgo rape, robbery, murder, and other atrocities?[22] When Greg Bahnsen debated Gordon Stein at the University of California Irvine, he pointed out the problem of moral absolutes near the end of the debate. He suggested to Dr. Stein that the debate could be resolved if Bahnsen pulled out a gun and shot the atheist. He then asked Dr. Stein to give a reason as to why he should not shoot him with a 357 Magnum. Dr. Stein only had two options. He could either give no argument claiming there to be no moral absolutes, or he could say murdering a debate opponent is immoral or evil. If a person truly believes in no moral absolutes, he must admit it is perfectly all right to win a debate by shooting the opponent. However, if the atheist argues that it is wrong

---

[22] Even the word "atrocity" presupposes an objective moral standard. Some unbelievers claim relativism as their moral view, but the vocabulary that comes from their mouths (like the word atrocity) betrays their position.

to murder one's opponent, then the atheist has to admit there is more to the universe than just matter in motion. The atheist will have to appeal to something beyond the material cosmos, namely, the moral law C.S. Lewis argued all people intrinsically believe in.[23] Ultimately, if he does not want to be arbitrary, he would have to appeal to the God of creation, but if he refuses to do so, he will most likely appeal to some abstract, moral absolute beyond the physical world by which to condemn someone for murder.

All atheists are trapped in this dilemma. The atheist believes that people should do certain things and not do other things. Some atheists claim that people ought to live by reason rather than faith. Besides the apparent contradiction in that position,[24] how can the atheist tell people what they ought to do if there are no absolute right standards? In an atheistic universe, people should be permitted to do whatever they want, even have faith in religious doctrines. Ultimately, people would not be justifiably able to condemn rape, murder, thievery, etc.

The Christian does not even have to appeal to extreme acts of evil as mentioned above, but instead can point out that the atheist cannot even be trusted to do academic work. With no absolute morals, what is wrong with falsification of lab reports to acquire funding for research or to gain fame and admiration?[25] All departments within the university system assume the honesty of the researcher and assume the accuracy of research reports. It is for this reason that it often takes years, sometimes decades, before it is discovered that embellished statistics were used to falsely support an accepted hypothesis. After all, it takes many months and dollars to replicate many experiments. Atheists have no reason to condemn dishonesty in science, since according to their worldview there are no moral absolutes to condemn lying in order to gain wealth and fame. Yet, universities that publish such false reports are often embarrassed when the truth is exposed, as are the people who blindly accepted the "research." Why be embarrassed? Such embarrassment is not consistent with the rejection of absolute morals, which only serves to demonstrate that atheists do believe in absolute morals.

---

[23] C. S. Lewis, *Mere Christianity* (HarperSanFrancisco, 2001), 3–8.

[24] Since reason depends on logic and functions of the mind, it is beyond the material world and cannot be sensed empirically. Thus, the atheist has faith in reason. When atheists claim people should believe things based on reason, and the Christian asks them how they know reason is reliable, they often appeal to reason as its own proof. This is begging the question and is arbitrary. The Christian has a reason to believe in reason and logic, but the atheist does not. The Christian worldview sees logic and reasoning as stemming from the mind of God, and humans as His image bearers can analogically utilize logic.

[25] These types of frauds are more common in the university system than people would think.

Back when I was an undergrad student working on my B.A. in History in the California State University system, I had to take a class promoting feminism and homosexuality. One of the feminist professors boldly claimed there was no such thing as moral absolute truth and invited students to challenge the position. Most of the students that tried to refute her failed, but then again, maybe that was why a professor with a PhD picked a fight with undergraduate students of which many were only about twenty years old. I wished that on the day of the final exam, I would have blatantly walked over to other students and in plain view copied their answers for my test. She most certainly would have been angry and possibly failed me. If that were to have happened, imagine if I would have moved in for the kill and publically said, "You are a hypocrite. You taught us that there are no moral absolutes, and so how can you judge me? I chose to pass this class by stealing another person's answers." Be certain that neither the university system nor the professor that allegedly believes in relativism would allow a student to get away with this. This goes to prove that they cannot even live according to their own worldview.

In chapter three, it was mentioned that the unbeliever effortlessly moves back and forth from atheism to idolatry in order to avoid absolute morals in some occasions and then to cling to absolutes in others. It is inconsistent, and the Christian must point this out. For example, many atheist liberals were opposed to the War in Iraq[26] and considered it evil and oppressive on the part of the American government. Yet, if a Christian were to question the liberals on the immorality of homosexuality, adultery,[27] or any other matter, the response would often be an appeal to relative morality. Hopefully it is apparent what they were trying to do. When it suited their purposes to be able to declare something as absolutely wrong (the War in Iraq) they somehow had the right to do so, but when it suited their purposes to deny absolute morality to defend their liberal positions, they also somehow had the right to do so. Not only is this inconsistent and unacceptable in academic thinking, but their appeal to moral standards to condemn the war was arbitrary. On their worldview they have no right to condemn any government action, whether it is mass killings, war, oppression of the poor, or any other government abuse. This is one more example that demonstrates deep down everyone knows the biblical God. Since humans cannot live without absolute moral standards anywhere in the world, the reality of the

---

[26] Mainly they were opposed to anything President George W. Bush did. The outcry vanished as soon as President Obama took office. This demonstrated their concern over the war to be fickle, but that is a different subject altogether.

[27] Many defended President Bill Clinton to the bitter end concerning his sexual indiscretion while in the White House.

biblical God is the only way to meet the necessary preconditions of moral standards in the first place.

There are many different options that the Christian can use to make this argument. Shooting an opponent and cheating on the test are but two easy examples. The point is rather simple. Despite what the atheist may say with his mouth, he lives as though moral standards are absolute. He will get angry when a reckless driver cuts him off on the road. He will demand the arrest of the criminal that mugged him. He will demand of the resignation of the politician caught laundering millions of dollars of taxpayer money. He will declare the mega-church pastor caught in adultery to be a hypocrite. The list can go on and on, but the point is simple.

An internal critique of their worldview proves them to be arbitrary and inconsistent when they appeal to absolute standards of right and wrong. Yet, with the Christian worldview, the preconditions for moral absolutes are met. The things that contradict God's perfect nature are evil, and the things that are in accordance with His nature are good. Our consciences are hardwired to know which is which, and what things are appropriate for the creator, but not for the creature (such as the receiving of worship). Since safe human interaction would be impossible on the meaningless atheist worldview, the argument from morality reduces their position to absurdity.

Consequences

In terms of consequences, the Christian merely needs to point out the murder count performed by atheistic communist governments in the last century, and he will have shown that atheists in one century have probably killed more people than all of the religious wars of history combined. When one looks just at the consequence in America of pulling Christianity out of the public school system, he will notice greater violence, much more frequent premarital sex, out of control statistics regarding teen pregnancy, the growth of violent gangs, exponential increase in usage of illegal drugs, and gross amorality. The atheist is hard pressed to defend his worldview in pragmatic terms.

Summary of Atheism's Weaknesses

At this point, then, it has been demonstrated that if materialistic atheism was true, people could not do operational science (inductive inference), nor could they use logic (deductive inference), nor could people trust their random, chemically operated brains, and they could not trust people in general since absolute morality is non-existent. The fact that the atheist performs science, uses logic (often incorrectly), has a reliable brain with reliable sense experience, and expects academic honesty in lab reports only serves as proof that deep down he does believe in the biblical God since he borrows from the Christian worldview just to get by in this world. The Christian needs to point out to him that he cannot have it both ways. The atheistic position needs to be driven into the ground and buried by the internal critique.

Unfortunately, just because the atheist sees his position demolished does not guarantee he will convert to Jesus Christ. Sometimes atheists do come to Christ because God has been working on them through life events, and the apologetic discourse pushes them over the top as the Holy Spirit grants them life. Often this is not the case. They will still reject the truth. They will insist that the Christian is wrong about this all because atheists do perform science and logic and so on. Thus, even though the Christian argument makes sense, it cannot be true since unbelievers do the things that Christians claim are impossible apart from the Christian worldview. At this point, we must insist that their use of science and logic simply prove that in their heart of hearts they do believe in the Christian God. In so doing, we can direct the argument straight from their intellect right down to their conscience.

The words of their mouth do not reflect what they believe deep in their heart, since their actions betray their worldview. Their actions prove Romans 1:21. They do know of God and His standards, but they suppress it in their hearts. In other words, the unbeliever is self-deceived. It is here that the Christian really needs to reach hard for conviction by appealing to the truth that we know that they know deep within their hearts, a truth that they have been suppressing by rebellion since the day they were conceived in the womb. Perhaps this part is where the apologetic approach will sting the most. It will either bring conversion, or at the least, it may shut their mouth in opposition to God.

Argument from Truth and Argument from Folly

Truly, the Christian should not be fearful of the atheist. When apologetic dialogue begins, the model provided by Proverbs 26:4-5 works magnificently. For example, I got involved in an Internet debate when a friend of mine posted on a popular social networking site something favorable about providence. An atheist immediately responded by claiming providence does not exist; instead, true reality is that of randomness. I then responded with an immediate argument from folly concerning randomness. How can randomness account for predication and uniformity? How can randomness make sense out of logic? It seemed clear that this atheist never thought about these questions previously, and quite honestly, it went right over his head on the first firing. He and I then privately continued the debate for the next few months responding to each other's arguments with long letters.

He immediately fired off refutations of the typical classical Christian defenses, but I continued to hammer him on the preconditions of intelligibility. He could not counter these arguments; instead, he offered more and more reasons why atheistic evolution, and all that goes with it, is true. At times, I removed the legitimacy of his ability to use evidence and facts but then later responded to his facts and offered evidence of my own just to prove that he is arbitrary and I am not. Often, when I demonstrated to him that his worldview failed to meet the preconditions of intelligibility, I then immediately followed up with how the Christian worldview explains all intelligibility. By my consistent evaluation of his arguments from a standpoint of both truth and folly, he was not able to win the debate. He even admitted that he was no match for these types of arguments and invited me to debate some atheists on a television show. I respected his honesty, and to this day, I respect the man greatly and appreciate his attempts at honesty in debate.

Another instance happened at a going-away-party for a Christian friend of mine. A mutual unbelieving friend was present, and he apparently had moved from nominal Christianity to staunch atheism. During dinner we ended up in a debate that went on for two hours and pulled the attention of just about everyone in the house onto us as we dialogued back and forth. True to my personality, I argued from folly first, demonstrating his evolutionary positions to be false. I also demonstrated to him the nature of presuppositions and how they color both his interpretation of evidence as well as mine. He really had no defense against the TAG, and might I add that this person is extremely intelligent. Near the end, the argument from morality just about silenced him. During the debate, as we moved from subject to subject, I continued to weave into it using the PIA technique to show his worldview's folly and the Christian worldview's veracity.

Some may wonder how exactly to do this naturally. The key is to rely on the Holy Spirit and to learn to think biblically. You can never prepare in a scripted manner for an apologetic debate or dialogue. So do not even try. In martial-art competitions, you cannot preset a specific attack combination of ten moves and then successfully use it on a live opponent. It does not work that way. The fighters have to respond to each other's movements thus making it to where no two fights are exactly alike.

The same principle applies to apologetics. If you learn to immediately ask and answer what the necessary preconditions are for any given argument to be true, then you will always be ready to give a defense for the hope that is in you. I did not have to prepare a response when the person on the social media site attributed reality to randomness. I simply asked and answered whether or not randomness could meet the preconditions of intelligibility. As the argument progressed and subjects changed, my basic strategy remained the same. Learn to think this way. Learn to think dependently upon God's revelation so that you will always have a grasp on the epistemological futility of autonomous human reasoning. This will allow the Christian effortlessly to force the unbeliever to justify his "knowledge." With enough pushing, he cannot justify his knowledge with his worldview.

Conclusion

Atheism is nothing for the Christian to fear. When one honestly thinks about it as a worldview, it becomes evident that atheism is groundless. It is groundless because it cannot account for the uniformity of nature. The very science that they claim disproves the Bible would not be possible if the worldview that the Bible sets forth were not true in the first place. Furthermore, nothing in science disproves the Bible, but instead, unbelieving scientists with faulty presuppositions and theories attempt to undermine it. Yet, the preconditions of intelligibility tear to tatters their theories. Atheism is also groundless due to its inability to account for the laws of logic. In a materialistic/atomistic world of matter, how can one believe in universal immaterial laws of logic? Even if one were to deny that such logic exists, they still use that logic every day of their lives just to reach basic conclusions on everyday matters.

Atheism is further hindered in that it cannot account for the reliability of the brain nor properly make meaningful distinctions between the mind and brain. Atheists cannot articulate in a meaningful way how a material brain processes immaterial logic, thoughts, and information, especially if everything that exists is supposed to be material. Atheism is proven groundless again when one considers that all humans live as though morals are absolute. Trying to live in an amoral world would be impossibly absurd, yet atheism cannot account for morals or ethics. Matter in motion has nothing to say about what people "ought" and "ought not" to do. Finally, atheism is groundless from a pragmatic perspective. It has wrought mass murder, immorality, the breakdown of families, and many other negative results since it attempts to remove man's accountability to God, thus also removing man's true dignity.

For these reasons, a Christian should never fear the atheist's arguments. Truly, they are folly.

Stephen Feinstein

Chapter Seven

Macroevolution

Introduction

In the previous chapter, atheism was dealt a multifaceted deathblow. In keeping with a martial-arts analogy, atheism's legs were shattered by a series of devastating round kicks, causing the entire system to fall with it. Well, in this chapter, we are going to deal with a particular style of combat that atheists appeal to, namely, the theory of macroevolution. Bear in mind that their entire worldview was crushed in the last chapter, but many atheists feel justified in their unbelief because they believe the theory of macroevolution provides an alternative explanation of origins. In fact, many people take macroevolution for granted, assuming it is a scientific fact that was proven true decades ago.

The truth be told, most people, even many Christians, automatically assume the universe is billions of years old, humans started out as unintelligent cavemen, and that secular scientists have good reasons to believe in macroevolution. Yet, the theory of macroevolution is a flawed idea indeed. It fails against the PIA technique and would not even be possible without the uniformity of nature and yet that very precondition contradicts the "time and chance" formula postulated by most evolutionists.

It is safe to say that the most prevalent atheistic attack has come in the form of the theory of macroevolution. Many are convinced that scientists have proven this theory and therefore have discredited the biblical account of creation. This has led to a variety of responses from the Christian community. Some moved to a strict fundamentalism and fideism and others have conceded to the evolutionists and proposed theistic evolution.

However, Christians have nothing to fear from the theory of evolution since ultimately it is groundless. The purpose of this chapter is to prove this. In this chapter, the discussion will include a brief history and description of macroevolution, followed by an explanation of its philosophical nature. Afterward, the PIA offensive will be applied to demonstrate the folly of the theory. Also, a brief refutation of theistic evolution will be in order as well. Finally, the political controversy caused by the theory exposes the true heart behind its opposition to the truth. When it is all said and done, the Christian should have no fear of this worldview.

History and Description of the Theory of Evolution

Charles Darwin did not invent the theory of biological evolution, but in fact it is quite ancient. The Greek philosopher Anaximander (610 BC–546 BC) opposed supernaturalism and instead believed that natural physical/material forces governed the universe. As a result, he postulated an ancient theory of evolution for the origin of mankind. He was not the only ancient materialist, for history records for us the atheistic philosophies of the Epicureans, Sophists, and Skeptics of the ancient Greco-Roman world. Such theories never took hold of the masses.

However, emerging geological theories in 18th and 19th centuries gave the notion of evolution its lucky break. Dependence on a uniformitarian view of earth history led many geologists to propose the earth was very old. Uniformitarianism is the theory that geological processes have been uniform throughout earth's history; therefore, the present day rates and conditions uniformly apply to the past.[1] Naturalists would then assume that with enough time, natural processes alone could account for life on earth. In addition to that, early biologists like Jean Lamarck proposed a theory of evolution, even though it was at first rejected. The idea continued to grow in the minds of some, until finally, Charles Darwin created a version of the theory that most naturalists would accept. Since the time of Darwin, the theory has captured the hearts of all secular universities, the public school system, museums, science fiction stories, and beyond. The theory has been modified many times, and even today, there is disagreement among evolutionists as to the details of the theory, but they all are in agreement that evolution must be true.

In its most basic form, the theory states that billions of years ago, the universe originated through a big bang causing space, time, and energy to expand from an original and infinitesimal point at an extremely fast rate. As energy cooled down, it formed into matter, which over time condensed into stars and galaxies.[2] The stars, in turn, produced heavier elements, which then condensed into planets. Our solar system is supposed to have emerged in this manner, with the earth possessing the

---

[1] Terry Mortenson and Thane H. Ury, eds., *Coming to Grips with Genesis: Biblical Authority and the Age of the Earth* (New Leaf Publishing Group, 2008), 85.

[2] Jason Lisle, *Ultimate Proof of Creation* (New Leaf Publishing Group/Master Books, 2009), 33.

right conditions for biological life. On earth, living matter emerged from nonliving matter in a pre-biotic soup, which under the right conditions made spontaneous generation possible. Through cell division, these early organisms multiplied, eventually evolving in a macro manner into something entirely different, and over millions and millions of years, life evolved from lower to higher complexity throughout the course of various geological ages. Human beings are simply one of the more recent products of this chance-based, random circumstance of earth history.

Darwin proposed that evolution occurred through natural selection (survival of the fittest), while later on, others proposed it occurred through a combination of beneficial mutations with natural selection, and yet others have proposed many other ideas since. Allegedly, support for the theory comes from the fossil record, which supposedly creates for the evolutionist a picture of the biological history on earth. Since the theory proposes that random natural processes account for all of what we see on earth, there is no need for God or the supernatural. In fact, evolutionists define an appeal to the supernatural as unscientific. In a nutshell, this is the theory of macroevolution.[3] The question for the Christian is, "How well does the theory hold up?" Truly, it does not hold up at all.

Yet, the Christian must evaluate the theory from the proper perspective. As argued throughout the pages of this book, it would be foolish to argue evolution in a piecemeal fashion. Instead, it should be judged for what it is—another philosophy.

Evolution = Philosophy; Evolution ≠ Science

The theory of macroevolution should be judged as a philosophy more than a science. In fact, evolutionists need to drop the myth that they are merely using unbiased scientific proof as their primary means to reach their conclusion. Instead, they have presuppositional and unproven convictions that control their reasoning, just like the creationists. Both positions are philosophical worldviews whose philosophies dictate how they interpret any and all evidence. When the theory of evolution is placed against a presuppositional argument, it has no ability to stand because it cannot meet the preconditions of intelligibility, and ultimately, is not even

---

[3] Macroevolution is the idea that one species evolves into a completely different species and can no longer reproduce with the members of the original species. This must be distinguished from microevolution, which simply is the idea that change occurs within a species over time (such as skin color, height, etc.). Christians do not dispute the reality of microevolution. Creationists believe in microevolution quite ardently. Unfortunately, evolutionists have the bad habit of citing examples of microevolution as evidence for macroevolution, and unsuspecting people buy into the faulty argument. More will be said on this later.

a scientific theory. Furthermore, it is highly arbitrary and inconsistent, and its consequences upon history have been disastrous.

Thus, the theory of evolution is not truly a scientific theory, but instead it is a philosophy. It does not even have scientific credentials since it lacks the traits of a scientific theory as well as real evidence. In actuality, it is an old worldview that was given a scientific veneer with some scientific vocabulary. But from a truly academic perspective, it is just another worldview. As such, the best way to refute it is to compare worldviews. Apologists waste so much time arguing over the veneer that they miss the point of the real issues. People have been told the opposite of this (namely, that evolution is scientific) for so long that they may not accept it at first glance, but hopefully, as this chapter progresses, this truth will become obvious.

With that said, it would be beneficial to test the theory of macroevolution against the PIA technique. Like atheism in the previous chapter, the worldview of macroevolution fails.

PIA Technique

The transcendental argument against macroevolution is pretty straightforward. By the theory's very presuppositions, it cannot meet the preconditions of intelligibility, thus failing the "P" section of the technique. Many years ago when I was an undergraduate student working on a history degree, I had to take Biology 101 just like everyone else. Near the end of the semester, the instructor presented the theory of evolution; a man who seemed to believe the theory was valid. He began by writing on the board, "Time + Chance = Macroevolution." As an eighteen-year-old young man unfamiliar with epistemology, logic, and transcendental logic, I was unable to immediately see a problem with the present formula. In that moment in time, the instructor was sharing with the class the basic assumptions of the theory. He did so only for a brief moment and then he moved onto to the "evidences" for evolution, spending days on it. As a result, I am sure most of the students forgot about the assumptions and instead focused on the impressive number of arguments advanced in favor of the theory.

Yet, had I possessed a keener mind at the time, I would have demanded for him to stay on those assumptions for a while longer. Time plus chance equals macroevolution? How can one ever prove that assumption? Can it be observed in real time that this is true? Did my teacher personally observe that time and chance made macroevolution happen? Obviously not! Instead, he began with the assumption that macroevolution really did occur and that time and chance was the foundation for it. Yet, by doing this, he assumed what he was trying to prove, namely, that time and chance make evolution possible. Surely an honest, Philosophy 101 instructor would declare him to be guilty of the fallacy of begging the question. We do not know if time and chance would eventually cause or even allow evolution to happen. Evolutionists simply insist that evolution did happen and time and chance must account for it. They claim evolution is the fact that proves time and chance created the universe, and then when you ask them how is evolution even possible, they answer with, "time and chance." This is narrow circularity of the worst kind.

Apart from the clear fallacy, the real question that I should have asked was, "If your assumption is that the ultimate reality is time and chance, then would you affirm that the governing principles of the universe are randomness and chaos?" In order to be consistent, he would have to answer yes, and it is there that his position disintegrates. After all, there were at least 100 students who sat in his classroom all semester engaging in rational and meaningful discussion, learning about biology and yet the very basis of the science of biology is the uniformity of nature. A predictable universe with consistent and uniform laws of physics are necessary for both the existence of the science of biology and our ability as students to learn the material. How can the universe be uniform and predictable if it is allegedly random and chaotic? Uniform is an antonym for random, and predictable is an antonym for chaotic! This is the worst type of contradiction for the atheistic evolutionist. In order for evolution to even be possible, there must be uniformity in nature, yet there cannot be uniformity of nature in a random-chance based universe governed by chaos! In other words, if atheistic evolution is true, it is false. Thus, the theory fails the test of the preconditions of intelligibility.

Of course, the Christian must be ready to deal with the counterargument from the evolutionist that we too are guilty of circular reasoning. The presuppositionalist does not deny this. The truth is everyone reasons off of presuppositions, and therefore, everyone reasons in a circular manner. This is why seeking the preconditions of intelligibility are so important. Evolutionists assume time and chance account for all that we see, but we just destroyed that possibility in the previous paragraph. So their circular reasoning leads to folly since their presuppositions contradict the preconditions of intelligibility.

The biblical creationist does not have this problem. Our presuppositions are the items of the Christian worldview, and these presuppositions account for the uniformity of nature, the laws logic, the reliability of the brain, and absolute morality. Thus, the Christian is never stuck in the type of contradiction that the atheistic evolutionist is. We will never be forced to say that if Christianity is true, then it is false. Therefore, we welcome the charge of broad circular reasoning, because then it gives us the chance to show that everyone does it, but only we can do it and leave the preconditions of intelligibility intact. This is the beauty of the transcendental argument for the existence of God.

As previously stated, the atheistic evolutionist assumes time and chance make evolution possible. Through the transcendental argument, we just saw that this is philosophically inconsistent and impossible by definition. Yet, at this point the Christian can also offer evidence in order to demonstrate to the evolutionist his arbitrariness. The evolutionist assumes that time and chance solves his problem, but he fails investigates whether or not the assumption is true. Does he ask and answer through the science of probability if time and chance truly could create life? Most do not. If he were to ask this question, he would find that not only is his presupposition philosophically impossible via TAG, but it also is mathematically impossible due to the science of probability.

Laying aside the transcendental argument for just a moment, we can ask the atheistic evolutionist whether or not they have considered the odds of spontaneous generation.[4] In 1967, Eden Murrey wrote an article called "Inadequacies of Neo-Darwinian Evolution as a Scientific Theory." Bear in mind that he was not a Christian nor was his work published by a Christian organization. Instead, he was a mathematician evaluating the theory of evolution from the standpoint of probability theory. He wrote, "It is our contention that if the word random is given a serious and crucial interpretation from a probabilistic point of view, the randomness postulate is highly implausible and that an adequate scientific theory of evolution must await the discovery and elucidation of new natural laws—physical, physico-chemical, and biological."[5]

In other words, if a person wants to believe that life on earth came together randomly, he has an enormous problem since the probability of randomness makes randomness impossible for accounting for what we see in the universe. For the word random to have any true meaning, it must be understood in terms of probability and chance, and from that very standpoint, random origins are statistically impossible. Even though the evolutionists postulate the age of the universe to be 14-15 billion years old, the probability studies prove that to be nowhere near enough time for random origins of life to even be remotely possible. It would take a whole new set of

---

[4] This is the idea that life arose spontaneously from non-living matter through natural means.

[5] Eden Murray, "Inadequacies of Neo-Darwinian Evolution as a Scientific Theory," *Mathematical Challenges to the Neo-Darwinian Interpretation of Evolution*, editors Paul S. Moorhead and Martin M. Kaplan, June 1967, pg. 109.

natural laws to make evolution possible. The hard science of probability effectively demonstrates that evolution is not scientific.

If this information has been around since the 1960s, why have so few people heard of it? The evolutionist and the secular universities ignore it. This is not very scientific of them, now is it? It would make sense that if someone truly believed that random chance could account for the universe and life in it, they would at least undertake a study to discover whether or not chance can truly account for it statistically. Yet, most evolutionists do not ask the question, but instead they are content to assume their presupposition is correct. Not all atheists are this foolish, however. Eden Murrey was not writing from a Christian perspective but from a scientific perspective. His conclusion was that Darwinian evolution is mathematically impossible unless new laws of physics are discovered. Thus, this unbeliever, that was brave enough to study whether or not random origins were even possible, tossed the theory of evolution in the garbage can when he realized it was not mathematically possible. If all evolutionists were this honest, the theory of macroevolution would be nothing more than a footnote in history books.

So what are the odds? Different scientists give different numbers, but there is one thing that they all have in common——spontaneous generation is statistically impossible! For example, Michael Denton, a molecular biologist, in his book *Evolution, A Theory in Crisis* elaborated more upon the mathematical problem. The spontaneous generation of a living cell by chance would require the simultaneous appearance of 100 functional proteins in one place and time. The probability then for each of the 100 proteins is 1 in 10^{20}. Imagine adding the odds of the 100 proteins together and the impossibility becomes even greater since it brings us to 1 in 10^{2000}.[6] No rational person would bet anything of value to them on such low odds. Many people have trouble betting on a football game when the odds are roughly 1 in 2. How much more so with a number as ridiculous as 10^{2000}?

James Coppedge presents it a little differently. He writes, "Even if we take the simplest large protein molecule that can reproduce itself if immersed in a bath of nutrients, the odds against this developing by chance range from one in 10^{450} (engineer Marcel Goulay in *Analytical Chemistry*) to one in 10^{600} (Frank Salisbury in *American Biology Teacher*)."[7] Mechanical Engineer Walt Brown helps us appreciate

---

[6] Greg Bahnsen, "Types of Worldviews," *Defending the Christian Worldview Against All Opposition, Series One*.

[7] James F. Coppedge, *Evolution: Possible or Impossible?* (Grand Rapids: Zondervan Publishing House, 1973), 71-72.

these numbers when he says that the visible universe is only about 10^{28} inches in diameter.[8] He goes on to write another probabilistic analogy:

> From another perspective, supposed we packed the entire visible universe with a "simple" form of life, such as bacteria. Next, we broke all their chemical bonds, mixed all atoms, then let them form new links. If this were repeated a billion times a second for 20 billion years under the most favorable temperature and pressure conditions throughout the visible universe, would one bacterium of any type reemerge? The odds are much less than once chance in $10^{99,999,999,873}$. Your odds of drawing at random one preselected atom out of a universe packed with atoms is about once chance in 10^{112}—much better.[9]

Almost as devastating, Fred Hoyle in his 1981 book *Evolution from Space* claimed that there are roughly two thousand enzymes, and the chances of getting all two thousand randomly is one in $10^{40,000}$! The entire universe could be one prodigious, organic soup and still the odds of one in $10^{40,000}$ render the evolutionary hypothesis as impossible. The numbers do not look good for the evolutionist.[10] Evolution requires a person to believe that macroevolution happened despite these odds. It is for this reason that Hoyle asserts that the belief in spontaneous generation is psychological rather than scientific.[11] It is fairly inconsistent if an evolutionist leaves the umbrella at home if there is only a 10% chance of rain but then at the same time places all of his faith in something that is mathematically impossible. Probability studies prove then that evolution is something that is believed on faith alone and a very unlikely faith indeed.

Of course, some evolutionists have attempted to escape the dilemma caused to them by probability studies. Perhaps the most notable is Richard Dawkins, the current generation's champion of atheistic evolution. He attempted to turn the probability argument around by agreeing that this universe is absolutely improbable due to its complexity, yet if it were created, then its creator would have to be even more complex than it. Therefore, the existence of this creator is even more improbable than the existence of this universe, therefore He most likely does not

---

[8] Walter T. Brown and Walt Brown, *In the Beginning: Compelling Evidence for Creation and the Flood*, 7th ed. (Center for Scientific Creation, 2001), 15.

[9] Ibid.

[10] Fred Hoyle and N. Chandra Wickramasinghe, *Evolution From Space: A Theory of Cosmic Creationism* (New York: Simon and Schuster, 1981), 24.

[11] Ibid., 130.

exist, and if He does, this creates more questions than answers.[12] There are obvious problems with this argument. Besides the fallacy of special pleading, [13] the presuppositional nature of this argument is completely ignored by atheistic evolutionists. First, they are presupposing that since the universe does exist, it must have occurred by chance, and therefore, regardless of the probabilistic impossibility of this, it is true by default. Rather than allowing the evidence to render the conclusion, the presupposed conclusion forces them to play gymnastics with the evidence. Without the presupposition that spontaneous generation is true, a person would be forced to conclude via the figures mentioned earlier that spontaneous generation did not occur since the odds are too greatly stacked against it.

Furthermore, these insane improbabilities only exist in a universe governed by chance. If the universe is specially designed by the God of the Bible and is under His control at all times, then the probability of life existing as it does is 100%. Randomness is not involved, and probability has no real meaning when applied to the creation made by a creator with omni-characteristics. The Christian presuppositions make complete sense out of the universe.

If anything, the point of the probability studies is to show that spontaneous generation is even impossible in an atheistic universe that somehow possesses the uniformity of nature. Also, bear in mind the fact that the uniformity of nature cannot exist in a universe of true randomness. Thus, the atheistic evolutionists' presuppositions are impossible, and even if we granted them a free pass on this, the probability studies still demonstrate their position to be futile.

From the standpoint of presuppositional apologetics, what is the point of this information? It is not to defeat the evolutionists with evidential reasoning. Instead, it is meant to demonstrate to them the unscientific nature of their position and to convey that it is a worldview like any other that is based on assumptions and presuppositions that are unproven. It is meant to show them that their entire position is guilty of the fallacy of begging the question since they arbitrarily assume that their theory is factual or even plausible. In other words, they assume what they are trying to prove, namely that 14 billion years of random chance can produce an orderly universe and an earth with complex life. They take for granted that assumption, and they argue as though it is true, yet they do not submit that assumption to scientific inquiry. It is difficult to take a theory scientifically serious if its fundamental assumption is scientifically impossible! Thus, the end goal of the probability problem

---

[12] Richard Dawkins, *The God Delusion* (London: Transworld Publishers, 2006), 138-141.

[13] Edgar Andrews, *Who Made God? Searching for a Theory of Everything* (EP Books, 2009), 24.

for evolution is to demonstrate its arbitrariness and even its inconsistency since it is not truly scientific.

Another problem with macroevolution is its assumption of uniformitarianism. As mentioned earlier in this chapter, this theory was used as the basis in the 18th and 19th century to reject belief in a young earth. It was also used to explain geological conditions apart from believing in a global flood. Uniformitarianism stresses that rates and conditions on earth do not change. For example, if scientists can measure current rates of carbon 14 decay in our own time, then they can project into the past how long ago the process began. In other words, the present is the key to understanding the past. Often, these measurements yield extremely old dates for objects. Such dating methods are believed to give macroevolution enough time in favorable conditions to occur.

Is this assumption warranted? Quite frankly, no. Scientists have no way to know or prove that the rate of decay in objects is the same now as it was in the ancient past. Records of decay rates have been kept for only a little more than a century, and from a purely empirical standpoint, the most that can be said is that for the last century the decay rate for some things have remained constant. Therefore, they must assume that 1 billion years ago, the decay rates were the same as they were in the 1800s, but there is absolutely no way to verify this. As a result, if their assumption is wrong about decay rates, then all modern dating methods instantly become worthless. For example, when the evolutionist sites the main dating methods—argon-argon, fission track, lead-lead, lutetium-hafnium, uranium-lead dating, samarium-neodymium, potassium-argon, rubidium-strontium, uranium-thorium, optically stimulated luminescence, etc.—every single one of them measures rates of decay. Yet, we only have records of such decay rates for a very limited time. It is impossible to *scientifically* prove that what has been true for only the last 100 years has also been true for the last 4.5 billion years, especially when the earth is in a state of constant change.

So from the very outset it can be shown that the very uniformitarianism that is necessary to support an old earth could never be proven or established as fact. Furthermore, the evolutionist is inconsistent in his application of uniformitarian principles. For example, if we were to assume for argument sake that certain rates and conditions do not change, but remain constant, then some phenomena actually demonstrate an old earth to be impossible.

One such phenomenon is topsoil. It takes about one thousand years for the earth to produce a single inch of topsoil by means of wind and erosion from rain. If the earth was over 4.5 billion years old, then the topsoil on the earth's crust should be extremely thick, however, the average topsoil depth around the earth is only six to nine inches. There is nowhere near enough topsoil to account for an old earth; rather, there is only enough to account for an earth younger than ten thousand years. Where are the naturalists when it comes to things like this? Since it does not fit into their needed model of deep time, they simply ignore it. Of course, a few will attempt to offer an answer by appealing to erosion into the ocean. Currently, 27 billion tons of river sediment enters the oceans each year with loose topsoil. At that rate, the present depth of ocean sediment would have accumulated in only 30 million years, a far cry from the 4.5 billion years that evolutionists appeal to.[14]

Another example of this can be found in meteor dust since it hits the earth's atmosphere frequently, disintegrates into the atmosphere, and then gently falls to the earth as dust particles. If the current rate of meteor dust accumulation on earth were constant over a period of over 4 billion years, then there should be 16 feet of such dust all over the earth.[15] Add to this that meteor dust is rich in nickel; the earth's crust should have an abundance of it, yet it does not. Furthermore, there is less than one inch of meteor dust all around the globe. Thus, where is the 4.5 billion years? Did the rates change for meteor dust but not for the measuring tools of the evolutionists? If they argued this, then that would be another case of special pleading.

Perhaps a better case study for meteor dust would be the moon. Given that it has no atmosphere to protect it, there should be an even higher concentration of meteor dust there. In fact, prior to the moon landings, scientists were very concerned that astronauts would sink into a sea of dust. Yet, when they arrived, the soil was only about an inch deep, and only 1/67th of it came from meteors. Given the current rate of meteoric bombardment of the moon, if it was 4.5 billion years old, then the dust should be 50 times thicker.[16] The only way for an evolutionist to escape this dilemma is to assume that bombardments are more frequent now than in the past, but there is no basis for such an assumption. In fact, it is safer to assume the opposite since every meteorite that struck the moon in the past is one less meteor flying around in space now.

The moon poses another problem for the evolutionist as well. The laws of physics require that the moon recede from the earth in terms of distance. If the moon began orbiting near the earth's surface, at its current rate of recession, it would have reached its current distance at best after 1.2 billion years, far less than 4.5 billion

---

[14] Brown and Brown, *In the Beginning*, 31.
[15] Ibid., 32.
[16] Ibid., 308.

years.[17] Some evolutionists assume that the earth may have captured the moon during that time into its orbit, but this scenario is unlikely due to its circular rather than elongated orbit. And if such did happen, it would have caused geological catastrophes all across the globe, thus changing rates and conditions, which would render uniformitarian dating methods as useless. Rather than accept the moon recession as a natural time clock, the evolutionists simply advance possible explanations that solve nothing other than diverting attention away from the fact that they tend to do this with items that contradict their presupposed views concerning the age of the earth. Once again, they are very selective in what type of evidence they use for determining deep time.

As a final example among many choices, the earth's magnetic field also can be used as a natural clock that points to a young earth rather than an old. Over the course of the past one hundred and forty years, direct measurements of the strength of the earth's magnetic field have demonstrated it to be in a state of rapid and steady decline. It is believed that there is an electrical current within the earth that produces this magnetic field, and based on the current rate of magnetic decay, just twenty thousand years ago, the electrical current would have been so prodigious that the earth's very structure could not survive the heat it would produce.[18] Since evolutionists prefer to date the earth based on current rates of decay, why do they ignore this decay of the earth's magnetic field? Could it be that an earth younger than twenty thousand years old does not fit with their already presupposed view? Thus, just like with the other natural clocks mentioned, they offer a trivial explanation and then ignore the evidence.

Perhaps my reader is wondering, "What is the point of this evidence?" After all, presuppositionalism is not evidentialism in terms of apologetic methodology. First, the manner of using this evidence is not to convince evolutionists with fact after fact that we are right and they are wrong. Instead, the evidence is used to demonstrate their arbitrariness and inconsistency. If they truly believe that rates and conditions do not change, and therefore the earth can be dated from that basis, why then do they ignore these numerous natural clocks that damage their view of a 4.5 billion year old earth? The answer is simple. These clocks do not fit with their presuppositions, and therefore, in an arbitrary manner they are picking and choosing what measurements to accept. In the process, they are also demonstrating themselves to be inconsistent since they truly do not believe rates and conditions have been the same. After all, most of their attempts to explain away the aforementioned arguments require them to

---

[17] Ibid., 304.
[18] Ibid, 32.

assert that rates and conditions have changed but only when it comes to the phenomena that disagrees with their presupposed deep time. This demonstrates them to be guilty of special pleading yet again.

Ultimately, the goal is to demonstrate that evolution does not have a ton of great evidence that embarrasses Christians, but to the contrary, there is a lot of counterevidence that discredits the theory. Evolutionists ignore the evidence because their presuppositions and philosophical commitments have no place for such evidence. This fact alone demonstrates why evidential apologetics is futile. The atheist has never lacked evidence for creation, but instead, he suppresses it. It is for this reason that we begin our argument at the presuppositional level with TAG and then we utilize evidence to demonstrate to them their failure against the *I* and *A* portions of the PIA technique.

This then proves that they do not believe in evolution because the abundance of scientific evidence shows that it "probably happened," but instead, they believe it because they want to believe it. It does not honor God to act as though the atheist gets to sit in judgment over God and decide if there is enough evidence to support God's existence. No, instead it honors God to assert that the God of the Bible does exist, the atheist already knows it since he operates in God's universe, and TAG proves it since atheism is groundless. Presenting evidence to then show the unbeliever's arbitrariness and inconsistency honors God since it is not used to affirm human autonomy; rather, the goal is to shatter it by showing its almost schizophrenic character in practice.

With spontaneous generation debunked via presuppositional reasoning and probability studies, and uniformitarianism debunked through presuppositional reasoning and counterexamples, the Christian can be satisfied in the fact that macroevolution is foolish. However, there is no need to stop here. In chapter five, it was noted that all the Christian needs to do in order to discover arbitrariness and inconsistency is to listen to the unbeliever explain his position. When this is employed in the case of macroevolution, it becomes apparently clear that there are numerous internal problems within the theory.

Greg Bahnsen was quick to spot one gigantic inconsistency with evolutionary theory when he appealed to the synergistic nature of our organs.[19] For example, mammals have hearts, lungs, and kidneys that work synergistically together, which is definitely a difficulty to a theory that claims organisms develop gradually over time. After all, in mammals, a heart is worthless without functioning lungs and both of

---

[19] Greg Bahnsen, "Types of Worldviews," *Defending the Christian Worldview Against All Opposition, Series Two.*

those without functioning kidneys. If each organ developed gradually over ages of time, it would be impossible for an organism to live, since all three organs would have to appear instantly. If that were the case, then the idea of slow gradual change goes right out the window, and the theory of evolution with it. Yet, this very fact that these organs had to appear instantly, completely, and simultaneously is totally inconsistent with the widely accepted evolutionary view of gradual change.

According to the evolutionist, every change in an organism is preserved due to a favorable interaction with the environment. If we were to take the complicated human eye as an example, how could it gradually develop into what it now is? Gradual changes would only be preserved if there were a favorable interaction with the environment, but what possible favorable interaction could an incomplete human eye possibly have? It would be blind! The partial eye is worthless to the organism since the beneficial function of the eye is sight, the very thing a partial eye does not possess. Furthermore, the eye is wired to the back of the brain, which makes no sense from an evolutionary standpoint, since the quickest and easiest place for it to connect to is the front of the brain. Add to this that it is reverse-wired thus causing images to come in upside down, and the brain then converts the images to right-side up. How is that favorable? It seems liked added and inefficient steps from an evolutionary standpoint. In other words, what can be observed within complicated life actually serves to undermine the theory of macroevolution.

Even Charles Darwin understood how damaging something like the eye could be to his theory. He wrote, "If it could be demonstrated that any complex organ existed which could not possibly have been formed by numerous, successive, slight modifications, my theory would absolutely break down."[20] Given that the eye is absolutely useless except in its final, complete form, how could have the gradual changes been selected and passed on over millions of years in the first place? This very notion is inconsistent with the theory of evolution since it claims that nature only selects the useful adaptations.

Related to this is the problem of irreducible complexity. Microbiologist Michael Behe elucidated the problem as it related to Darwin's aforementioned dilemma. Behe wrote:

> By *irreducibly complex*, I mean a single system composed of several well-matched, interacting parts that contribute to the basic function, wherein the removal of any one of these parts causes the system to effectively cease

---

[20] Charles Darwin, *The Origin of the Species*, 6th edition (New York: Macmillan Publishing Co., 1927), 179.

functioning. An irreducibly complex system cannot be produced directly (that is, by continuously improving the initial function, which continues to work by the same mechanism) by slight, successive modifications of a precursor system, because any precursor to an irreducibly complex system that is missing a part is by definition nonfunctional. [21]

In other words, even the simplest cell is comprised of numerous biochemical machines working together synergistically, and if even one of these parts did not work, the cell would die. Therefore, the cell is irreducibly complex, meaning that its complexity cannot be reduced without destroying the functionality of the cell.[22] This damages the theory of macroevolution because irreducibly complex systems cannot come into existence via evolutionary processes, but instead must appear instantly in their complete form. Given that both the simplest of all living cells and every multi-cellular system are irreducibly complex, macroevolution could not have occurred.

Another difficult question for the theory of evolution concerns sex. We know that human babies come from sexual intercourse. Yet, according to the theory of evolution, life began as little amoebas that emerged from the prebiotic soup. The amoebas did not reproduce through sexual intercourse, but instead by asexual cell division, a process far more efficient than sexual intercourse. So how do you get from one extreme to the other? With gradual development, what good is a partially developed genital? Why would an organism develop it in reaction to the environment when such development has no environmental advantage? After all, it is so much easier to simply produce another life form through cell division. The theory makes no sense, especially when one really thinks of how we moved from cell division to copulation. To be quite honest, the theory is arbitrary. It asserts that the gradation from cell division to sex must have happened, but has absolutely no idea of how or why, other than explanations that amount to fairy tales with academic vocabulary. Some evolutionists are honest about this and admit it is a great difficulty for their theory, but they then ignore it believing an answer will one day be discovered. That sounds a lot like the misguided faith they often ridicule.

More can be said on the difficulty of sex for evolution. To better appreciate the problem, consider what Walt Brown wrote on it:

---

[21] Michael J. Behe, *Darwin's Black Box: The Biochemical Challenge to Evolution* (New York: Touchstone, 1998), 39.

[22] Lisle, *Ultimate Proof of Creation*, 20.

If sexual reproduction in plants, animals, and humans is a result of evolutionary sequences, an absolutely unbelievable series of chance events must have occurred at each stage.

a. The amazingly complex, radically different, yet complementary reproductive systems of the male and female must have *completely* and *independently* evolved at each stage at about the *same time and place*. Just a slight incompleteness in only one of the two would make both reproductive systems useless, and the organism would become extinct.

b. The physical, chemical, and emotional systems of the male and female would also need to be compatible.

c. The millions of complex products of a male reproductive system (pollen or sperm) must have an affinity for and a mechanical, chemical, and electrical compatibility with the eggs of the female reproductive system.

d. The many intricate processes occurring at the molecular level inside the fertilized egg would have to work with fantastic precision—processes scientists can describe only in a general sense.

e. The environment of this fertilized egg, from conception through adulthood and until it also reproduced with another sexually capable adult (who also "accidentally" evolved), would have to be tightly controlled.

f. This remarkable string of "accidents" must have been repeated for millions of species.[23]

Considering these facts, it makes absolutely no sense to believe sexual reproduction and sexual diversity arose through evolution and survived. Evolutionary theory cannot account for this, and the very nature of sexual reproduction is inconsistent with their theory yet again. Their theory should expect natural selection to favor asexual reproduction.

Cell division itself also presents a difficulty for evolutionary theory. The first cells or amoebas allegedly were cell dividers. When they first emerged, they were all identical. What caused the cell division process to cease utilizing identical cell division in favor of diversification? It is tough to grasp how single cells that can only make identical copies of themselves could then produce something entirely different.[24] Do people take a single-typed page to a copy machine and after pressing

---

[23] Brown and Brown, *In the Beginning,* 16 (emphasis original).
[24] Bahnsen, "Types of Worldviews." *Series Two.*

the copy button expect an entirely different page with different words to emerge? Even if you set it to make one billion copies, it still would only make duplicates of the original. An evolutionist may appeal to mutations, but this is a faith-based appeal since no known mutation has ever produced a life form with greater complexity and survivability than its ancestors.[25] Yet, off of this faith assumption, the evolutionist rests his entire theory of forward moving biological change.

In addition to these problems, the theory of evolution cannot account for morality either. Supposedly, the original language using life forms did not have moral notions in the previous stages in evolution, but then at some point in time this changed. What from natural selection would cause this leap in self-conscious beings to move from the realization of what is to what ought to be?[26] All attempted explanations from evolutionists are nothing more than arbitrary words. From a purely natural selection standpoint, ideas like eugenics[27] would make sense, but for some reason, most scientists consider it wrong. Why? This is yet one more inconsistency in their worldview.

Remember, the more the Christian allows the evolutionist to talk, the more rope the unbeliever grants for his own hanging. Evolutionists tend to explain their theory one piece at a time in order to hide its ridiculousness, but when the theory is stated in its broad and general terms, it sounds so ridiculous that no rational person can truly claim to believe it.

In a nutshell, their position is that there was once nothing but disorder all compressed into a tiny dot, and the universe then somehow exploded from that, creating an orderly realm of inorganic material. Then that inorganic material somehow came to life, bringing order from disorder, beginning as efficient cell division but then jumping to less efficient sexual reproduction, and then evolving into intelligent, moral beings. This is not a caricature, but instead this is their theory. The Christian has the right to ask why and how disorder became order from the principle of true randomness, and how the inorganic began to live despite the mathematical impossibility. Evolutionists cannot give a good answer. Their theory contradicts every pattern that has ever been observed in the actual scientific process. Life from non-life, disorder to order, cell division becoming sex, etc., have never been observed and ultimately are irrational when compared to the things that are

---

[25] Brown and Brown, *In the Beginning, 5.*

[26] Bahnsen, "Types of Worldviews." *Series Two.*

[27] Eugenics is the notion of improving the human species by only allowing reproduction for its members that have the genetic characteristics that are deemed desirable for evolutionary progress. Perhaps the most infamous eugenicists were the Nazis in the 1930s-1940s.

observed. Therefore, their position is riddled with inconsistency, arbitrariness, and the impossibility of meeting the preconditions of intelligibility.

Of course, the Christian still will be asked to deal with the fossil evidence. After all, evolutionists claim that the fossil record proves that evolution occurred. Furthermore, we have all looked in biology textbooks and have seen the drawings that demonstrate a progression of ape-like animals leading upward to modern man. Are not these drawings based on hard and factual fossil evidence? The answer is an emphatic no! To the contrary, the fossil record demonstrates that life appeared abruptly with systematic gaps between various kinds of creatures. Furthermore, there are literally hundreds of millions of fossils in museums all across the world, and yet not a single one of them is an actual missing link (intermediate life form) between two species. In terms of human origins from ape-like ancestors, this problem is even more prevalent. The pictures in textbooks are nothing more than artist conceptions, and they are not based on fact at all but instead on presuppositions.

Even unbelieving evolutionists sometimes admit their peril in terms of real evidence. Lord Zuckerman admitted in *Beyond the Ivory Tower* there are no definitive missing links between man and earlier species. He wrote that if man did evolve gradually from ape-like ancestors, then it occurred, "without leaving any fossil traces of the steps of the transformation."[28] There are evolutionists that disagree with his pessimistic view and attempt to see evidence of evolution in ape skulls, but the fact of the matter is that these are just interpretations offered by people who presuppose macroevolution, and as such, these ape-skulls do not constitute real evidence; especially, given the fact that many unbelieving and believing scientists disagree with the interpretations. Lord Zuckerman was absolutely insulting to the evolutionary interpretations of some of these bones, pointing out that they were just apes!

With the grim reality of the lack of fossil evidence, evolutionists have only two options. The first option is to deny reality and claim certain fossils to be missing links even if they are not. This is probably the more common route taken by staunch evolutionists. The second option is to come up with a different interpretation of how evolution happened so that it would fit with the current evidence. Of this second option, the late Stephen Jay Gould was the champion. He was a Harvard professor, and was perhaps the United States' premier paleontologist.

His answer to the lack of fossil evidence is a relatively recent theory called punctuated equilibrium. Rather than seeing life over long periods of time evolve into

---

[28] Solly Zuckerman, *Beyond the Ivory Tower* (New York: Taplinger Publishing Co., 1970), 64.

more complicated newer life forms, punctuated equilibrium is the idea that such changes occur in short durations of time. For extremely long periods there is no change, and then all of sudden in a short period of time there is rapid evolutionary change that is then followed by another long period of no major change. The purpose of this hypothesis is to explain why the fossil record indicates the abrupt appearance of life forms rather than the long, gradual changes macroevolution originally argued for. With such abrupt changes happening in a short period of time, there is not enough time for fossil remains to be formed. In short, the reason there is no evidence for macroevolution is because evolution occurred in such a way that it did not leave any evidence! This is blind faith.

Truly, Stephen Jay Gould's insistence on a punctuated equilibrium is one of the most telling truths against macroevolution. The evolutionists like Dawkins offer empty bravado as they insist the fossil evidence is entirely abundant, yet a pillar like Gould betrays their confidence by showing the evidence is so scant, a new theory must be advanced that explains why there are no missing links. Gould writes, "All paleontologists know that the fossil record contains precious little in the way of intermediate forms; transitions between major groups are characteristically abrupt."[29] In other words, the truth is that the fossil record really does not offer the evidence that evolutionists need to support their theory. Concerning what is found in the textbooks, Gould writes, "The evolutionary trees that adorn our textbooks have data only at the tips and nodes of their branches; the rest is inference … not the evidence of fossils."[30] Given the fact that men of the stature of Zuckerman and Gould dispute the fossil evidence of evolution, it should cause many to question the confidence, or perhaps arrogance, of men like Dawkins.

People like Gould should serve as a lesson that evidence will be interpreted in accordance with one's presuppositions. The evolutionists assume evolution is true, and so they interpret these problems in such a way to nullify their ramifications. Gould noticed that the fossil record shows life appeared abruptly and completely just as creationism demands, yet rather than arriving at that conclusion, he postulated that evolution occurred without leaving evidence. Someone like Dawkins ignores the lack of fossil record evidence, and due to his presuppositions, he insists against reality that there is evidence for all to view, even if such evidence is nonexistent. The extremes of Gould and Dawkins are why the debate cannot center on a comparison of evidence; instead, they must occur at the presuppositional level.

---

[29] Stephen Jay Gould, "The Return of Hopeful Monsters," *Natural History*, vol. 86, June-July 1977, 23.

[30] Stephen Jay Gould, "Evolution's Erratic Pace," *Natural History*, Vol. 5, May 1977, 14.

Evolutionists may claim that the Christian is equally guilty in interpreting the facts according to the Christian worldview and that should be an invited challenge. At that point, the Christian can then simply ask which of the two worldviews meets the necessary preconditions of intelligibility, and thus rip their position to pieces in same manner as was done to the atheist in the previous chapter. To reemphasize, the scientific evidence is meant to demonstrate the unscientific nature of the evolutionary worldview in order to lead the argument to where it belongs, namely, a philosophical comparison of worldviews. Once there, the theory of evolution has no chance of survival.

Thus, wrapping up the PIA offensive, the Christian should take this information and ask the evolutionist a question. Are we supposed to really believe that an irrational universe governed by random chaotic chance caused a step-by-step process of irrational changes that brought about an orderly, inorganic universe, then identical organic forms, followed by the diversified and then the intelligent, and finally, the moral forms of life that we now call humans? This question is designed to show how foolish this theory really is. Yet, this philosophy of evolution—for it is not qualified to be called a science—is veiled in academic and scientific vocabulary in order to make it sound reasonable.

Furthermore, the evolutionists confuse people by offering microevolution (change within the species) as evidence for macroevolution. Change within a species does not, and cannot, prove the change from one species to another. Talking about moths changing colors in London is entirely different than proving the moths transformed into a new life form altogether. Evidence for macroevolution would require an example of the latter, not the former, yet the former is what is often offered.

Doing such is either poor argumentation or deliberate deceit. Either way, it does not constitute a sound and valid argument. If every evolutionist in the world stopped giving dishonest slices of microevolution and instead told people the full theory in summary, rational people would probably not actually believe it.

At least Roger Lewin of *Science* magazine admitted that the offering of microevolution as evidence for macroevolution is fallacious when he wrote, "The central question of the Chicago conference was whether the mechanisms underlying microevolution can be extrapolated to explain the phenomena of macroevolution. At the risk of doing violence to the positions of some of the people at the meeting, the answer can be given as a clear, No."[31]

The bottom line is that macroevolution, as a theory, has no right to be regarded as a science. It is nothing more than an ancient philosophy repackaged with scientific

---

[31] Roger Lewin, "Evolution Theory under Fire," *Science*, Vol. 210, 21 November 1980, 883.

vocabulary to offer unbelievers an intelligent sounding excuse to reject God. The truth of the matter is that the theory cannot account for the preconditions of intelligibility. The transcendental argument absolutely kills macroevolution since the theory ultimately depends on a materialistic-atomistic presupposition governed by randomness. The uniformity of nature, the immaterial laws of logic, and the definite existence of moral absolutes land a crushing blow to the theory. Furthermore, the arbitrariness of using uniformitarian ideology on matters that provide an old earth, but then ignoring the ideology on tests that demonstrate a young earth is one more reason to reject the theory of macroevolution since it clearly is incoherent.

At numerous points, the theory assumes what it is supposed to prove (i.e., time and chance allow for macroevolution), and it cannot account for what it seeks to explain (how gradual evolution accounts for irreducibly complex organs such as the eye). Riddled with fallacies, macroevolution fails the coherence theory of truth; the fact that it does not comport with reality causes it to fail the correspondence theory of truth; its horrific consequences such as eugenics, mass murder, and justified abortion bring it to its knees under the pragmatic theory of truth; and logically, it can be dismissed rather easily under the semantic theory of truth.

So why do people believe it? Macroevolution is what post-Enlightenment secular man needs in order to try to understand and interact with the world without God. Even Darwin's Bulldog, Thomas Huxley, admitted this when he said, "When we come up against Moses telling us we can go no further by order of the Creator, we need to breakdown the sign and proceed on. The value of the theory of evolution is it enables us to dispute the biblical view of man's origins."[32] As a result, it is the first refuge of those who do not want to agree with what the Bible says, and therefore, they use it as an alternative view of our origins. It is just one more attempt of fallen man to suppress the truth in unrighteousness. The theory is not scientific since as a whole, it is not falsifiable. It cannot be tested in a lab, observed by scientists, and proven or disproven by the scientific method. As a result, it is just another metaphysical theory concerning origins. Christians would do well to remind evolutionists of this. Christians need to bring the theory back to the presuppositional level so that they can cast it straight into the abyss from which it came.

What About Theistic Evolution?

Due to the effects of compromise, many liberal "Christians" believe that macroevolution occurred. Sadly, it was many men that claimed Christ as their savior

---

[32] Bahnsen, "Types of Worldviews.", *Series Two*

that initially undermined the Bible with their uniformitarian geological theories in the 18th and 19th centuries. By the time Darwin published *Origin of the Species*, many in the church had already abandoned a literal interpretation of Genesis 1-11, and as Darwinism gained momentum among the scientific community, many theologians adopted the theory into their theology. Christian liberalism soon grew from this and has been a plague ever since.

In the 20th century, numerous scientific challenges to Darwin's theory led to a revitalization in a literal interpretation of the Bible. Young earth creationism grew among evangelicals and of course the battle has continued to rage on. Yet, there are still many who claim to believe in Christ, and yet they also believe that macroevolution occurred. Their position is called theistic evolution.

Most theistic evolutionists agree that a causeless random universe, spontaneous generation, and some parts of macroevolution are impossible. Instead, they argue that God created the matter of universe and directed it to form into galaxies, solar systems, and planets, but then He allowed them to naturally age for billions of years. Once the earth naturally developed an atmosphere and seas, God then stepped in and caused life to form in the prebiotic soup. He then stepped away and allowed it to evolve on its own. Natural evolution occurred, with occasional interventions by God. Finally, when the time for man came, God intervened and made humans far greater from other animals by giving them a soul. God's interventions are said to be a divinely orchestrated punctuated equilibrium.

A view like this really meshes well with liberal Christians, since in their mind it allows them to fit in with the views of modern scientists. They can claim to believe in most of the details outlined in typical biology textbooks, and yet they can also claim to believe in the parts of the Bible that pass humanity's judgments. Of course, this compromise does not make them tolerable in the eyes of atheists. If it was just a matter of believing in evolution, then they would be tolerated, but since at its heart it is a philosophical issue instead, the atheists cannot accept a universe that is not based on random chance and chaos. Quite honestly, theistic evolutionists often alienate themselves from both atheistic evolutionists and young earth creationists.

The question at hand then, is how does our apologetic deal with the theistic evolutionist? After all, their view removes the problem of the uniformity of nature, the laws of logic, and moral absolutes. Rather than the arbitrary and groundless punctuated equilibrium of Stephen Jay Gould, the theistic version calls for design. With that said, can the presuppositional arguments work against theistic evolution? The answer is a resounding yes.

Presuppositionalism argues not for any God, but the God of the Bible as revealed in the Bible.[33] Only the biblical God meets the preconditions of intelligibility and is non-contradictory in His attributes. That God revealed Himself in the scriptures, which are beyond contestation. The theistic evolutionist stands against God's direct statements, but instead sits in judgment over God's revelation using man's autonomy to declare what parts of the Bible are true and false. By claiming to believe in the biblical God, but then rejecting what the Bible says, they are guilty of inconsistency. Their basis for holding to that inconsistency is the finite and non-exhaustive knowledge of man, thus rendering them as arbitrary. Furthermore, they too assume uniformitarian principles even though there exists only a century's worth of records. Additionally, they ignore the measurements that hurt deep time such as the magnetic field, meteoric dust, sediment, etc. Both of these points also make them arbitrary.

Given that they agree to the unproven assumptions of the atheistic evolutionists, and yet ignore the indications that point to a young earth, it seems clear that their motive is to be accepted by the world. They did not arrive at their conclusions from their own inductive reasoning since doing so is impossible anyway, but instead it seems they are purposefully acceptant of atheistic theories. The atheists are right about one thing. If macroevolution could occur by natural processes, then God is not needed. Hence, theistic evolution serves them no purpose and deserves no secular respect.

Yet the greatest problem with theistic evolution is its theological consequences. If all humans did not originate from an originally immortal Adam and Eve, and if death did not enter the world through Adam, then the rest of the Bible is untrustworthy. Jesus declared Adam and Eve were literal people, and Paul declared that death entered the world through Adam. Without this, the entire theology of redemption crumbles, and there is no purpose to Christianity.

Since theistic evolution makes death natural, rather than a product of the curse, then Christ's death could not be substitutionary, but would also have been natural since He would have died anyway. With no substitution, the doctrine of justification disappears since it depends on double alien imputation[34] and vicarious penal

---

[33] Our theology informs our philosophy, rather than it being the other way around.

[34] Double alien imputation is the simple biblical doctrine found in verses like 2 Corinthians 5:21 where Christ has our sin, which is alien to Him, imputed to His account where He then paid its consequence in full. We, on the other hand, have His righteousness, which is alien to us, imputed to our account, therefore leading to our justification. Our sins are forgiven due to Christ's payment for them, and we are declared righteous, or justified, because we receive the credit for all of Christ's righteous deeds. This gift is received through faith.

substitutionary atonement.[35] Truly, theistic evolution is a mess that forces its adherents (if they are consistent) to see the world like every other worldview; sin is normal, but if a person tries harder (works-righteousness) then they are good people meeting divine standards. The entire book of Galatians demonstrates such a view to be anathema.

Theistic evolution is an unacceptable compromise that is unnecessary. Christians must have a presuppositional commitment to the truth of the scriptures, and rest on this commitment since the Christian worldview, as described in the Bible, is the only worldview that meets the preconditions of intelligibility. A constant focus on the scriptures along with an application of TAG to all aspects of reality demonstrates the biblical worldview to be true beyond contestation, and it renders all opposing viewpoints as arbitrary and inconsistent nonsense. Furthermore, it assures the Christian that any "new" discovery that supposedly undermines Christianity is nothing more than an anti-Christian interpretation of the discovery based upon faulty anti-Christian presuppositions. Christians should honor God and sanctify Christ in their hearts, since doing so would guard them from unbiblical compromises with the world.

The Political Controversy

Undoubtedly, the evolutionary debate provided the largest cultural opposition to Christianity in the 20th century. The nature of the battle in the courtrooms began with the Scopes Trial[36] in 1925 and has continued with the evolutionary worldview continually winning the right to teach evolution in nearly every American State, while at the same time prohibiting the teaching of creationism. The secular university system, Hollywood, public education, and many politicians jeer at creationism and speak and write pejoratively against it. Innumerable times Christians hear the argument that the Bible is untrustworthy because scientists have proven evolutionary origins.

With success in the courts and the media, and with a monopoly in the public educational system, the evolutionists have been quite evangelistic in their efforts to convince people of their theory. With their control of the educational system, they prevent the introduction of arguments against their viewpoint. In fact, many atheists

---

[35] Vicarious penal substitutionary atonement simply means that Christ vicariously (for us) suffered the penal or legal consequences for our sin in our place (substitution), thereby removing our sin from God's record permanently (atonement).

[36] Even though the Christian side won the Scopes court case, overall the trial has been seen as an ideological victory for the evolutionist.

call themselves "free thinkers," yet they absolutely seek to silence all opposition. Such tactics betray free thinking, but instead are reminiscent of the tactics of the Nazis in 1930s Germany, or the Red Bolsheviks of the USSR. Democracy is built upon the open exchange of ideas and debate; dictatorship is built upon using media and education to support only one view.

Often Christians are accused of being narrow-minded. Yet, many Christian schools teach both sides of the issue. Do the public schools? The Christian schools have no fear in this because the truth should never have any fear of alternative viewpoints. If a view is false, it is false. It does not matter how clever the debater is since the critical mind can detect his folly. It is somewhat ironic that the mentality of fundamentalist Christians during the Scopes Trial is now that of atheistic evolutionists today. In the 1920s, the fundamentalists wanted to prevent evolution from being taught in the schools, perhaps from misguided fear. Yet, today the evolutionists will fight to the bitter end to keep intelligent design out of their institutions. One only needs to watch Ben Stein's documentary *Expelled* to see this in action.

The tenacity of the courts, the ACLU, and many universities in their attempts to silence those who advocate intelligent design demonstrates the controversy to be far more than a difference of opinion. Instead, there is something spiritual at work here. Many universities tolerate religions like Islam, and even have students preferably read great pieces of Islamic literature. Yet, when it comes to Christianity, they mock it. Universities typically support the feminist movement and homosexual rights, and yet in Islamic countries women are executed for being raped, and homosexuals are murdered for their lifestyle. Where is the outcry against Islam? Where are the liberal giants on issues like this?

The answer is simple. Wide is the path that leads to destruction, but the path that leads to salvation is only as wide as the Savior's arms stretched upon the cross! The feminists may have an opposite view from the Muslims, but they both work together to undermine Christianity because ultimately they are on the same side. The political controversy over evolution is just another example of this dichotomy of truth and error. All types of error are permitted and promoted, but the only view that is absolutely forbidden is the Christian one. This certainly should make people wonder.

Argument from Truth and Argument from Folly

Just as with atheism, the Proverbs 26:4-5 strategy works well with evolution, or any other worldview for that matter. This chapter provided only a handful of the many arguments against evolution to demonstrate its fall due to the PIA technique.

However, reading books from Answers in Genesis, the Creation Research Institute, and many other organizations dedicated to the same purpose, allows for the Christian to fill his arsenal against macroevolution. The information from these sources is most excellent, as long as they are used in a manner that glorifies God.

In terms of engaging in dialogue or debate, there are many scenarios in which the subject can come up. When the subject does come up, the Christian can start with the argument from truth or folly. I most likely would start with the argument from folly, and would immediately begin to demonstrate through the PIA technique why macroevolution would make intelligibility impossible. Given that many evolutionists are atheists, I would probably combine some of the arguments from this and the previous chapter.

A recent example from my own life occurred when a relative claimed to be starting a diet called the Paleolithic diet (nicknamed the paleo diet) that was supposedly eaten by hominids from 2.5 million years ago until about 10,000 years ago. In other words, it is the caveman's diet. It assumes that men in this era mainly ate fish, grass-fed meats, certain vegetables, fruit, nuts, and roots, but they did not eat dairy, grains, salt, or anything processed. Since this allegedly occurred prior to agriculture, they were limited in what was available to them. This relates to evolution because this diet's proponents claim that we inherited our genetic adaptation to food from these cavemen (as they adapted it from earlier hominids), and as a result many food items common today cause us harm since we are not genetically adapted to them.

Of course, this is just one more fad diet that is popular because it has passed the test of pragmatism. Sedentary people lose weight and feel healthier when they eat lean meats and stay away from simple carbohydrates. Once a scientific sounding explanation is added to the diet, it then sells like oil, regardless of the fact that no one knows what cavemen ate since cavemen did not leave any written records! Instead, a person only needs to assume that this is the way it was, use the right vocabulary in explaining the idea, and then the masses buy into it.

Well, when my relative mentioned this diet, I objected to its name, and asked how he could know whether or not there even was a Paleolithic man, and second how he could know what he ate. Of course, he looked puzzled and gazed condescendingly at his religiously fanatical kin. I then continued by asking what kind of evidence is necessary to prove that a Paleolithic group of humans moved from place to place eating these foods. After all, they did not build cities, and so they left no evidence there. They did not plant fields and thus stay put in one place. There was no written language to leave a concrete record. And since they were constantly on the move, we would not even expect to find footprints indicating their travels due to rain-fed erosion. So we are left in a position like Gould's punctuated equilibrium. In other words, my relative would be forced to say, "Paleolithic men lived in such a way that left no evidence that there ever really were Paleolithic men!" Fortunately, he saw my point and conceded temporarily.

This example is just one more illustration of the deceptiveness of evolutionary thought. It is not built upon arguments with lines of true evidence, but instead it is a technical explanation riddled with unproven assumptions, but due to the impressive sound of it, people assume it rests on solid evidence. Had my relative pushed the issue further, we could have dived into the entire theory of macroevolution. My point, however, is that there are many scenarios in which the argument over evolution will come up.

I knew a woman who took a biology class at a local junior college, and when her instructor started his "ponds to people" speech, she kept asking him how he knew this, and demanded that he prove it. He became frustrated and simply asserted his educational credentials (which was an MA or MS degree). This freshman in college frustrated the evolutionary instructor simply by demanding proof. Scenarios like this occur frequently. The Christian must always be ready to demonstrate the folly of macroevolution, and at the same time advance the Christian worldview.

Conclusion

In summation, the theory of evolution is a failed worldview that is both arbitrary and inconsistent. It is completely arbitrary since there is no real evidence that supports it. Microevolution is falsely touted as evidence for macroevolution, the science of probability proves the impossibility of spontaneous generation, the fossil record lacks the alleged missing links, and the theory is inadequate to account for the complex nature of life on earth. Therefore, the theory is arbitrary and without justification. Additionally, the theory is inconsistent as evolutionists themselves cannot agree on how it occurs, or how to interpret the fossil record. Furthermore, chaos to order or randomness to orderliness is opposed to actual verifiable scientific laws.[37] Thus, it is inconsistent with other fields of science. It can be assumed that most evolutionists are opposed to murder, thievery, adultery (especially if they are

---

[37] The Second Law of Thermodynamics is a classic example of this. Of course, evolutionists will offer explanations such as multiple universes, but truly this is not falsifiable and amounts to more arbitrariness. The Christian must remember that an explanation is not the same as evidence. Crafty atheists can offer really scientific sounding explanations, but epistemological questions (how do you know?) prove them to be arbitrary.

victim), and a host of other vices, but from a standpoint of natural selection these things are not wrong, but instead favor the stronger members of the species. This demonstrates more inconsistency since people cannot live according to the principles of the evolutionary worldview.

Evolution also fails to meet the preconditions of intelligibility. As a philosophy, it depends upon impersonal chance and randomness to produce a universe with life in it. Yet, operational science depends on the uniformity of nature, predication, logic, and dependability. Randomness cannot create uniformity and predictability, but instead should only lead to the opposite. Furthermore, observation has only demonstrated personal beings creating impersonal objects such as a factory worker producing a tractor, and never has the opposite been observed such as a tractor producing a factory worker. Living in a universe with both personal and impersonal things, and never observing the personal coming from the impersonal, but only observing the opposite, runs counter to everything the theory of evolution argues. Natural selection cannot account for morals, yet all humans live by them. The more a person ponders about what actually exists in the world, the clearer it becomes that evolution did not and could not create what we see.

Finally, the consequences of the theory of evolution have been too much to bear: racism, eugenics, abortion, communist regimes, Nazi ethnic policies, the sexual revolution, degradation of morals, and the list could go on and on. The theory of evolution is an unscientific philosophy that is plagued by arbitrariness, inconsistency, and malicious consequences. Truly, it is not a reasonable alternative to the Christian worldview, but instead it is nothing more than a weak theory readily accepted by those who suppress the truth in unrighteousness.

Chapter Eight

The Problem of Evil

Introduction

Perhaps the most common objection to the existence of the biblical God is the problem of evil. From the standpoint of unbelievers, this is often their ultimate attack. They believe it to be the unanswerable dilemma of the Christian worldview. If God is good, then why would He allow evil if He possessed the omnipotence to stop it? On the surface this appears to be an example of incoherence in our worldview. Thus, how is the Christian to respond?

For many Christians, the problem of evil is the argument most feared. It is my hope that by the end of this chapter, the fear will be entirely gone. Continuing with the martial arts analogy, the problem of evil at first glance appears to be an athletically fit and professional trained opponent. Yet, on further analysis, it turns out to be a poster boy with no skill, weak knees, and a glass jaw. One good PIA and its over!

Ultimately, the problem of evil is summed up in Job 40:8. God asked Job, "Would you really challenge My justice? Would you declare Me guilty to justify yourself?"[1] Fallen man will do anything to justify himself, and the problem of evil represents his most blasphemous attempt. To declare his own righteousness and autonomy, he declares God to be guilty, and then uses that as a basis to deny His existence. Truly, it is not an intellectual problem, but instead it can be reduced down to the fallen, rebellious heart.

In order to strengthen our understanding and answer to this problem, a number of issues will be addressed in this chapter. First, a quick definition and analysis of the typical responses offered by Christians will be given, along with an explanation as to why they all fail. Second, a somewhat lengthy discussion concerning the problem of

---

[1] Holman Bible Editorial Staff, ed., *HCSB Study Bible, Brown/Tan Duotone Simulated Leather* (Holman Bible Publishers, 2010), 872.

evil is necessary in order to understand at the core what the problem reduces down to. After that discussion is complete, the PIA method can be applied to the problem to show the Christian that there truly is nothing to fear from this argument. When it is all said and done, it will indeed be clear that the argument as advanced by unbelievers is just a poster boy with no skill, weak knees, and a glass jaw.

Faulty Answers to the Problem of Evil

Due to the fact that the problem of evil is such a prevalent thorn in the side of most Christian apologists, many different philosophical explanations have been advanced against it. Holding true to the unbiblical forms of apologetics, these defenses do not first seek what the Bible says on the issue, but instead their first recourse is to turn to human philosophy and ethical theories to answer the problem. When they do so, they imitate unbelieving epistemology, thus rendering their solutions to the problem of evil as groundless.

The Lord knows that I have been guilty of this. There would be times that I would offer a defense for the problem of evil feeling as though I did God a great service, but upon later reflection, I realized the defense was weak. Whether it was the free-will defense or the unreality of evil (these were my two favorite), a child repeatedly asking "why" or "how do you know" could have demonstrated the untenable nature of these arguments. Due to my own experience, I anticipate that my readers also have used arguments like these. Therefore, before giving a proper and biblical answer to the problem of evil, it would be beneficial to quickly discuss the commonly used philosophical defenses. John Frame did an excellent job of introducing and evaluating these defenses;[2] therefore I will follow his lead in the following presentation.

The first unbiblical and untenable defense is the *unreality of evil defense*. The manner in which this defense is typically offered is as follows. Since everything God made is good, evil then must be in a category of non-being. Thus, evil in and of itself is not a real entity, but instead it is the privation of the real entity of goodness. Apologists often appeal to cold and heat as an analogy. They claim that cold is not truly a real thing, but instead it is a word that merely represents the absence of a real thing, namely, heat. Applying this to evil, the apologists claim that evil is merely the absence of good. Thus, if God tells us to do a good thing such as love our neighbor, then adultery with our neighbor's wife is the absence of that good, since it is unloving to steal intimacy with another man's wife.

---

[2] John M. Frame, *Apologetics to the Glory of God: An Introduction* (P & R Publishing, 1994), 155–170.

The problems with this defense are manifold. First, it must be noted that this is an attempt absolve God from the responsibility of the existence of evil. If evil does not really exist as a true thing, then supposedly God's responsibility disappears. The first problem with this is that it does not take into account scripture. In scripture, evil is a real thing that God Himself labels of certain actions.[3] A second problem with this defense is that it does absolutely nothing for the person who suffers. What difference does it make if evil is only a privation of good? A person who saw their entire family murdered is not going to feel any less indignant toward the concept of God's goodness if it turned out that evil was not real. The pain is real, thus leading one to conclude that the evil is real as well. The third problem is that God never defends Himself in this manner, and who are we to presume upon God? God had His chance to use this defense on Job, but nothing even remotely like this was found in God's discourse with the suffering man. Thus, the *unreality of evil defense* should not be appealed too as an answer to the problem of evil. It is unbiblical, it ultimately boils down to semantics, and it offers the suffering human no comfort or answer that would point them towards faith in God.

The next unbiblical solution is the *divine weakness defense* defended by process theologians, or open theists. The idea behind this "solution" is to deny that God possesses omniscience and omnipotence, therefore absolving Him of responsibility for the existence evil since He lacks the power to stop it. Those who hold this view are so devoted to the idea of human freedom, that they deny the freedom of God in order to permit or allow evil. Therefore, God does all that He can to stop evil, but since He does not know the future, He lacks the power to prevent evil from happening.

Besides being blasphemous, this defense against the problem of evil fails on the same grounds as the last one. First, the scriptures clearly disagree with this view of God.[4] Their philosophical commitment to total human freedom causes them to

---

[3] Genesis 2:17 has God tell Adam not to eat from the tree of the knowledge of good and evil. Before evil even entered the world, God already contrasted it from good. Thus, God treats evil as a real thing. In Genesis 6:5, God saw that man's heart was focused on evil all of the time. Once again, God treats evil as a real entity. In 2 Samuel 11:27, God calls David's actions concerning Bathsheba and Uriah as evil. In fact, in the ESV, the English word "evil" appears 520 times. It would seem that those who appeal to the "unreality of evil defense" did not bother to consult the Scriptures. This is the chief problem, thus guaranteeing the inadequacy of this defense.

[4] Psalm 139:9-12 and Jeremiah 23:23-24 demonstrate God's omnipresence. Psalm 90:2 and Jude 1:25 show that God is unlimited by time, which relates both to omnipresence and omniscience. Psalm 147:5 clearly proclaims that God's understanding (or knowledge) has no limits (thus it is not limited by time). There are literally dozens of verses that demonstrate God possesses the omni-characteristics and sovereignty.

overlook clear scriptural teachings. Second, what value is their defense to anyone? How is it a solution to the problem of evil to say that God has no ability to stop it? It would mean that evil has no solution since God is powerless to stop it. What is the point of prayer to a God that is not omnipotent? Finally, philosophically, this position creates a god that fails to meet the scriptural description of God: an absolute personality that is distinct from creation, and a God that is sovereign and triune. This God is the necessary precondition of intelligibility. The god of open theism cannot provide the transcendental requirements of intelligibility.

Another defense to the problem of evil is the *best possible world defense*. On the surface, this defense seems fairly pleasing to Christian sensibilities. It argues that this is the best possible world God could have created after He considered all of the logical possibilities. The best possible world required the existence of evil. For example, unless there is suffering (an example of evil) how could there be pity and compassion (examples of good). Thus, evil is necessary for the world in order to produce the optimal level of good, which was ultimately displayed in the salvation of sinners by God.

Although there are aspects of this defense that have merit, ultimately it is not derived from scripture. God did not offer this explanation for the existence of evil. Instead, God's response to Job was to show him that if mortal man cannot understand the complexities of creation, how can he ever hope to understand the even greater complexities of how our good God works all things (including evil) for the good of those called according to His purpose (Romans 8:28). We should not presume to offer an explanation that compromises what God indeed has said. Of course, it is true that God does use evil to bring about good, and thus there is some merit to this idea. However, it is wrong to presume that God could not have made a better world without evil. Prior to the Fall, the world was created good with no evil, and to say that evil is necessary for the world to be even better forces God to depend upon humans to meet that end. God does not need anything from man.[5] Also, in the end state, God will create a new heavens and a new earth that will last for all eternity, and yet there will be no evil in it.

Thus, evil is not necessary for an optimal level of good and the scriptures do not support the *best possible world defense*. Christians should consult the scriptures first rather than immediately appealing to philosophical explanations. God's very existence as the ultimate standard of perfection and goodness proves that evil is not necessary to create a more complete good. Otherwise, how could God, having no evil in Him, be the ultimate standard of goodness? When we consider that point, it is

---

[5] Acts 17:25.

clear that this defense is also weak philosophically. Does God use evil events and work them for good? Yes, but that does not support this particular defense. It simply shows that God is sovereign over everything, including the evil that exists in the universe.

The most prevalent defense against the problem of evil is that of the *free-will defense*. This particular position holds that evil came about by the rational free-will decision of creatures such as Satan, demons, Adam, and all humans. Since the choice was not foreordained, God is thought to be absolved of responsibility for the existence of evil. Often, the Arminian philosophers that champion this view offer the cliché, "Love demands a choice," as an argument in favor of this position.

How well does the *free-will defense* hold up? On one hand, the scriptures do teach that man possesses freedom, but the question is to what extent are we free? Adam was free to choose between good and evil prior to the Fall, but we as his fallen descendents have no such freedom. Instead, the scriptures affirm again and again that unregenerate humans, spiritually speaking, can only perform spiritual evil.[6] Regenerate humans have the original freedom restored, and even greater freedom through the indwelling of the Holy Spirit. We also have the scriptures thus enabling us to put to death the deeds of the flesh.[7] However, unregenerate man cannot even come to God unless he is effectually drawn and called by God.[8] So we must conclude that scripturally speaking, there is not a truly free-will. Humans possess a will that is both limited by their finitude[9] and nature.[10] God's will is far freer than ours, and He can and does impose His will on the inferior wills of man; just ask Jonah. Yet, man has a will and is responsible for the choices he makes, as many scriptures demonstrate.

The correct defense against the problem of evil must start with scripture. If the Christian apologist were to look at scripture first, rather than immediately offering philosophical speculations, then he would not offer the free-will defense. There are a number of reasons for this. First, the position assumes that God does not foreordain the willful actions of volitional creatures. Yet, Genesis 50:20, 2 Samuel 24:1, Proverbs 16:9, Acts 2:23, and a prodigious number of other passages clearly teach that God ordains specific evil actions of men, yet He still holds them responsible.

---

[6] Genesis 6:5; 8:21, Isaiah 64:6, Romans 3:10.

[7] Romans 6:6-18 and Ephesians 4:17-32.

[8] John 6:44,65 and Romans 8:29-30.

[9] I cannot cause the moon to explode by willing it in my mind, thus demonstrating my will's limit by finitude.

[10] Sinful man cannot choose to do good because his nature is that of sin due to the Fall. The nature must be changed first through regeneration (i.e. John 3:3-8).

The scriptural position is that of compatiblism, where volitional creatures make choices, but it works in a compatible way with God's decreed sovereign decisions. The scriptures do not tell us exactly how this works, but this truth is affirmed many times within the Bible. With that said, the *free-will defense* loses its primary assumption, namely, that the choices of volitional creatures are uncontrolled and are not foreordained by God. Clearly the scriptures say otherwise.

Second, in the passages that address the problem of evil—Book of Job, Psalm 37, Psalm 73, and Romans 9—not a single one of them offers anything resembling the free-will defense. To the contrary, they offer statements of God's sovereignty! Clearly, then, the proponents of the free-will defense are not basing their answer on scripture, but instead on an unbiblical devotion to a non-existent free-will. The cliché, "Love demands a choice," is a line found nowhere in the pages of the Bible. Instead, it is philosophically assumed due to a commitment to the idea that man possesses uncontrolled freedom. Christians would do well to judge their philosophy by scripture rather than judging and interpreting the scripture by their philosophy.

The simple truth is that love does not demand a choice. Once the eternal state begins, and all saints live with God in the new heavens and earth, there will be no more sin, hence no more choice to rebel. By our nature, we will only be able to do what is good. Is that unloving of God? Furthermore, the cliché can be reduced to absurdity when applied to another scenario. If a rebellious child is playing near the road, and then wanders out into the street as a diesel truck is heading his way, what should the father do? Should the father merely proclaim to the child, "Get out of the road now!" and then allow the child the freedom to choose to stay behind? No, we would call that parent negligent, and unloving. Given that certain death awaits the rebellious child, the parent would run out to the street and snatch the kid out of the road against his will. That is love! Love does not demand a choice, but instead it demands that the one who loves does what is best for the one who is loved.

Of course, this invites the charge that God then loves some more than others, and this is a welcome charge because it agrees with scripture. God has a special love for the elect, and a common love for the non-elect. Some may object to God's right to do this, but humans do the same. Does not a man love his wife and children more than he loves his neighbor's wife and children? Why are humans allowed to have such freedom over their love, but God cannot? Who has the right to limit God? Deuteronomy 7:7-8 teaches that God chose Israel out of all of the nations of the world because He loved them. It had nothing to do with their worthiness at all, but instead He had a special love for them that He did not have for the other nations, otherwise He would not have given Israel a special place. Concerning true

Christians, Ephesians 1:4-5 says, "In love he predestined us for adoption as sons through Jesus Christ, according to the purpose of his will." Not all people are adopted sons of God, but only those who believe,[11] yet those who believe were predestined for divine adoption. So clearly this effectual love that predestined people to adoption was not given to all humans, otherwise all humans would be saved. Thus, God has a special love for His elect that leads to their salvation, but towards the rest of humanity He has a providential love where He provides rain and harvest,[12] and the opportunity to repent even if they refuse.

Romans 9:13-23 is perhaps the textus classica concerning this:

> As it is written, "Jacob I loved, but Esau I hated." What shall we say then? Is there injustice on God's part? By no means! For he says to Moses, "I will have mercy on whom I have mercy, and I will have compassion on whom I have compassion." So then it depends not on human will or exertion, but on God, who has mercy. For the Scripture says to Pharaoh, "For this very purpose I have raised you up, that I might show my power in you, and that my name might be proclaimed in all the earth." So then he has mercy on whomever he wills, and he hardens whomever he wills. You will say to me then, "Why does he still find fault? For who can resist his will?" But who are you, O man, to answer back to God? Will what is molded say to its molder, "Why have you made me like this?" Has the potter no right over the clay, to make out of the same lump one vessel for honorable use and another for dishonorable use? What if God, desiring to show his wrath and to make known his power, has endured with much patience vessels of wrath prepared for destruction, in order to make known the riches of his glory for vessels of mercy, which he has prepared beforehand for glory.

In verse 13, Paul quotes Malachi 1:2-3 demonstrating that God does not love all people the same, but instead in the case of the twins Jacob and Esau, God loved one and yet rejected the other. Yet, anticipating that someone may accuse God of being unjust, Paul quotes what God said to Moses, namely, that He would have mercy and compassion on those He chooses. Notice also that Paul does not try to advance a philosophical argument to defend God, but instead he simply appeals to scripture. Moving then to verse 16, Paul makes it clear that God's love, mercy, and compassion do not depend on "human will or exertion," but upon God Himself. Concerning the evil that happened to Israel through Pharaoh and the subsequent

---

[11] John 1:12-13
[12] Acts 14:17.

judgment of Egypt, God said in Exodus 9:16 that He caused all of this to happen so that He could make His power known in all the earth. This sounds like a sovereign God with certain control and foreordination over the will of man.

Paul ends the argument by concluding that in God's sovereignty, "he has mercy on whomever he wills, and hardens whomever he wills." Expecting another objection, Paul answers one last time proclaiming that as creatures we have no right to question God and His actions. He is the judge and creator, but we are just finite creatures in no position to put Him on trial with our limited reasoning. Ultimately, God uses evil to "show his wrath and make known his power" concerning those who are doomed due to their sin, and He also uses it to "make known the riches of his glory for vessels of mercy … prepared beforehand for glory."

Truly, there is nothing in Romans 9, or anywhere else in scripture, that supports the free-will defense. Humans have a will, and they freely make choices, but above it God is sovereign and has declared the end from the beginning,[13] demonstrating ultimate control even over the evil that exists in the world. Even more puzzling is that God causes it to work for the good of those who love Him and are called according to His purpose.[14]

There is one more consideration in this that must be addressed. Most who hold to the free-will defense believe God to be omniscient. If God has perfect knowledge of what will occur, then it means that His knowledge can never be incorrect. So if God knows all of the free-will decisions that all men would make, why would He still create those that He knew would be condemned? Why would He allow a murderer to be born if He knew in advance that the person would commit murder? That is no different than a judge letting a pedophile go free, knowing that the pervert will molest more children. Would we expect that judge to justify this by declaring, "Love demands a choice?" The truth be told, most fallen humans would hold that judge just as accountable as the pedophile. Are the *free-will* proponents so naïve that they think unbelievers would not consider the same of God? So no matter how the Arminian apologists attempt to rid themselves of this dilemma, they cannot absolve God of responsibility for the problem of evil unless they deny His omniscience.[15] No matter how we look at the issue, the problem of evil cannot be answered according to the free-will defense.

---

[13] Isaiah 46:10

[14] Romans 8:28.

[15] This exactly what the open theists do. Yet, their solution is no better since they offer a non-biblical God that cannot meet the preconditions of intelligibility.

C.S. Lewis promoted a different type of answer for the problem of evil, known as the *stable-environment defense*.[16] In this simple defense, it is argued that man needs a stable environment (i.e., a uniformity of nature) to live and function, but the existence of such an environment necessarily allows for the possibility of evil. For example, gravity must exist, otherwise we would fly off the earth and suffocate in space, but gravity also opens up the possibility that a person can fall when climbing a mountain, and thus die.

This defense brings the Christian apologist no closer to a biblical answer since it too fails the test of scripture. In Genesis 2, God created Adam in a perfectly stable world, and there was no evil or pain. Thus, a stable environment only can cause evil in a world where death already exists. The fact that there was a stable world prior to the Fall, and the fact that there will be a stable world on the new earth is enough reason to reject this defense. Also, this defense does nothing to explain how a stable environment produces the evils found in the human heart. How did it cause man to volitionally rebel against God? Although some evils may be traced to a stable environment, certainly this cannot be said of all. John Frame rightly concluded that this defense allows men to blame evil on creation itself rather than on their own wicked hearts.[17] Thus, the *stable-environment defense* cannot adequately answer the problem of evil.

Many Reformed theologians appeal to the *indirect cause defense* as an answer to the problem of evil. For example, if I was bowling and sadly ended up with a split-eight, I would have to hit one pin in such a way that makes it fly across the lane into the other pin. If it worked, then I would be the ultimate cause of both pins falling, but I would be the direct cause of the first pin, and only the indirect cause of the second pin. In the scriptures, God's relationship to evil is indirect as He never commits evil Himself. The serpent tempted Eve, not God, but God is the one who placed the forbidden tree in the middle of the garden and created Eve with the volitional capability to rebel against Him. Since God is not the direct cause of the temptation, He is absolved of responsibility, whereas the serpent was the guilty party since he directly provided the temptation. However, God is still the indirect or ultimate cause of it. From this standpoint, proponents of this view believe that only if God were the proximate cause could He be responsible for evil.

On the surface, this response is better than some of the other ones since it accurately assesses the scriptures as they speak of God's relationship to sin. However, it ultimately does not relieve God of responsibility. After all, when Julius

---

[16] Frame, *Apologetics to the Glory of God*, 164.
[17] Ibid., 165.

and Ethel Rosenberg passed on secret nuclear information to the Soviet Union in the 1940s, they were not the ones who then created and detonated an atomic bomb. Yet, they were the indirect cause of Joseph Stalin getting his hands on such a destructive weapon, and as a result they were found guilty of espionage and executed. Likewise, Hitler probably never killed a single Jew himself, but instead he ordered Heinrich Himmler to oversee the Final Solution. Yet, when we speak about the Holocaust, it is common to say Hitler killed six-million Jews.

The *indirect cause defense* by itself cannot answer the problem of evil, however, it can at least be stated that it is a true observation that God is never the proximate cause of sin. As James 1:13 teaches, God cannot and does not tempt anyone to sin. However, a greater answer is needed than this.

Some appeal to an *ex Lex defense*, which means God is outside of the law. In other words, He does not have to abide by the same laws that we do since He is divine and transcendent. There is some merit to this since it is true that the creator-creature distinction renders certain things appropriate for God (such as worship) that would be inappropriate for man to receive. Murder is wrong for men, then, because by God's sovereign determination, which is in accordance with His nature, He does not like to see one creature made in His image murder another. Yet, God is above humanity, and therefore as the sovereign judge He has the right to end life as He chooses. From this standpoint, evil exists in the world because God can both directly and indirectly cause it, and as the sovereign Lord this is appropriate for Him to do. Since scripture forbids human criticism of God's actions, there clearly is an element of truth to this defense.

Yet, there are problems with the *ex Lex defense* too. The law is said to reflect God's own character. In Leviticus 11:44, God commanded Israel to be holy since He is holy, and the manner in which they would show themselves as holy was by keeping His law. Therefore, the law must be a reflection of God's own holy character. This then means that God will act in accordance with the same standards of holiness that He prescribes for us, but there are obvious exceptions when it comes to matters in which His responsibilities differ from ours due to the creator-creature distinction. This is why there is some truth to this defense, but the claim that God is completely outside of His law fails the scriptural test since the law flows out from God's nature.

Looking back at all of these solutions to the problem of evil, there is one thing they all have in common. They all seek to answer the problem first philosophically, and second scripturally, if that at all. Furthermore, they all assume that an easily understandable answer exists. Yet, later in the chapter it will be argued that God never actually directly answers the question for us as to why evil exists. A truly biblical answer to the problem of evil is to address it the same way that everything else has been addressed thus far. What are the preconditions of the existence of evil, can unbelievers justifiably advance this argument without destroying their own position, and what should be the Christian's response? Before addressing this, however, a general discussion about the problem of evil is in order.

Discussion of the Problem of Evil and a Biblical Answer

The problem of evil is usually the most difficult problem that believers have to answer for. The suffering and evil that exist in the world seem to cry out against the existence of the biblical God since He is both omnipotent and benevolent. Often, the problem of evil is presented as a logical difficulty to the Christian worldview. Ultimately, every person's life has been touched by it through natural disasters, birth defects, diseases, tyranny, war, murder, poverty, and every other tragedy known to man. When unbelievers look at the laundry list of evil happenings, they believe there is good reason to doubt the existence of God, or at the least, the goodness of God. Why is there so much misery and why is it allocated in an apparently unjust fashion?[18]

Such questions are difficult to answer. When a person confronts the Christian with these problems, it is probably because they have personally been affected by some of the horrible happenings in this world. We must take into account the emotional and psychological state of our opponent and understand that they are probably angry over a tragedy or a set of tragedies.[19] The Christian cannot assume that he is merely going to refute the intellectual and philosophical aspect of the problem of evil, but instead he may be ministering to a person hurt by suffering. We must also remember, and even remind the unbeliever, that we too have been hurt by the problem of evil, lest we seem insensitive to a person's emotional pain.

Even Christians want to cry out to God with the question of why. We see Psalmists often make this cry, and ultimately even the Lord of Glory, Jesus Christ, shouted the question of why while he was suspended upon the cross. Jesus Christ, as God, knows all things, and yet even He could ask why He was forsaken by the Father. He knew why, but it did not make it any easier for Him to bear the greatest evil of man in conjunction with the righteous wrath of the Father all poured out upon

---

[18] Greg L. Bahnsen, *Always Ready: Directions for Defending the Faith*, ed. Robert R. Booth (Covenant Media Press, 1996), 164.

[19] Greg Bahnsen, "Types of Worldviews," *Defending the Christian Worldview Against All Opposition, Series Two.*

Him on the cross. If even the Son of God could ask the question of why, then we too are not in sin when we cry out to God.

As long as the Christian remembers these things, he will have the proper perspective when confronting the problem as unbelievers advance it against Christ. Thus, the problem of evil is not always brought up as an attempt by an arrogant unbeliever to logically make a fool out of a Christian,[20] but sometimes is advanced by a person in pain. With that said, this discussion is not an intellectual debating game, but instead we must insist on the reality and serious nature of evil. The Christian cannot downplay it, ignore it, or even try to make the ridiculous argument that evil does not exist. Evil is real, it is ugly, and so we need to take it seriously, especially since the unbeliever wants to condemn it.

Since the problem of evil is often brought up in college classes as a logical problem, it would be beneficial to answer the logical problem of evil first. Christians allegedly hold to a series of premises that when taken collectively are inconsistent. For example, believing that 1) God is all good; 2) God is all powerful; and 3) evil exists, are said to be in conflict. If God is all good, He would not want evil to exist, and if God is all powerful, then He could eliminate evil; therefore if God exists, He is either not all good or not all powerful. This is the logical problem of evil since there is apparently incoherence within the Christian worldview. This logical dilemma is actually pretty easy to answer. The Christian only needs to add a fourth premise: 4) God has a perfectly moral reason for allowing the evil that exists.[21] The logical problem is now solved since all the premises hang together coherently.

More importantly, when the unbeliever advances this argument, the Christian needs to evaluate the argument via the PIA technique, thereby finding arbitrariness, inconsistency, and the failure of non-Christian worldviews to meet the necessary preconditions of the existence of evil. The Christian has every right to ask the unbeliever, "For whom is evil logically the problem, me or you?" In other words, based on a worldview comparison, for whom does evil really pose the problem? A closer reflection reveals that the unbeliever cannot use the problem of evil against the Christian unless the unbeliever has the justification to assert that evil exists in the first place. If there is nothing that truly counts as evil, then there is no problem of evil that the Christian has to account for. Thus, the unbeliever's case depends upon the existence of evil as a real thing that can be evaluated. It also requires that some particular event in time and space qualifies as evil (such as the Holocaust). The atheistic unbeliever does not have a worldview that meets the preconditions for evil

---

[20] Though often it is.

[21] Bahnsen, *Always Ready*, 171–172.

to exist as a real thing in the first place. So their insistence upon it actually is self-defeating.

By what standard can the unbeliever determine what is good and evil? The unbeliever has only a few possibilities in meta-ethics. Perhaps they view good and evil as to whatever the majority of people approve of or disapprove of. Of course, this would make the declaration of things as good and evil as senseless. After all, by definition it could never be true that the majority participated in an evil deed since evil is defined as what the majority disapproves of. Thus, the Holocaust in Germany, racial segregation in the United States, and host of other injustices could not truly be seen as injustices. Truly, ethics does not reduce to statistics.[22] This fallacy is known as *ad populum* and is unacceptable in logic.[23]

Many people are quick to recognize the problems with such a view of good and evil, and so most people think of goodness as something that inherently receives their approval because it already is good, and evil inherently receives their disapproval because it already is evil. In this sense, good and evil are real things with understood properties, and therefore exist irrespective of the beliefs people have concerning them. In other words, the Holocaust was wrong because it possessed the properties of wrongness, and such properties did not change just because the majority of Nazi's were in favor of it. However, this view of good and evil could be reduced to relativism since it is possible to reduce good and evil down to individual opinion. In other words, not everyone will agree upon what the inherent properties of good and evil are. Often people disagree with each other in ethical judgments, especially if they reject the notion of objective moral truth that applies to all people in all circumstances. This would make concepts of good and evil nothing other than the arbitrary opinions of individual men, thus rendering the concepts as useless.

Others may argue that good is defined by the consequences that are brought about by an action or belief. For example, utilitarianism stresses that an action is good if it achieves a certain end, which in most cases is the greater happiness of the majority of people. Yet, this is also useless since it is impossible to rate and compare happiness in order to decide what things are good.[24] For example, a single action can bring happiness to some and misery to others. If you take a person that is disliked by a crowd and inflict pain upon that person, many who do not like the person may be happy by his pain, but he will not be happy. So how does a person weigh and

---

[22] Ibid., 168.

[23] This fallacy states that an opinion must be true because a majority of people believe it. For obvious reasons in history (i.e. Holocaust), this type of argument is patently false.

[24] Bahnsen, *Always Ready*, 169.

measure his great misery from the intense pain over against the small satisfaction of each person in the crowd? This cannot be quantified. How can one prove the added joy of the crowd is larger than the sum of his individual pain?

Truly, utilitarian ethical theories make it impossible to make moral judgments. Instead, people would be left to guess what would make the greatest number happiest since we cannot calculate the consequences and compare pains and pleasures. Thus, it is arbitrary. Yet, there is an even greater problem with utilitarianism. If something is good because it produces a particular end, you would have to know ahead of time what a good end is to be able to declare a particular end as good. This is begging the question. Rather than discovering what things are good by pragmatism, they arbitrarily assert what is good and then declare something to be good if it agrees with their arbitrary declaration. A good example to illustrate this is Libertarianism. Libertarianism is the belief that something is good if maximizes freedom for people, but to be able to declare this they would have to prove that freedom is what is good for people.[25] This is something that they cannot prove, thus making it arbitrary.

Of all of the meta-ethical views espoused by unbelieving philosophers, none of them are workable. This truth is important for the Christian because when unbelievers say that Christians have an inconsistency in their worldview due to the existence of evil, the Christian has the right to ask, "Can you prove that anything is evil?" On their worldview, they cannot prove any given action to be evil. Of course, if they asked if the Christian was denying that something like the Holocaust was evil, the Christian can say, "Yes it is evil, but I can say it is evil because the Christian worldview accounts for that judgment. The existence of a living creator that is holy, immutable, and sovereign declared such things to be evil since they are opposed to His perfect nature. The question is can you, the unbeliever, call anything evil?"

The unbeliever has to be able to justify with his worldview the ability to authoritatively call anything evil. If his justification is arbitrary or relative, then he loses the argument. If he claims good is what makes people happy, well in the case of child molestation, the molester was happy to commit the action. If there is no God, then there is no such thing as evil, and everyone can do what is right in his own eyes and no one should be able to condemn anyone else for any action. The irony is that if the unbeliever points to the existence of evil to disprove the existence of God, he is attempting to be rid of the necessary precondition for the existence of evil itself. It is a self-defeating argument.

This just goes to show that when the unbeliever claims people should be able to do what makes them happy, he does not really mean it. What the unbeliever really

---

[25] Bahnsen, "Types of Worldviews."

means is that people should be able to do whatever that particular unbeliever thinks is permissible, which amounts to arbitrariness. Without objective morality, we must ask, does the molester have the right to do what he wants to do? If not, why not, and if he does have the right to be happy, then why try him in court? Obviously, as Christians, we believe molestation is heinous and deserving of the maximum penalty, but we have a philosophical and justifiable right to declare it as evil. The unbeliever will claim that the molestation is wrong and deserving of the punishment, but he cannot account for it being evil or justify it as such.

By the unbeliever trying to argue against the Christian worldview by appealing to evil, he is taking evil seriously, but it is impossible to do so unless there are moral absolutes. Yet, moral absolutes are unintelligible except on the Christian worldview. So the unbeliever borrows from the believer's worldview to advance the objection against God in the first place. His very argument does not disprove God's existence, but instead it serves to prove it since it demonstrates that evil truly does exist, and all people intrinsically know and believe this, even if their lips say otherwise. The Christian is obligated to point this out to the unbeliever that tries to use the argument of evil against the Christian worldview.

At this point, the argument is not finished. After all, we still seem to have a paradox within the Christian worldview that must be resolved. Yes, adding the fourth premise that God has a morally good reason for the evil that exists does solve the logical problem as advanced in a syllogism, but people still want to know how we can add that fourth premise. The answer is found in the fact that all people reason from presuppositions. Christians presuppose that what God has revealed about Himself in scripture must be true. Since He has revealed that He is both all good and all powerful, but also that evil exists, then the Christian must conclude based upon his biblical presuppositions that there is a morally sufficient reason for the evil that exists.[26] This is perfectly logical within the framework of the Christian worldview. It is only when you reason from a different set of presuppositions that you may come to a different conclusion, but transcendental reasoning solves the problem when it clearly shows that the Christian presuppositions are the only ones that meet the preconditions of all intelligibility.

The unbeliever claims that the problem must be evaluated in a neutral fashion, but neutrality is a myth as shown in previous chapters. His claim to neutrality is not even itself a neutral claim, but instead it is a presupposition that neutrality is possible and that man can reason apart from presuppositions! It actually is self-defeating. If the Christian agreed to the unbeliever's rules of "neutrality," the Christian is weighing

---

[26] Bahnsen, *Always Ready*, 171–172.

God with anti-Christian presuppositions, and so of course it will make it seem as though there is an inconsistency! Yet, when the Christian reasons according to the Christian presuppositions, all inconsistency disappears, the logical syllogism is repaired by the added premise, and the Christian is leaning on the only worldview that makes logic intelligible in the first place. The unbeliever, has no such luxury, especially since his presupposition of neutrality is self-defeating and irrational.

The Christian would do well to realize that the real problem of evil is a psychological problem rather than a logical one. The existence of evil is only a true logical problem for unbelievers since they cannot account for its existence in the first place. Yet, evil does exist, and it causes a great amount of pain to just about everyone. Therefore, the true problem is psychological since people find it emotionally difficult to believe in and trust the goodness and power of God, when He does not give us the reason why evil things happen to us and others. Greg Bahnsen put it well when he said, "The unbeliever presents the problem with the underlying demand that if there is a morally sufficient reason, then I need to know what it is."[27]

Truly, both believers and unbelievers internally cry out for an answer, but God rarely provides an explanation to humans who question why the evil they personally experience occurs. Job is a perfect example of this. Being afflicted for reasons that he did not know or understand caused him to question God's goodness and to demand an answer from God. When God finally granted Job an audience, He did not answer Job's question, but instead He asked a series of questions meant to demonstrate to Job how little he as a human could actually comprehend. If Job could not understand basic matters about creation, then how could he be expected to comprehend the mysteries of God's will? Job repented of his bad attitude and realized his error.[28]

Man is in no position to judge God, and if He allowed us to place Him under our courts and place Him on trial, that would be a surrendering of His sovereignty. In the case of Jesus Christ, the second person of the Trinity did voluntarily allow Himself to be placed under the trial of man, and fallen man did exactly what was expected—found Him guilty and killed Him! Even if God gave the full answer to mankind in a way that was understandable, man would still reject God since it is his fallen nature to do so.

Ultimately, Deuteronomy 29:29 tells us that the things God has revealed to us belong to us, but the secrets that He has not revealed belong to Him alone. Even if God told us why evil things take place, and exactly how it works into His greater glory and our greater good, there is a strong likelihood that we would not understand

---

[27] Bahnsen, "Types of Worldviews."
[28] Job 42:1-6.

it. It is rather arrogant for any mortal human to demand that God answer to us. God says in Isaiah 55:8-9 that His ways and thoughts are not our ways and thoughts, and that His ways and thoughts are higher than ours. Perhaps God is doing things with the evil in our lives that are so entirely complicated that they are beyond our ability to comprehend. For the Christian, this is where true biblical faith comes into the picture. Faith is not a simple belief in the God of the Bible, but instead it is a surrendering trust to Him. It is an admission that as humans, we do not have the answers or the power to make the wrongs in this world right. It is a confession to God that despite the pain we may feel, we know He is working it for our good since He has promised such in Romans 8:28.[29] The psychological problem of evil, therefore, can only be solved by trusting God.

The unbeliever absolutely hates this idea. He wishes that God could be put on trial. If God was obligated to answer us concerning this problem, it would be akin to saying that God must tell us why bad things happen and then we, with our limited human judgment and wisdom, will independently judge whether or not God's reason is just. Philosophically, this is absurd. The idea of God not owing us and not being judged by our own rationality is absolutely intolerable for the unbeliever's pride. Such a person refuses to believe in a God that will not tell him why evil things happen. The unbeliever is upset that God will not allow him to sit as judge over Him to assess His answer. No amount of proof, evidence, logic, rationale, etc. that a Christian offers will ever be enough to satisfy the unbeliever's demand. Simply put, the unbeliever will not trust God unless God will subordinate Himself to the intellectual authority and moral evaluation of man. Thus, it all boils down to authority. The unbeliever thinks that he should be the judge of God rather than God being the judge of the unbeliever. Humans are the guilty party and God is the one we owe restitution to, yet the unbeliever demands that God trade places with the guilty and allow the guilty to judge Him. In grace, this is exactly what God did when 2,000 years ago He was born of virgin and was then tried and crucified three decades later. Man's quest for rebellion was not satisfied.

Whenever classical apologists, evidentialists, and cumulative case advocates appeal to a neutral testing of God and the Bible, they are giving in to the sinful and rebellious demands of fallen humanity, and in so doing they dishonor God. Their apologetic method is doomed to failure since they allow men to put God on trial and to judge Him according to their disagreeing and arbitrary opinions as to what is good

---

[29] It must be noted that God is not working "all things" for the good of unbelievers. This promise is only for believers. Ultimately, all things will work to curse those who are God's enemies.

and true. The only God-honoring and logical approach is to maintain that only God has the right to declare what is true and false, and good and evil. The Christian must demand that the unbeliever submit through saving faith by actually trusting God.

According to Genesis 15:6, Abraham believed God, and it was counted to Him as righteous. What did Abraham believe? He believed that God had the right to command his life and the power to do the humanly impossible—to grant an old man and his wife a son. Abraham could have questioned God's ability, or even His goodness since no child had yet been given, but instead he trusted God and was justified. After tearing down the false pretenses of the unbeliever's worldview, this call to faith and dependence upon God is perhaps the most difficult thing for an unbeliever to accept. In fact, only by the miracle of regeneration will the unbeliever change his mind.

This then brings us back to the fact that the problem of evil is psychological. It is not merely so due to the pain that evil causes in the lives of people, but ultimately it is a huge psychological example of a lack commitment and trust. In fact, the manner in which unbelievers struggle with the problem of evil and demand an answer from God is nothing more than a continuation of the sin of our first parents. Eve should have trusted God's Word, but she relied on her own independent reasoning. Humanly speaking, the consequences were not worth it. The very evil that unbelievers protest came into the world and ravaged it due to Adam and Eve thinking in a manner similar to how the nonbelievers think at this very moment. It all comes back down to authority. Should man trust God and what He says simply because He says so, thereby trusting that He has a sufficiently good reason for what He commands? Or should man evaluate God and what He says on the basis of his own "independent" intellectual and moral authority?[30] Eve chose the latter. Christians choose the former.

The final aspect of the problem of evil that must be addressed is that often unbelievers accuse God of being evil. This goes one step beyond claiming that the existence of evil is incoherent with the Christian worldview, but instead it accuses actions of God such as the Flood and the command of the Canaanite genocide to be evil. Thus, the Christian may hear the objection as follows: "How could a good God order the killing of the women and children of the Canaanites?" Too many Christians are stumbled by this because it is difficult to answer when appealing to unbelievers from a "neutral" approach. However, the presuppositionalist will deal with this question the same way he deals with anything. First, is the unbeliever even justified in asking the question? After it is made clear that he is unjustified in even asking the

---

[30] Bahnsen, *Always Ready*, 173–174.

question (not answering him according to his folly), the believer should then answer the question to show him how this problem is not a problem within the confines of the Christian worldview.

When the unbeliever advances the question, it must be pointed out to him that the question itself presupposes an absolute standard of justice that God is subject to and will be judged by. This is the very thing that the unbeliever's worldview cannot presuppose! How could there be absolute standards if God is not the one who stands behind the standards? How could these standards be objective and true if they are not reflective of God's very nature? Therefore, the unbeliever's question proves the inadequacy of his worldview yet again. He has no right to advance the question, nor does he have any ability to say it is logically inconsistent within the Christian worldview since the existence of logic also depends upon the Christian worldview.

With that said, the believer can then answer the question within the framework of the Christian worldview. The Canaanites were evil people who set their children on fire for the gods Molech and Chemosh, and they committed just about every detestable sin known to man. In addition to that, God knows the fallen condition of man, and so His command served two purposes. First, He was using the sword of Israel to execute judgment on a very wicked people. God, being sovereign and distinct from creation, has the absolute right to serve as judge, jury and executioner, and He may use whatever means He determines in His own will. Second, God was protecting Israel knowing that in their fallen nature they would copy the practices of the Canaanites. Since Israel failed to destroy them, this is exactly what happened as both the Bible and secular history have demonstrated widespread idolatry and polytheism in Israel prior to the exiles to Assyria and Babylon.

Concerning the babies and children, all people including babies are guilty before God. Psalm 51:5 teaches that even in the womb we were brought forth guilty with iniquity. Romans 5:12 says that death spread from the first man Adam because "all sinned." The "all sinned," is in the constative (summary) aorist active indicative tense,[31] thus demonstrating that the "all sinned" is something that we all did with

---

[31] A.T. Robertson, *Word Pictures in the New Testament*, Vol.V c1932, Vol.VI c1933 by Sunday School Board of the Southern Baptist Convention. (Oak Harbor: Logos Research Systems, 1997), Ro 5:12. The Greek grammar is to be understood as follows: The aorist tense conveys a completed action rather than a continuous action. The indicative mood simply indicates something, but when it is present with an aorist verb, it makes the aorist/completed action something that is past tense. The active voice indicates that those being spoken of are the ones that actively performed the verb. Given that this completed past action of "all sinned" is tied to Adam earlier in the verse, this must be understood as saying that when Adam sinned in the past, thus causing the Fall, all humanity actively sinned in this action as well. This is as clear a teaching

Adam when he sinned in the Garden. No one has to teach children to sin, but all are born with the propensity to sin, and are born guilty of Adam's sin. From that standpoint, God is perfectly just in ordering the death of any human, regardless of the age. It is never a question of justice when a guilty party receives their legal sentence. God in His perfect holiness and righteousness has declared the wage of sin to be death (Romans 6:23). Fallen man is in an epistemologically unjustified position to declare what is either just or unjust for God to do and therefore cannot call God's decree wrong.

Concerning the eternal salvation or damnation of the children executed by Israel, the Bible does not directly say. However, the Christian can be confident that since Deuteronomy 1:39 claims that small children do not yet know good and evil, and that Romans 2:14-15 claims the conscience (knowing good and evil) is what makes all people guilty of violating God's law, then the children probably were not held guilty by God for their sin. Additionally, Romans 5:13 says sin is not imputed where there is no law, and Romans 7:9 has Paul claim that he was alive (spiritually) prior to coming into contact with the law, but died upon contact. Putting these truths together, infants and children are guilty of sin, but God does not eternally impute such sin to their account until they come in contact with God's law, which, according to Romans 2:14-15, occurs when they develop the conscience, which teaches them the difference between good and evil. God, then, is completely just in eternally damning children, but in His mercy He chooses not to do so. However, God reserves the right to use human means or natural disasters to end the physical lives of both adults and children for judgment of sin. In such a case, I believe the infants, small children, and the mentally retarded will receive spiritual salvation since sin was not imputed eternally into their account. The blood of Christ will cover such people.

Answering objections against the Flood can be accomplished in the same manner as the Canaanite genocide was answered. God is the holy and righteous judge, and all men (regardless of age) were guilty of sin and depravity. Therefore, God judged the earth in His righteousness to set a precedent and example of a future judgment that will be even worse. Rebellious humans will ignore such a judgment by either claiming it never happened, or using it as a reason to question God's goodness. The end result is they doubt the future judgment to come, and therefore they do not repent. In contrast, those who are regenerated by God look to the past and see the holy and righteous judgment of God being justly poured out upon humanity, and

---

of original sin as is possible. Although there are different theories among evangelicals as to how each human has shared in Adam's sin, Paul's use of grammar clearly teaches that we did.

therefore they trust God's promise that since His nature is immutable the future judgment is inevitable. They choose to repent.

Another complaint that unbelievers advance against God is that billions of people will end up in Hell, and how can a loving God do such a thing? Or it is sometimes asked how God could send those who have never heard the gospel to Hell. First, the same problem applies for the unbeliever as with the previous case. Their question presupposes that there is some absolute objective standard of goodness that the doctrine of Hell defies. Their worldview cannot justify the existence of such a standard. Therefore, the Christian must demonstrate to them the futile and contradictory nature of their question. The truth of the matter is that God will not send anyone to Hell because they did not hear the gospel. Instead, He sends them to Hell because they have all sinned.

When people present the question in this way, they are really accusing God of arbitrariness since He is judging someone who "never had a chance" to repent. It needs to be pointed out that God sends people to Hell for violating His law that they know from within their hearts and the natural order as presented in Romans 1:18-32 and 2:12-15. Even if an unbeliever never heard the gospel, he still violated God's perfect and holy standard, and for God's attribute of justice to be true, He must punish those who sinned. Grace, then, is not an obligation that God owes anyone, but instead it is something that God gives freely to those He chooses. People should be thankful that He saves any since strict justice demands that He save none. Through the work of Jesus Christ on the cross, it allowed for God to be both the just and the justifier since the punishment of the saved was cast upon Jesus. Meanwhile, the righteousness of Jesus is imputed to the account of those who are saved.

God has the obligation to condemn sin wherever it may be, but He has the right if He so chooses to justify sinners since He Himself bore the penalty of sin. People miss the point because they do not take sin serious enough. If humans took it as serious as God declares it to be in His Word, and if they properly understood God's holiness, then Hell is not inconsistent, but rather it is totally consistent with a God who is both good and holy.

In conclusion, the problem of evil does not truly present an intellectual basis for unbelief in God. The logical problem is not truly a problem for the Christian, but instead is a problem for the non-Christian who cannot logically believe that evil is real. The unbeliever simply uses the problem of evil as a personal reason to not believe in the God of the Bible. Due to the fact that it is a psychological problem, it is not a justification for a lack of faith, but instead it is merely the expression of a lack of faith. Humanity is unable to epistemologically justify the belief in moral absolutes. Some claim they do not exist, until they are treated according to their own stated belief; at that point they seem to quickly believe in absolutes. The demand that God justify or prove everything to us is sinful and proves that humanity does not trust God and therefore places no faith in Him. Like our first parents, unbelievers try to be their own authority even though they have no grounds to do so, and in the end, they make their condemnation sure.

PIA and Argument from Truth and Folly

Given that the problem of evil is so often used by unbelievers as an argument against the existence of the biblical God, the Christian must be ready to provide a God-honoring answer. If one were to listen to a number of high profile debates between Christian apologists and atheists, they would notice just how frequently this objection comes up. Ever since the Enlightenment, this has been a favorite objection advanced by unbelieving intellectuals, and today even non-academic atheists are well-acquainted with this objection and use it quite often. With that said, it is important to utilize the PIA technique to take down this objection.

It is important to keep in mind what was written in the previous section of this chapter. Sometimes the problem is advanced in a snooty manner as an intellectual argument, and at other times it comes from a person crying out due to the psychological impact that suffering has personally had on them. The apologist needs to take this into consideration since it does affect how to answer, at least concerning tone. The snide intellectual simply needs to be shut down intellectually, but the hurting victim needs to see how the evil in the world proves God's existence and ultimately points us to Him for salvation.

In either case, all versions of the problem of evil require the same general strategy. The Christian should ask for the preconditions of intelligibility regarding the ability to declare anything as evil. For example, if a student in a junior college philosophy class says, "I reject the Bible because a loving God would never ask the Israelites to kill women and children," the Christian has the right to ask, "How do you know that it is wrong?" This is not meant to make light of death, but instead it is designed to force the atheist to justify the idea that killing women and children is wrong. The conversation might continue as follows:

Atheist: You don't think it is wrong to murder women and children?

Christian:	Sure I think it is wrong to murder, but I disagree with you that we are talking about murder here. But, I do not want to move to that point right now. I want to know how you, the atheist, know that murdering women and children is wrong?
Atheist:	It just is.
Christian:	No, how do you know it? I want to know how you can call anything wrong?
Atheist:	What do you mean? We all know that some things are wrong!
Christian:	On your worldview nothing can be said to be wrong. We are just evolved animals in a world of natural selection where might makes right. In nature, we don't call it wrong when a lion rips its prey to shreds. So if we are just animals that exist via accidental evolution, then you tell me how anything is wrong? Murder is just another expression of natural selection. Rape helps expand the species through greater chance of leaving offspring. So tell me, how is murdering women and children wrong?
Atheist:	That is not fair. We just know that some things are wrong, and we don't have to be able to explain it.
Christian:	That is very arbitrary of you. You believe something called evil exists, but you have no justification to believe it. I guess all I have to say is that we Christians know that God exists, and it was not wrong for him to order the execution of the Canaanites. I don't have to prove it, but I can be just as arbitrary as you are.
Atheist:	No, you can't do that. You just can't assume God exists, and it is okay for Him to command the murder of women and children. You are wrong.
Christian:	Prove it! Please, tell me how I am wrong. For you to even make the statement that I am wrong means that there must be some objective standard of right and wrong that exists that we are all bound by. What is that standard? Can you show me it? Where is it to be found? Your atheistic worldview of random chance cannot account for an ordered system of right and wrong.

Atheist:	The standard of right and wrong are determined by societies, and through upbringing we learn that some things are wrong according to our culture.
Christian:	That doesn't help you. On that standard of morals, Hitler and the Nazis cannot be condemned for killing Jews because their culture was fine with that. The Israelites could not be condemned for killing Canaanites because their culture was fine with it. You are judging another culture with yours, and since you are saying morals are culturally relative, your statement against God is meaningless.
Atheist:	Well, there are some things that are just wrong. Plain and simple!
Christian:	Your mere assertion is not an argument, and it is not proof. It looks like you are unable to justify the declaration of anything wrong. In your frustration, you are simply saying things are the way they are because you said so. That sounds like blind and arbitrary faith. It is also inconsistent since you only grant this freedom to your opinions.
Atheist:	Okay Christian, why don't you tell me how there can be right and wrong?
Christian:	The God of the Bible created the universe, and made man in His image. Right and wrong are not abstract concepts with an independent existence, but instead they are grounded in the nature of God. Good things are good because they are in accordance with His nature, and evil things are evil because they are in rebellion against His nature. Lying is wrong because an attribute of God's nature is veracity or truthfulness, and lying is an act of rebellion against that. God gave us a conscience to know the difference between right and wrong. That is why you know deep down some things are wrong, but you give up the ability to account for it when you deny the existence of God. You are like a person arguing that air doesn't exist all the while you are breathing in air to make your argument.
Atheist:	I still think your position is wrong because my conscience is telling me that murdering women and children is wrong, and a good God cannot command such a thing.
Christian:	Your perspective is wrong. God gets to define who is innocent and guilty. You are just a man with a three pound brain, and you are in no position to declare what is true. God is an omniscient, omnipotent,

and omnipresent being with exhaustive knowledge of everything. He gets to declare what is true, and His declaration about humanity is different than yours. All people, including woman and children, are actually guilty of sin, which bears the penalty of death, and God as the just judge has the right to carry out the sentence whenever He chooses. In that case, He chose Israel to be His agent of justice. You may disagree with God all you want, but you will have to live in a state of total inability and groundlessness to justifiably disagree. You cannot account for evil without God, and therefore you cannot use the concept of evil to declare God guilty and yourself righteous.

This dialogue demonstrates the hopelessness of the unbeliever's use of the problem of evil. By appealing to this argument, he actually defeats his own position and inadvertently offers an argument for the existence of God since God is the necessary precondition for there to be standards of right and wrong. The atheist may or may not accept the argument, but the Christian will have honorably defended God nevertheless.

The argument of evil clearly fails before the PIA technique. Without the God of the Bible, we lack the preconditions for moral standards, thus failing the *P* portion of the critique. The atheist's insistence on the existence of evil cannot be justified by the atheistic worldview, thus rendering it arbitrary and failing the *A*. If the Christian insisted upon being arbitrary himself, the atheist would never accept it, thus showing the atheist as inconsistent, which fails the *I* part of the technique. Furthermore, the consequence of the problem of evil argument is it encourages atheism which carries with it the horrific consequences mentioned two chapters ago.

Concerning a person who advances the argument due to personal pain, the Christian needs to equally demonstrate that God is the necessary precondition of moral absolutes. So the same style of argument applies. However, this needs to be done with sensitivity to their suffering and perhaps an admission of one's own bouts with suffering. Sharing your own pain and suffering and how it has pointed you to God and served to actually strengthen your faith carries powerful weight as a testimony. After all, the unbeliever has no peace in his agony caused by personal suffering, and yet the Christian's demonstration of peace in equally agonizing circumstances can leave the emotionally distraught unbeliever wanting. This is well illustrated by the church of the first three centuries. Tertullian was able to boast that the blood of the martyrs was the seed of the church since persecution caused Christianity to grow. The Romans could not explain how the Christians died so peaceably during the most torturous circumstances. They were so impressed by the martyrs that they continually converted in mass numbers thus finding that same peace for themselves.

Conclusion

As persistent as the problem of evil is, it is not a great threat to Christian theism. In fact, it presupposes that Christian theism is true, thus offering people one less excuse for unbelief. Logically, the problem is solved through the added scriptural premise that God has a sufficiently moral reason for the evil that does exist. All that we are left with is the psychological nature of the problem, namely, that fallen man demands an answer from God that he can put on trial and independently accept or reject. God never gives man an answer like this, nor will He. Job demanded an answer from God, but all he received was a rebuke and a divine prosecution proving the impossibility of mortal man to even understand the answer if it were given.

Paul informs us in Romans 9 that God is sovereign and that the evil that does exist will inevitably lead to God's glory. His justice and holiness will be observed through the vessels of wrath, and His mercy, grace, and love will be observed through the vessels honor. On one hand, then, we can say that evil exists so that God will get more glory. We have to settle for this answer since God tells us no more. He is the creator, and we are the creatures. Therefore, we cannot judge Him or find Him guilty. When fallen man tries to judge God, Paul answers in Romans 9:20, "But who are you, O man, to answer back to God? Will what is molded say to its molder, "Why have you made me like this?"

Fallen man will not accept this. Yet, this is not a justification for his unbelief, but instead it is merely a manifestation of it. Ultimately, he will be confronted with the same question God asked Job. "Would you really challenge My justice? Would you declare Me guilty to justify yourself?"[32]

---

[32] Holman Bible Editorial Staff, ed., *HCSB Study Bible, Brown/Tan Duotone Simulated Leather* (Holman Bible Publishers, 2010), 872.

Chapter Nine

Secular Dualism/Idealism

Introduction

Back in chapter three, I introduced the various categories of unbelieving thought. Much of what the Christian will battle against in our time is materialistic atomism and all of its variants. The previous three chapters addressed that category in such a way that if applied to any of its variants, they too would fall to the Christian apologetic attack. The category of pragmatism would also be savaged by the Christian critique, since it cannot withstand the PIA, for as pointed out elsewhere it is guilty of begging the question. With that said, it is time to move onto the remaining two categories: dualism and spiritual monism. The latter of those two will actually be addressed in the chapters refuting competing religious claims, thus leaving for us in this chapter the subject of secular dualism.

Secular dualism affirms the existence of both spirit and matter, and assumes that the two interact with each other. Some forms of dualism are fairly articulate, while others are rather haphazard. Most people in the United States operate off of dualistic assumptions, whether they know it or not. As will be pointed out later, even materialistic atheists act as though some aspects of dualism are true, even if they deny such with their mouths.

In terms of martial combat, facing dualism can be intimidating because in some ways it is like looking in the mirror. It is a troubling thought for a fighter to enter the ring or cage, only to see that their opponent moves in a similar manner and mirrors his own style. Secular dualism can have this effect because Christians are dualists too. We also believe that reality consists of both physical and spiritual components that are related to each other. In fact, dualism is a necessary precondition of logic and concepts, since they are not physical. Thus, it might seem like Christians will have a more difficult time with secular dualists since on the surface they do not have the same weaknesses of the materialist.

However, it must be noted that secular dualists will fall by the same technique. The PIA will cause the dualist to crumble because ultimately, all forms of non-Christian dualism are arbitrary and inconsistent. Furthermore, on closer evaluation, it cannot meet many preconditions of intelligibility, thus rendering it moot before the TAG. The secular dualist's ability to mirror some movements of the Christian apologist will not spare him from being defeated. His worldview is the like the person who learned to fight by copying kung fu movies. Such people are all flash with no substance.

With that said, secular dualism will be explained in both its sophisticated and popular variety, and will then be evaluated by the PIA technique. Afterward, the argument from truth and folly will be applied against it.

Explanation of Dualism

Some unbelievers do not reject the existence of spiritual reality, but instead they believe that reality consists of both mind and matter. In most instances, these dualists are not sophisticated or articulate in their belief, but instead they simply assert it and take it for granted. Yet, there are others, though perhaps few, that hold to a form of dualism and can philosophically articulate it. The beauty of presuppositional apologetics is the same internal critique applies to all forms of unbelief, and thus secular dualism fails against the Christian critique just as easily as atheism, evolution, or any other non-Christian worldview.

Perhaps the most famous and articulate secular dualist was the great philosopher Plato (428-348 B.C.).[1] He rejected the notion that the material world was the ultimate reality, but instead he argued that it was secondary. Due to its changing nature, the physical world could not be the object of knowledge, since knowledge itself seems to be of universals, or unchanging forms. From that standpoint, Plato believed that the primary world cannot be a world such as this one that changes, but it must be a different world that does not change. Since the material universe within time and space seems to be in constant change, the primary world must, by definition, exist outside of these dimensions where change occurs.

Summarizing Platonic idealism then, above this secondary world of matter exists a primary and perfect world of forms, and as such, most things that exist in our world have a corresponding universal in the world of forms. In the world of forms, there

---

[1] Plato et al., *Essential Dialogues of Plato* (New York: Barnes & Noble, 2005), xvii. The introduction in this book was written by Pedro de Blas.

exists all universals, and in the world of matter, there exists all particulars.[2] Any human reading this text is a particular, but humanity itself is the universal.

Of course, the question at hand is how did Plato know there is another realm beyond our senses since that realm cannot be observed? Although his answer was quite arbitrary (it will be discussed shortly), he appealed to the rational necessity of such a world. In other words, if no such world of forms or ideals existed, then humans would not be able to make any sense out of our experience.

On one hand, he understood the failure of materialism, but his proposition amounted to nothing more than faith. He was able to clearly see that material atomism cannot meet the preconditions of intelligibility, and so he created an explanation that he thought would account for such preconditions. However, it was by faith alone that he accepted his dualistic explanation. Because of his faith, the Christian scholastics of the Medieval Era argued that Plato possessed a Christian worldview, but lacked the special revelation of the Bible, and therefore he did the best he could. Unfortunately, this was a disservice. Prior to the Scholastics and afterward, too many Christians have suffered heresy due to their respect offered to Platonism, such as the idolatrous love affair that many "Christian" thinkers had throughout the centuries with Neo-Platonism.[3]

With certainty, Plato was right for insisting that this world does not make sense if there is not something more than just this physical world. Yet, when a person honestly evaluates how he tried to make sense out of this world, the conclusion must be that Plato failed catastrophically. Ironically, the first man to refute Plato was his most talented student, Aristotle (384-322 B.C.).

Aristotle argued that the world of forms is a useless explanation since we never encounter such forms. Given their opposite nature to the particulars, they can teach us nothing about such particulars. Furthermore, can the world of forms explain motion? Aristotle saw motion as the most pervasive characteristic of the world we live in, since it was the cause of change.[4] If the world of forms cannot account for

---

[2] Francis A Schaeffer, *The Complete Works of Francis A. Schaeffer: A Christian Worldview.* (Westchester, Ill.: Crossway Books, 1985), 306–307.

[3] Neo-Platonism was the idea that the ultimate reality–the Demiurge–emanated out of self-love, thus creating a similar being known as the Nous, or mind. The Nous then copied the Demiurge and emanated from itself thus creating the World Soul. The World Soul then did likewise, thus creating the world of matter and all of the particulars that corresponded to the universals in the thoughts of the Nous. Some Christian thinkers from the early centuries up through and past the Renaissance held to this view, and identified the Father with the Demiurge, the Son with the Nous, and the Holy Spirit with the World Soul.

[4] Aristotle and Louise Ropes Loomis, *On Man in the Universe*, Classics Club Edition edition. (Walter J. Black, n.d.), 32-33

motion, nor explain what happens in this changing world, then it is useless to philosophy.[5] Although the realm of forms can answer how we have laws of logic, morality, justice, and so on, it has no real relationship to this world.

Of course, Plato was not without an answer. His answer to this problem was that the particulars do relate to the forms by participating in the function of the form. As a metaphor, Plato compared it to actors participating in a role. Many actors act out the part, but ultimately there is only one role. All of the dogs of the world are trying out for dogness and are thus playing the part.[6]

Although many people today would not advance Plato's explanation, or use his exact reasoning, the fact is that this is a pervasive way of thought. Many people assume that there are absolute standards of right, wrong, justice, beauty, and so on, and when pressed concerning that standard, they appeal to a non-material abstract absolute standard. They may not offer an explanation of how that standard exists, or how we as humans know about it, or how it interacts with the physical world, but they live with this dualistic conception nevertheless. Many materialistic atomists unknowingly do the same when they condemn one action as unjust and promote another as a virtue. Others, hold to a form of dualism where they assume the soma/sema (soul and body) distinction, and yet they cannot say how they know there exists an immortal world of spirit. Instead, they arbitrarily assume such a world exists, that our souls come from there and return to there, and this physical life is either a character building test, or an endless chain of reincarnation.

Truly, dualism is a popular concept that many people take for granted. If Plato's version of it can be dismantled by the PIA technique, then how much more so these other inarticulate varieties? With that said, let us answer Plato according to his folly so that secular dualism cannot be seen as wise in any person's eyes.

PIA Technique

Platonic idealism, or any form of secular dualism for that matter, is going to be riddled with arbitrariness, and this is where its greatest weak point is. It can be argued that Plato's theory can in some way explain the uniformity of nature and reliability of the brain, and it can account for the laws of logic and morals. From this standpoint, it holds up much better than materialistic atheism does. However, Plato's explanation only weakly accounts for these things, and has much larger problems, such as logic and morality being the function of persons, and yet he would see them

---

[5] Ibid., 33.

[6] Greg Bahnsen, "Types of Worldviews," *Defending the Christian Worldview Against All Opposition, Series One.*

as impersonal abstract concepts. It goes back to the issue of the impersonal being grounded in the personal, not the other way around. So he has no sovereign absolute personality that is distinct from creation ruling over it and sustaining it, thus his view leaves us with a meaningless existence. Furthermore, his system failed to stand successfully against Aristotle's materialistic critiques.

When dealing with a case like Plato, sometimes it is best to focus heavily on the A of the PIA technique. After all, if a worldview is entirely arbitrary, then it is irrational to believe it, and that alone would cause it to fail to meet preconditions of intelligibility such as rationality. Remember, there are four types of arbitrariness that we can look for when evaluating a worldview: mere opinion, relativism, prejudicial conjecture, and unargued philosophical bias. Platonic dualism is guilty of arbitrariness since it is ultimately justified by mere opinion, as will be demonstrated shortly.

Recall that Plato answered objections by appealing to a metaphor of actors playing a role. The first thing that the Christian should notice, then, is that the most brilliant proponent of secular dualism was forced to resort to a metaphor when attempting to figure out the very basis of reality. A metaphor is not proof, and it certainly is not a strong argument. In fact, Plato believed that the answer as to how the first particulars came into the physical world from the world of universal forms was unknowable. In other words, as technical as Plato's theory sounds, the simple epistemological question of, "Sir, how do you know this, and if it is true, how did it happen?" totally stumps both the man and his worldview. The end result is he leaves us with a metaphor!

Bahnsen explained it with a comical illustration of cookie dough.[7] He asked his listeners to imagine that cookie dough is the matter, and a duck shaped cookie cutter is the form. Thus the form (cookie cutter) is used to cut identical shapes out of the matter (the dough). Plato understood reality in these terms, but once again the question is how did the forms first impose themselves on the matter to create the particulars? A cookie cutter does not move itself! Thus, Plato's answer was to invent a myth.

He argued that there existed the Demiurge, a somewhat benevolent cosmic craftsman,[8] who fashioned the material world, and then made the immaterial universals into material particulars.[9] Yet, the Demiurge could not make the

---

[7] Ibid.

[8] Thomas R. Martin, *Ancient Greece: From Prehistoric to Hellenistic Times*, 1St ed. (Yale University Press, 1996), 180.

[9] Plato, *Timaeus*. Penn State Hazleton.
   http://www2.hn.psu.edu/faculty/jmanis/plato/timaeus.pdf (accessed March 26, 2014).

particulars perfect like the universals since by definition (according to Plato), matter is by nature imperfect. Thus, since Plato had no philosophical explanation, he resorted to giving a type of creation story that he apparently believed was true. Yet, his story did not come from revelation from the Demiurge or any divine or spiritual force. Instead, it was the arbitrary invention of his mind that he needed in order to bridge the gap of epistemology that made his worldview impossible. Therefore, Plato's best answer as to how the forms of logic, moral absolutes, and class concepts entered the world was to go with a self invented myth, and in so doing, Plato defeated himself.

It is irrational to hold to a worldview that arbitrarily says reality is like an actor playing a role or the Demiurge cutting cookies! This can easily be reduced to absurdity when applied to another example. Imagine a primitive tribe of hunter-gatherers whose ancestors decided to live near a large meteor crater. The current generation knows nothing of space rocks crashing into the earth, and so they need some sort of explanation for the crater. The wisest man of the tribe one day says, "Although we do not know how this giant hole got here, I have deduced that a giant dragon named Godzilla battled a giant gorilla named King Kong, in which the latter slammed the former into the ground at this very point, thus creating the hole." If the smallest child in the tribe then asked how the wise man knows this, what can he say? He did not see it with his own eyes. No dragon skeleton was found in the hole. The wise man would be left with only one honest answer: "I do not know for sure since I did not see it, but it must be true because it explains how the hole got here."

Truly, this is arbitrary. The hole did not get there due to a fight between monsters. An explanation does not equal an argument, evidence, or proof. This is the same problem the theory of macroevolution faces. Offering an explanation for what is seen without being able to prove it is arbitrary. Both macroevolution and Platonic dualism are in the same type of situation as the crater story above, with only one difference. Plato and evolutionists seasoned their arbitrary explanations with academic vocabulary, thus making it sound more reasonable. Yet, absurdity is absurdity, no matter how technical the language to describe it is.

Aristotle was not satisfied with his teacher's arbitrariness, thus causing him to move in an entirely different direction towards a type of theistic materialism.[10] Both philosophers would agree that to know something, a person must have a justified true belief, as mentioned in chapter four. Yet, Plato could not justify his belief of reality from either revelation or evidence, and neither could Aristotle do so with

---

[10] Aristotle and Louise Ropes Loomis, *On Man in the Universe*, xxv.

materialism. Thus, neither of them could know their beliefs were true. As a result, they were both guilty of arbitrariness.

Plato appealed to mere opinion for his entire theory. Observation showed him that materialism was inadequate since logic and abstract concepts were not material. Rather than accept his finite limitation and then seek a special revelation from God, he instead made up a story, supported it with a self-invented creation myth, and then acted as though he provided an acceptable view of reality. Mere opinion is nothing more than arbitrariness. Thus, Plato's dualism cannot be justified, and therefore it is irrational to believe it. It is ironic that he used rationality to invent an explanation that can only be accepted if one were committed to irrationality. Such irony demonstrates inconsistency within this worldview. Any system that cannot be justified and is inconsistent certainly cannot meet the preconditions of intelligibility since logic and non-contradiction are part of the observable real world.

Thus, the Christian should never be intimidated by the modern day Platonic idealist. Of course, who knows the odds of encountering such a person anyway? However, a Christian is most certainly bound to run into unsophisticated idealists who believe in universal ideals like fair play, love, etc. For example, the current political and moral issue of our day is the issue of homosexual marriage. Often the argument is, "People should be able to love whoever they want, and it is wrong to prevent love." Apart from the ease with which this can be reduced to absurdity,[11] its fundamental problem is it presupposes that their definition of love is a universal reality that all people should understand and recognize. Yet, how can they justify this? How do they know that people should be able to love whoever they want? Where did they find this universal law? Is it written in the stars, or did God reveal it to them, or is it something that all people intuit? The obvious answer is they do not know. They arbitrarily assume their position is absolutely true without any justification whatsoever. Thus they are arbitrary. They do not ask the creator and author of love whether or not He approves of homosexuality.

When a Christian begins to refute such people's beliefs, they will show themselves to believe in immaterial absolute standards, and the Christian must push the issue by asking how any concept can be absolute in their worldview. During the Vietnam War era, many hedonistic hippies declared President Johnson to be unjust

---

[11] Why are incest, consensual pedophilia, and bestiality wrong then? After all, should not people be able to love whoever or whatever they want? Yet, this notion is absurd, thus showing that there are necessary limitations on who should be our objects of love. Given that such limitations exist, it makes the gay-activists' argument that "people should be able to love whoever they want" as moot. They have to be able to prove that homosexual love should not be one of the limitations.

in sending American troops 10,000 miles away to war. How could the hippies justify an absolute notion of justice on their worldview? They could not. Instead, they arbitrarily accepted some things as being right and other things as being wrong, but it was based on nothing other than their mere opinion. Furthermore, they could never provide the preconditions of intelligibility in the first place that allow for the existence of absolute immaterial concepts. Only the Christian worldview meets that demand.

As alluded to earlier, most materialistic atheists are dualists deep down. They may profess otherwise with their lips, but their actions speak against their words. After all, if the material world is all that exists or all that matters, then all things are changing under the dominion of motion and thus nothing is objective, but instead all is subjective. Without objective justice, the world will end up as a wicked place since no one can legitimately condemn anything as wrong. Yet, even atheists declare certain things are wrong, especially bad things done in the name of religion, like Catholic clergy molesting children. Well, if only matter existed, then no ideals would exist that can be justified. In that case, Catholic clergy violating children could not be declared wrong, unless ideals do in fact exist. When pushed, many atheists will admit that some ideals do exist, yet doing so undermines their materialism.

Thus, whether a person realizes he is an idealist or not, the Christian must ask where these ideals exist and how does the unbeliever know about them. If he gives an arbitrary answer that demonstrates he has no justification in his belief, the Christian needs to nail that point to the ground. If he says it is not important to know where such absolutes exist or come from, then the Christian can ask what the relationship is between his ideals and the real world that we all live in. In other words, how did the ideals intrude themselves in a governing manner into the physical world? Just as Plato could not answer it, no other idealist can either. Deep down the idealist may believe in two types of reality, but he will always have to deal with the problem of how to bring the two realities into a relationship with each other.

In the end, dualism or idealism cannot stand because it is arbitrary. It rightly understands that immaterial absolutes exist, but it cannot account for them apart from arbitrary philosophical explanations and creation myths. Plato and all other idealists have no epistemological means to prove or support the notion of the existence of forms. Instead, they merely figured out why materialism cannot work since it cannot account for logic and deduction, but their own attempt to account for these things is no more justified than any other person arbitrarily creating their own story to explain it. Thus, believing in secular dualism as a worldview is irrational. Perhaps, this irrationality is the most obvious consequence, but even worse is the eternal judgment that follows.

In contrast, the Christian worldview accounts for all things (e.g., uniformity of nature, logic, the mind, morals, etc.) and is not based upon arbitrary man-created explanations, but instead is centered upon divine revelation given to man by the transcendent and immanent creator of all things, both spiritual and physical. Ideals exist because they reflect the character and holy nature of God. We know about them through our created status as the image of God, and though that image is broken by sin, God provides special revelation and illumination to believers in order to properly understand those ideals and to apply them in life.

Argument From Truth and Folly

As with the other application chapters, here too is advice on confronting the secular dualist worldview. As stated above, many people are not even aware that they are dualists. As any conversation with them progresses, and they begin to insist that any given subject is morally good or bad, the Christian can then ask them how they arrive at such a conclusion. It will ultimately be arbitrary, unless it is grounded in the Bible. Below is what it might look like.

Dualist: I think capital punishment is wrong because it is murder.

Christian: Why do you think murder is wrong? And why do you think capital punishment is murder?

Dualist: You don't think it is murder?

Christian: No, I think it is justice, and it is commanded in the Bible for those who commit murder.

Dualist: How can it be right to murder the murderer? It makes the state guilty of the same thing the criminal was guilty of, and is therefore hypocritical.[12]

Christian: How do you know it is wrong for the state to be hypocritical?

---

[12] At this point a classical apologist or an evidentialist would probably spend time trying to convince the person that all killing is not murder, and therefore when the state executes a murderer, it is different than when a murderer kills a victim. Although this is true, much time will be wasted, especially since the unbeliever has presuppositions that cause him to see capital punishment as murder. Therefore, the presuppositional apologist would wisely ask him to justify his indignation in the first place. The presuppositionalist would ask him to prove that murder and hypocrisy is wrong. Christians can justify it, but can the unbeliever? No. This is where we prove to him the folly of his way.

Dualist: Because hypocrisy is wrong. No one likes hypocrites.

Christian: But how do you know hypocrisy is wrong? Who says it is wrong?

Dualist: We all just know it is. Come on, you know it is wrong.

Christian: What if someone disagrees with you and says murder is good because it keeps the population down and hypocrisy is a tool of evolutionary survival?

Dualist: But we all know murder and hypocrisy are wrong!

Christian: Can you show me a science experiment in a lab where we proved this? Or can you show me where this absolute standard is written in the heavens? Can you show me any proof that this is right?

Dualist: Well, no. That is not how this works. But there just has to be standards of right and wrong, otherwise everything would be fair game and atrocities would increase.

Christian: Okay, so you are saying right and wrong must exist by necessity, otherwise we are all in trouble. Well, that still does not prove that it exists. I could say that a pink unicorn exists by necessity otherwise airplanes would all crash across the world. It doesn't mean that I am right.

Dualist: If there was no right or wrong, then Hitler's actions were justified and so were Stalin's. Do you really believe that?

Christian: No, of course not. My question to you, is how do YOU know what is right or wrong? Hitler and Stalin disagreed with you. What makes you right and them wrong?

Dualist: I guess I can't point to something tangible. But deep down I think everyone knows.

Christian: I agree. Let me explain why you have a problem, and then I will explain why I don't. You have a problem because your insistence that capital punishment is wrong is simply a mere opinion. It is not supported by objective evidence. You have not ascended into the heavens and found a divine word that says this. Instead, you think it, and you believe that everyone else should think it too. Yet, you are just a mere human, with a three pound brain, and you have only lived a limited time. You do not have perfect or exhaustive knowledge of anything. And so from that standpoint, it is impossible for you to justify your position as being anything other than your own arbitrary opinion.[13]

Dualist: Okay, how is it different for you?

Christian:[14]   Human beings are incapable of knowing things absolutely, but it seems clear that we do in fact know things. The reason for this is that we were created in the image of God, and as a result we possess intuitive knowledge of right and wrong. However, since the Fall, we are a cursed race tainted by sin, and so our moral faculties do not work with 100% accuracy. Thus, God gave us a written revelation that clears up what things are right and what things are wrong. We simply need to believe what He has written.

Dualist: How is that position any better than mine?

Christian: It is rather simple. Your position cannot account for ANYTHING being right or wrong. If all that exists is matter in motion, then there is no abstract absolute concept of right or wrong. Instead, we would be like animals acting upon other animals. We do not consider it murder when a lion eats a zebra. So why consider it murder when one human kills another? Yet, we know deep down these two scenarios are different. The reason for it is simple. Right and wrong exist as real and absolute things, only because God exists. That which is right is right because it agrees with God's holy and righteous nature. That which is wrong is wrong because it rebels against God's holy and righteous nature. Without God, we have no justification for believing that right and wrong exists. Yet, as you said, if right and wrong did not exist, then we would all kill each other in a massive post-apocalyptic nightmare. That hasn't happened precisely because right and wrong do exist, but they cannot exist in and of themselves, for how can an abstract universal yet impersonal concept exist with any authority?

Dualist: I don't know. But does appealing to God really solve the problem?

Christian: Yes. If we do not appeal to God, we are left with relativism. I have no more authority than you do, and we have no more authority than

---

[13] Thus ends the argument from folly.

[14] Thus begins the argument from truth.

Hitler. So we disagreed with him on the Holocaust, but how could we ever prove we are right unless a court higher than both of us exists? Yet, more than that, the God of the Bible provides the necessary preconditions for everything: logic, uniformity of nature, and moral absolutes. God exists because if He didn't then nothing in the real world would be knowable. A random universe would not have predictable uniform laws that allow us to adapt. Our brain's chemical reactions would not be uniform either, thus rendering thought as chaotic and useless. We could not even have this conversation. Truly, I could go on and on, but I think you get the point. Every single fact of nature depends upon the existence of God. It is no different for our moral absolutes.

Dualist: Okay, so I am forced to admit that I do not know why murder is wrong, but you in contrast can say murder is wrong because the God who created the universe declared it as such because it is contrary to His nature. Furthermore, humans generally know this because we exist in God's image.

Christian: Precisely.

Dualist: I will have to think more about this, but I will admit that you do not have the same problem as me. I want to think more about these preconditions.

Christian: If you do think about them honestly, you will see what I am talking about. Ask yourself if any single thing that you see can be accounted for by randomness. Also, concerning morals, I want to make one more point. You rightly believe murder is wrong, but you wrongly believe capital punishment is wrong. God, who is the definer of good and evil based on His nature, said that capital punishment is not murder, but instead it is justice, which is a virtue. You are a human with non-exhaustive knowledge. God is omniscient, lacking no knowledge. You are in a position in which it is impossible to disagree with God and be right in doing so.

Dualist: That is an interesting point, I'll have to think about that too.

Christian: Well, if you have a few moments, maybe we can pause this discussion and I can share with you about my Lord.[15]

Bear in mind, this scenario addressed secular dualism as it relates to moral standards. A dualistic mindset can be attached to many different subjects such as the soul, reincarnation, logic, etc. The same application of the answer from truth and folly applies. Show the folly with the PIA technique, ask epistemological questions to demonstrate arbitrariness, and point out the inconsistency of their position. Then demonstrate to them that Christianity has no such problems. It works every time!

Conclusion

Secular dualism is nothing to be feared. The sophisticated variants show more promise than materialistic atomism, but ultimately they are arbitrary. The popular variants can easily be demonstrated as folly as well. Whether we are arguing with Plato, or we are arguing with a local unbeliever at the coffee shop, their dualistic standpoint cannot be justified as the PIA demonstrates.

Hopefully, through this chapter the wheels have also begun to turn in your mind with regard to how we should answer competing religious claims. After all, we just saw how to deal with a worldview that believes in spiritual reality. In the same manner that secular dualism falls to the presuppostional critique, so too will competing religious claims. To that, the next two chapters are focused.

---

[15] In such a scenario, if a person seems softened due to the apologetic discourse, always follow up immediately with the gospel. You already broke the intellectual barrier, but ultimately it is far more important to break through his conscience with the law and the gospel.

Stephen Feinstein

Chapter Ten

Transcendent Mysticism and Immanent Moralism

Introduction

Now that atheism, evolution, and secular dualism have been dealt a deathblow, the Christian apologist must learn to refute the competing claims of other religions. An unbeliever might concede that a god exists, and that the problem of evil has an adequate answer. He may even reject evolution as being groundless. However, what happens if he appeals to other religions? He may ask how we do we know our religion is the one with the truth rather than the Jehovah Witnesses, or the Muslims. In fact, one might mistake the nature of presuppositional apologetics, and assume that it will not work against competing religious claims. Of course, such an assumption is erroneous.

Many of us have heard liberals advance the elephant analogy in such a way as to either dismiss religious truth altogether, or to promote a type of religious pluralism. It goes like this. Six blind men stumble upon an elephant, and they feel various parts of it in order to figure out what it is. One grabs the tail and declares it to be like a snake, another feels the body and calls it a pillar, and yet another touches the ear and thus declares it to be a winnowing basket. And so it goes. All are certain of what they think it is, but it is based upon each of their limited experience. Thus, this is what the world religions are like. We are all blind to the divine, and so with our limited and narrow experience, we dogmatically claim God is this way or that way, but in reality we are all wrong and right in our own way. The moral of the story then is that we each should learn from each other's experience and come to the realization that we all are talking about the same thing, only in different ways.

Of course, this analogy is presented as great wisdom, and if you are to be enlightened, then liberals strongly suggest you accept it. I remember hearing it numerous times as an undergraduate in the California State University system. It completely jives with the postmodern age where all views are tolerated as long as they believe every other view is equally correct. If a Christian were to stand up and protest, declaring that Jesus is the way, the truth, and the life, and no one comes to the Father but by Him, then the enlightened professor will simply correct him with the elephant analogy and claim the Christian is one of the blind men dogmatically blinded by his own limited experience.

Sadly, these academic minds are not very critical in their thinking when it comes to this analogy. After all, a simpleminded person can find many problems with it. First, an analogy does not prove anything, but instead it illustrates a point, which in this case is just a pluralistic opinion. This is no better than Plato offering a metaphor to answer his unanswerable dilemma. Second, the religious pluralism advocated by the analogy violates the law of non-contradiction, thus rendering it as inconsistent. Two contradictory statements cannot both be true at the same time. The analogy is self-defeating since it leads to the absurd conclusion that contradicting religions are equated with each other. Third, the analogy does not demonstrate that all religions are talking about the same thing, but instead it shows that all religions are wrong since they all have inaccurate perceptions. So it actually favors the opposite position of its intent! Fourth, it is guilty of the worse kind of contradiction, namely, that if God is unknowable, then the very knowledge that God is unknowable means that at least in one way He is knowable. In other words, if the analogy's point is true, then it is false.

Besides these obvious issues, there are other questions that render the analogy as absurd. For example, if they are all blind, then how do they know what a snake, pillar, and winnowing basket look like? If they can have accurate knowledge about those things, even with their limited experience, then why cannot the same be true of the elephant? What about the correspondence theory of truth? The truth of the matter is the blind men are examining an elephant. Therefore, their opinions about the object they are examining ends up being irrelevant since in reality it is an elephant. Also, how does the narrator know it is an elephant? What is special about the narrator to where he does not have the same blindness as the blind men? Why is it not possible that Christians are the narrator, and all other religions are the blind men? And finally, if the elephant began to communicate through roaring, then all the blind men would realize they are wrong. Thus, the analogy does not take into account divine revelation. If God spoke to prophets, and infallibly had them record His message to humanity, then those with His revelation are not blind concerning Him. The analogy assumes that the Bible is an invention of man, which is just another form of begging the question.

The reality of the situation is quite clear. All religions are not equal. Other religions fail to meet the preconditions of intelligibility just as bad as atheism. Likewise, they are arbitrary, inconsistent, and in most cases have led to negative consequences. The elephant analogy does not evaluate these religious faiths, and therefore it can say nothing meaningful about them.

One thing that must not be forgotten is that presuppositionalism does not defend *a god*, but instead with it we seek to defend a very specific concept of God. We seek to defend the biblical God as the only God and the only necessary precondition of all intelligibility. The arguments used thus far have nothing to do with a generic theism, but instead they only serve as a defense to Christian theism.[1] Only the biblical God provides a worldview that offers the preconditions of intelligibility and is free from arbitrariness and inconsistency. The gods of false religions and the false conceptions of God from the Christian cults fail to do this.

Therefore, the arguments used in this book cannot be used in favor of Islam or any other view. When a Christian defends Christian theism against an atheist, and a person of another religion (e.g., Islam or Mormonism) decides to jump in on the Christian's side,[2] the Christian must be quick to say that we are not on the same side, and our conceptions of God are as night and day. Since apologetics is a battle of worldviews, the false religious worldview is at just as much enmity with Christ as the atheistic one is. Ultimately, only Christianity will make sense out of science, law, morality, the human mind, human dignity, etc.

Greg Bahnsen, once again, provided a great service to Christian apologists concerning the task of refuting other religions. He did so by providing categories by which to understand the various religions.[3] In fact, he lumps all religions into three broad categories, and if the Christian understands how to refute each category, then any of the individual faiths that fall under that category are defeated in the same manner. The three categories are 1) Religions of Transcendent Mysticism, 2) Religions of Immanent Moralism, and 3) Biblical Counterfeits. Transcendent mysticism puts a broad emphasis on the notion that truth and reality are beyond human experience, and therefore can only be contacted in a mystical way. The most famous example is Hinduism. Religions of immanent moralism focus on this world rather than on matters outside of this world, such as life after death. They offer adherents a code to follow in order successfully get through this world. Famous

---

[1] i.e., Biblically defined Christian theism.
[2] I have actually had this happen to me.
[3] Greg Bahnsen, "Types of Worldviews," *Defending the Christian Worldview Against All Opposition, Series One and Series Two.*

examples are Confucianism and Buddhism. Finally, Biblical Counterfeits are false religions that have been influenced by the Bible, or in some way have conceptions that match the biblical God, but are counterfeits. Within this third category, there are three subdivisions: 1) Polytheistic; 2) Unitarian; 3) Pseudo-Messianic. Each of these will be explained and defined in clearer terms.

In this chapter, transcendent mysticism and immanent moralism will be discussed. First, we will deal with religions of transcendent mysticism.[4]

Transcendent Mysticism

Among the categories of world religion, religions of transcendent mysticism claim many adherents. Simply defined, this category of religion views true reality as something far beyond human experience, and therefore the only way to contact true reality is through a mystical way that is above regular rationality. Hinduism is the largest and best known example of a religion of transcendent mysticism. A basic understanding of Hinduism will assist the Christian apologist in refuting it, as well as all other forms of transcendent mysticism.

According to Hindu religion, all reality is ultimately one, and that one reality is spiritual, not physical. The physical world is a world of illusion, something often called Maya and is classified as Saguna.[5] In Maya, we observe many distinctions[6] (e.g., light and dark, life and death, trees and grass, men and beasts, etc.) but such distinctions are not truly real. It is all part of this massive illusion that we are trapped in. The true reality is supposed to be an impersonal divine spiritual essence called Brahman and is classified as Nirguna.[7] Thus, their worldview teaches that Brahman is god and god is everything.[8] You are god, I am god, and the trees and everything else is also god. Due to being trapped in this world of Maya, most people are tricked by the illusion, and therefore they do not experience the true reality of Brahman.

For the Hindu, sin is not the main problem of humans. Instead, individual existence—which is really an illusion—is the real problem, and the solution to the problem is to escape the illusion and realize you are really Brahman. The only way to

---

[4] In chapter three, one of the unbelieving philosophies was spiritual monism. Hinduism is the chief example of spiritual monism, and thus I reserved the discussion of it for this chapter as I refute religions of transcendent mysticism.

[5] Timothy C. Tennent, *Christianity at the Religious Roundtable: Evangelicalism in Conversation with Hinduism, Buddhism, and Islam* (Baker Academic, 2002), 41.

[6] Patrick S. Bresnan, *Awakening An Introduction to the History of Eastern Thought* (Prentice 2002 2nd Ed), 42-43.

[7] Tennent, 41.

[8] Bresnan, 38-39.

do this is through mystical means such as yoga and eastern meditation, by which a person separates their mind from the illusory world of Maya until they see reality for what it really is. At this point, they would reach enlightenment. This is the most basic understanding of the Hindu worldview, but it must be noted that Hinduism is not a monolithic religion of unified concepts. Instead, it is highly contradictory as different Hindu groups describe Brahman and Maya differently, and have different explanations for how one escapes the world of Maya. Many Hindus worship a variety of deities, who ultimately are also illusions of Maya,[9] believing that such will help them achieve enlightenment to see past the illusion.[10] Other Hindus trust the traditional Indian beliefs in karma to reach enlightenment and escape the world of Maya. At the end of life, if a person has more good karma than bad, it is thought he will be reincarnated to a higher position in society, until ultimately he no longer gets reincarnated but instead becomes one with Brahman. The ultimate goal of all Hinduism is the escape from this life and to no longer be reincarnated. Becoming one with god is called moksha.[11] Every nuance of Hinduism has this same end goal, and the philosophy behind it all is mysticism.

PIA and the Argument from Truth and Folly

With that very basic description of Hinduism in mind, how should the Christian evaluate it? We need to evaluate it the way we would evaluate any other worldview. We need to perform an internal critique of it looking for the preconditions of intelligibility, arbitrariness, and inconsistency. In other words, we need to use the PIA technique. Also, with Hinduism it is helpful to look at the social and political consequences that befell India for ascribing to this belief system. After evaluating Hinduism, it should be clear that it is an inadequate worldview that embodies irrationality and foolishness. As with secular dualism, it works well for the Christian to begin with the A of the PIA technique. In so doing, its arbitrary nature

---

[9] In Hinduism, the impersonal indescribable Brahman is classified as Nirguna. Below this is Saguna, where all distinctions exist. The millions of Hindu deities are said to be Saguna. This was developed by Hindu philosophers to deal with the contradiction between the devotion to many gods and the insistence that all reality is truly Brahman. Often, when Hindus are presented with the Christian God, they classify Him under Saguna since He bears personal characteristics and can be described. In their arrogance, they think their indescribable spiritual deity is far above the true God, thus they classify Him on the lower level of reality.

[10] Yes, they believe devotion to an illusion (gods) will assist them in being free from illusions.

[11] Winfried Corduan, *Neighboring Faiths: A Christian Introduction to World Religions* (IVP Academic, 1998), 199.

immediately reveals itself. Soon after, it becomes clear that Hinduism cannot meet the preconditions of intelligibility.

Transcendent mystical worldviews claim to be beyond our rationality. Remember, they see the world as an illusion, and thus rationality is limited to this world of illusion and is therefore useless in learning about the true nature of realty. Our first problem then, is if their religion is beyond human rationality and beyond human experience, then how do they know about it? If it truly is beyond human rationality or experience, then there is nothing they can tell us about it since it would have to be rational and based on experience in order to be put into words. Every single word an enlightened Hindu can tell you about Brahman depends on experience and the rational usage and understanding of words. After all, the sage through experience has achieved true knowledge. How is this possible if Brahman is beyond our rationality? So on one hand they claim through the mystical means of karma, yoga, and meditation (all of this is human experience) they know about Brahman (i.e., true reality), but then they say Brahman is beyond rationality and experience and cannot be known through such!

This is inconsistent for sure, but above all it is arbitrary. Since we cannot rationally know or experience the true reality, then anything said about it can be nothing more than an arbitrary guess that carries no authority. If a Hindu tells me I need to practice yoga and meditation to learn of true reality, I have just as much right to disagree and say barking like a dog will bring me into oneness with reality. After all, we are both being arbitrary since reality is beyond experience. Of course, the Hindu may argue that their methods were handed down by enlightened sages and are proven to work. The problem with this is that their own worldview's understanding of the ultimate essence does not allow them to claim this. If Brahman is beyond all human experience, then I have no reason to listen to the sages.

Hinduism, or transcendental mysticism, can be refuted just by briefly describing it. For example, Hindus claim our problems in life stem from us making distinctions, believing that there are millions of things when in reality there truly is only one thing.[12] There is no difference between the trees, waters, or anything else, and the way to see through the illusion is by meditation or some other mystical means. Through such means, enlightenment comes, and rather than being reincarnated, a person will enter Nirvana (personal extinction); the drop of water that represents the person as an individual will rejoin the giant shoreless ocean of being where there are no distinctions and no beginning and end.

---

[12] Heinrich Robert Zimmer and Joseph Campbell, *Philosophies of India* (Princeton, N.J.: Princeton University Press, 1969), 380.

So how did this mere description of the worldview serve the purpose of refuting it? Simply put, it is suspiciously interesting that for something that is supposed to be mystical and beyond human rationality and experience, there is a group of sentences that were just used to explain it! Words rationally put together somehow are accurately explaining something that is unexplainable! This is why the ability to describe Hindu belief ultimately refutes the presuppositions of the worldview itself. This is just one more example of inconsistency and the arbitrary nature of every single Hindu belief. After they describe their beliefs, we have the right to ask them, "How can you say that?" They cannot rightly justify their answer.

This all goes to show that the Christian's dependence on the Bible is not the same as Hinduism's use of its religious texts. There are a number of sacred religious texts to Hindus, such as the Vedas and the Bhagavad Gita, but their own worldview negates any ability to appeal to these texts as a personal revelation from God or even a text about God. The Christian worldview, in contrast, believes in the God who created the universe (and is thus distinct from it), who also is an absolute personality, triune, and sovereign over all things. As such, He can reveal Himself in a personal way through language, whether spoken directly to man, or written and preserved in a book (the Bible). Regardless of whether or not the Christian story is true, the story at least comports with itself, and it hangs together.

A Hindu book cannot be a personal revelation from God, since in Hinduism the ultimate divine essence is not personal. Therefore, it is incorrect when people try to view Hindu texts as analogous to the Bible. Although they are both religious in nature, the things the Bible claims are radically different. The Bible is not inconsistent with itself by claiming to speak the very words of the personal God to His created persons. Hindu texts are inconsistent when they attempt to explain the Brahman reality since Brahman cannot reveal anything to persons since revelation is a property of persons. If the Hindu texts do not present themselves as revelation from God, they are still worthless regarding the truth since Brahman is unexplainable with human experience or rationality. Thus, when Hindus speak their beliefs or read their texts aloud, the Christian has the right to ask and say, "How do you know that? You are being arbitrary. If they respond, "Brahman revealed it to the sages," you have the right to say, "The very statement 'Brahman revealed it to the sages' is a personal statement itself; something impossible for an impersonal *it*." Therefore, Christian texts and Hindu writings are not on equal footing, especially since consistency would demand that the Hindus not even have sacred texts.

This type of argument may also occur without appeal to religious texts. Greg Bahnsen illustrated this perfectly with a hypothetical conversation with a Hari

Krishna at the airport.[13] If a Christian bumped into one at the airport the conversation could go as follows:

Hari Krishna: You are not in Nirvana. You are in this world of Maya. You are on the wheel of life and if you don't get things right, you will be reincarnated and have to go through this whole life again. You need to get enlightened so that you can escape it with Nirvana.

Christian: Let me repeat your views back to you. My problem in life is that the world is an illusion, and I am drawing artificial distinctions that are not real since all is one, and the one is Brahman. When I do this, I block myself from enlightenment.

Hari Krishna: Yes, that is exactly what I am saying.

Christian: So I can't enter Nirvana because I will not be enlightened if I keep seeing these distinctions?

Hari Krishna: Yes.

Christian: Well, I draw the conclusion that I already am in Nirvana.

Hari Krishna: No, you are not. If you are still in this world, it means you still see things in an illusory way, which means you are not in Nirvana.

Christian: When you say this, you assume there is a distinction between Maya and Nirvana. If there is a distinction between Maya and Nirvana, then you are wrong that the ultimate reality has no distinctions.

At this point, it is already a checkmate in favor of the Christian. The argument is won because it has just been shown that the Hari Krishna's story is both arbitrary and inconsistent. After all, if there are no distinctions we must already be in Nirvana since all is one. If all is one, then all is also Maya since there are no distinctions. If everything is ultimately one, then it makes absolutely no sense for the Hari Krishna to have a sentence that distinguishes Maya from Nirvana, and the enlightened from the unenlightened. Of course, the Hindu will not be happy with this argument, and so let us continue.

Hari Krishna: There is your problem. You are committed to your Western logic and so you think you found an inconsistency in our truth. Well, our theology transcends your logic. It is beyond all logic.

---

[13] Greg Bahnsen, "Types of Worldviews," *Series One*. This is not a word-for-word transcription of what Dr. Bahnsen said, but is close and captures the essence of what he said.

Christian:	If you tell me that your religion doesn't follow the laws of logic, then I tell you that it does. After all, if a person rejects logic, then they have no right to insist on consistency.
Hari Krishna:	You are still using logic. I reject logic.
Christian:	No you don't.
Hari Krishna:	Stop it. I just said I don't believe in logic. You have no right to say I do.
Christian:	If there is no logic, then there is no contradiction. So I can say the opposite of you for the rest of the day and claim it is what you believe since you don't believe in logic, and therefore don't believe in contradiction. If you really reject logic, then I have the right to do this. Of course, you don't really reject logic. You prove it with your frustration whenever I contradict you. You are lying to yourself.

Once the Hari Krishna shows any frustration at contradiction, the Christian also has demonstrated that Hinduism fails to meet the precondition of intelligibility. In other words, what is the necessary precondition of contradiction? The answer is logic. Hinduism, if it rejects logic, does not even meet the fundamental precondition necessary for something as important to human survival as the law of non-contradiction.[14] In fact, the Christian can ask the Hindu to open up their sacred texts and justify in addition to logic things like inductive inference and moral absolutes. After all, their texts teach that there are no distinctions between good and evil (thus no moral absolutes) or between any physical objects (thus no inductive inference). It would be impossible to live according to Hinduism, especially with regard to no true morals. Can they complain if someone brutalized a Hindu priest and robbed him? No, because both the beating and the distinction between good and evil are illusory. Truly, this worldview is unlivable.

The Hindu religious option is no competition to Christianity whatsoever, especially to people committed to rationality. Those who are rational have to reject Hinduism due to its incoherent, inconsistent, and arbitrary nature. Those who claim to reject rationality do not really live day to day as though they did. Otherwise, they should not get angry if someone steals their wallet, murders their child, cuts in front of them at the grocery store, etc., since all is one, illusions are not real, and contradiction does not truly exist. There are those who will vocally give up rationality in order to be a Hindu, but then you can contradict them again one more

---

[14] Ibid.

time just to show them that they truly do not reject rationality. It may seem disrespectful at first glance, but in reality it is the Christian treating them according to their own worldview[15] in order to show them the impossibility of it.

The discussion may end with the Hindu storming away claiming he will no longer talk with that particular Christian. This is ok, and Christians need to be comfortable with this. We will not persuade everyone to be a Christian. The Holy Spirit's work is to change the heart, and He often uses our preaching to do so. The Holy Spirit has the job to change the heart; we have the job to destroy every lofty opinion raised against the knowledge of God.[16] Our hope and prayer is that the Holy Spirit would change our opponents' hearts, but if it is not His will, then our secondary prayer needs to be that our defense shuts their mouths, especially knowing that God can still reach them after they have closed their mouths.[17] Consider it a great victory if the Hindu opponent admits that in order to reject Christ he also has to reject rationality. In so doing, he has proven for us the truth of Romans 1:20-23, namely that fallen man knows the truth deep down, but willfully deceives himself. The human heart is in so great a rebellion against God that many do not want to be rational if being rational means accepting the Christian God.

Concluding our discussion of Hinduism, and transcendental mysticism, it should be clear that the worldview completely fails against the PIA. It is arbitrary, inconsistent, and it cannot meet the preconditions of intelligibility for anything experienced in the real world. If Hinduism were true, we could not know anything at all. It truly is a hopeless worldview.

Also, we need to look at the negative consequences, for Hinduism has much to be said against it. India's caste system oppressed peasants and outcastes for thousands of years. The disbelief in the reality of the world led to minimal scientific discovery as compared to the West. It could be argued that men bearing the name of Christ did horrible things such as the crusades and race-based slavery, but it must be noted that such men did not live in accordance with the Christian worldview, but their actions actually contradicted the Bible. In contrast, the caste system of Hinduism was created by the religion's belief in samsarra, dharma, and karma.[18] In fact, the reason why the

---

[15] Argument from folly.

[16] 2 Corinthians 10:3-5.

[17] Greg Bahnsen, "Types of Worldviews," *Series One.*

[18] Samsarra is the ongoing cycle of reincarnation and suffering in the world of Maya. Dharma is the duty that each caste member is expected to perform. Karma is the balance that weighs how well each caste member fulfilled their dharma or duty. If at death a person's positive karma outweighs their negative—meaning they fulfilled their dharma—they are reincarnated upward to the next caste on the list. Thus vertical mobility takes a lifetime and a reincarnation to the next

caste system is difficult to erase from India today is due to these beliefs. The consequences of Hinduism are apparent to any student of South Asian history.

The Christian worldview not only meets the preconditions of intelligibility, but actually is the necessary precondition of intelligibility. We can confidently say that if the Bible is not true, then nothing can be proven to be true. We can prove this. No Hindu can say this from any of their texts, since none of them can justify the laws of logic, scientific inference, moral absolutes, and so on. Therefore, Hinduism has been shown to be foolishness.

Immanent Moralism

The next broad category of religious ideology is immanent moralism. Rather than emphasize what goes on outside of the physical world, adherents of these religions focus specifically on this world and the here and now. They often do not concern themselves with notions such as life after death or the nature of God.

Two of the most prominent examples are Confucianism and Buddhism. In both, reality is not thought to be beyond mankind's experience, but instead reality is nearby. Therefore, they reject mystical living and instead favor moralistic codes. This is not to say that such religious viewpoints are atheistic, though some are such as original Buddhism, but instead even if they believe in the existence of a god or gods, such religious forces are close at hand and are not outside of the domain of our experience. In many cases, such deities matter little since the ultimate goal of these religions is to provide a moral code for humans to live by. In order to demonstrate the futility of this type of religious worldview, its two largest and most historically significant variants will be discussed: Confucianism and Buddhism.

Confucianism

Confucianism was founded by the Chinese philosopher K'ung fu-tzu, or better known in the West as Confucius (551-479 B.C.).[19] Confucius was born into the nobility, but due to hardships that befell his family, he entered the civil service at age fifteen, and ascended to the position of minister of justice at age fifty.[20] During this

---

position. If a peasant attempted to be an innovative artisan or merchant, then they would actually accrue bad karma since their dharma is that of a peasant. They would be reincarnated in the lowest caste —outcastes. So the caste system was justified by Hindu religion, and to rebel against it carried the threat of bad karma. This discouraged social improvement, education, and technological innovation.

[19] Bresnan, 128.
[20] Corduan, 292.

time, he spent much effort studying ancient history and philosophy. Yet, after only seven years of being at the height of his career, he was ousted due to court politics and was exiled from his home province. He then became a famous teacher having thousands of disciples by the time of his death.[21] Although he invented no new religious doctrine, he did believe in the abstract Chinese view of heaven ruling earth, and he believed that heaven, or T'ien,[22] called him to teach the precepts of Confucianism.[23]

Confucianism really is more of a socio-political ideology than a religion,[24] but it does demand that people live a certain way. He combined the concepts of *ren* (seeking the welfare of others)[25] and *li* (doing the right thing at the right time)[26] and created a moral code that was meant to fix the political, social, and moral chaos of China. All human interaction consisted of five basic relationships, and if all people did their part in each of the five relationships, society would be completely healed.[27] The five relationships in order of importance are as follows: 1) father and son, where the father shows kindness and the son shows obedience (filial piety); 2) elder brother and younger brother, where the older shows gentility and the younger humility; 3) husband and wife, where the husband shows righteous behavior and the wife responds with obedience; 4) elder and junior, with the elder displaying humane consideration and the junior deference; 5) ruler and subject, with the ruler leading in benevolence and the subject showing loyalty to the ruler.[28] The sacred text of his codified teachings is the *Analects*.

For observers of Confucianism, the emphasis is not ritual, meditation, or enlightenment since these are mystical and focused on the transcendent. Their focus is instead directed at living according to the teachings briefly mentioned. The *Analects* are sayings of Confucius, where he states how the noble man lives. For example, the noble man is to be a gentleman, who is educated, cultured, courteous, etc. If all people strived to live by the moral code, then they would have mastery over the real world. Thus, if a Christian were to appeal to the Confucian and preach the gospel, the Confucian is trained to see the transcendent realities of God and His

---

[21] Ibid.

[22] Wing-tsit Chan, *A Source Book in Chinese Philosophy* (Princeton, N.J.: Princeton University Press, 1969), 16.

[23] Corduan, 293.

[24] Ibid., 15.

[25] Bresnan, 136.

[26] Ibid., 133-134.

[27] Ibid., 135.

[28] Courdan, 294.

attributes as irrelevant. Instead, his code is all he needs to get by in the world. With that said, how does one refute this worldview?

PIA and the Argument from Truth and Folly

Bahnsen suggests that the most devastating refutation of any religion of immanent moralism is that there are so many of them.[29] At first glance, that may not seem like a refutation, but when one truly contemplates the implications of it, it savages any religion of immanent moralism. Who is to say that what Confucius says is right? How do we know he was right and the Buddha was wrong? Perhaps the Roman Stoics are the ones with the right code! How is anyone to know which code is true? So what if Confucius said the nobleman keeps the five relationships? In other words, it all comes back to authority. What authority does Confucius have? He was only a finite human being, with a three pound brain, living in a pre-scientific era, and therefore he had a non-exhaustive knowledge and he too was a slave to sin. If any regular man is ever appealed to as the authority, we are reduced to relativism since epistemological authority cannot be justified due to our finitude. Thus, the Christian has the right to ask, "Why should I listen to Confucius? Who is he that I should pay attention to him? He's just a man who only held a job for seven years, got fired, and then became a teacher!" It appears that Confucianism suffers from arbitrariness, or the *A* in the PIA.

Of course, the Confucian may try to reverse the question and ask, "Who is Jesus that we should listen to Him?" Are we at an impasse? Not in the least! The Christian's answer is that Jesus is the Son of the Living God, and He will be the judge of the whole world. As a result, He not only is infinite and possesses exhaustive knowledge, but He also is the one who created the moral standard (Law) based on His own nature, and He is the one with the authority to hold us all accountable to that standard. The Confucian may not accept this truth, but that does not matter. The Christian still can say, "In the Christian explanation of things, it makes sense for us to say Jesus is the authority. We are perfectly consistent. You, the Confucian, are not in such a position. In a world controlled by impersonal heaven or T'ien, what is so special about a mere man like Confucius?" If he answers that Confucius' wisdom is what makes him special, the Christian can reject that by asking, "Says who, other Confucians?" In other words, who was the person who held a contest that said all wise people can come forward to share their wisdom so that he could then judge (on his own authority) who the wisest was?[30] No such contest ever

---

[29] Greg Bahnsen, "Types of Worldviews," *Series One.*
[30] Ibid.

occurred, but even if it did, how could anyone know authoritatively who the wisest was, unless there already existed an objective standard of truth and morals that transcended humanity?

Since these types of religions do not have a transcendent authority to appeal to, they cannot justify their positions. Confucius could not explain how the impersonal T'ien put the right views in his mind. Instead, he arbitrarily asserted that he knew what was right, and when questioned as to how he knew this, his response was that it was his destiny to know and teach his code.[31] Truly, his code was nothing other than his mere opinion. He received no revelation from T'ien, and thus no divine words explaining true wisdom to him were given. As a result, Confucianism is incapable of proving itself superior to its competitors.

Christians have a personal transcendent authority that has given special revelation, and that special revelation commands us to listen to Jesus. Therefore, it makes sense in the Christian story that Jesus is the authority, that He is the only Way to the Father, and that every knee should bow. The Confucian may reject this, and therefore will face the consequence of such a rejection, but what he is left with is an arbitrary worldview that philosophically cannot be justified.

In addition to its arbitrariness, another great weakness is the inconsistency of immanent moralism in general. All forms of it, including Confucianism, will tell people that the problem of individuals and communities is that they do not live according to the right code. In fact, they will often admit that all humans have failed to live according to the code. Well, if all people have failed to live according to the code, then it must be a fact that something is wrong with all people. If there is something wrong with people, then it must be true that they need something to help them live by the code. In other words, if humanity is guilty of not following the right code, then before the code can do anyone any good, there must be a solution to change man so that he can follow the code and stop failing.

This proves then, that the Christian concept of redemption and deliverance is necessary, yet none of the moralistic faiths have redemption. Instead, they simply demand that mankind try harder to follow the code. If a person became a Confucian adherent tomorrow, it does not change the fact that he has previously spent his entire life breaking all of the rules of Confucius. What can he do about this? Confucianism's only answer is for people to start living by the rules, but that was the problem to begin with. What will make the person be able to start following the rules? There is no answer!

---

[31] Chan, 727.

Even worse, if by some miracle the person was able to live according to the code starting today, the guilt incurred from all past failures to live by the code would still not have been dealt with. If a murderer stopped murdering today, and lived peacefully for the next ten years, but then was arrested for the past murders, he would still serve the prison sentence for the past guilt. Thus, moralistic faiths not only cannot deal with the problem of man's lawbreaking nature, but they also cannot deal with the guilt of past lawbreaking. This great internal inconsistency exists in all forms of immanent moralism, thus making these religions useless. In a like manner, Judaism's emphasis on keeping the Law fails in the same way. Only Christianity offers a moral code that is not arbitrary, and in addition to that, it deals with the sin nature of man by regeneration, and the past guilt of lawbreaking through justification.[32] Only Christianity provides a coherent worldview. The *I* of the PIA demonstrates the bankruptcy of manmade moralistic codes.

Confucianism also cannot meet the preconditions of intelligibility. On one hand, it seems as though Confucius was unconcerned with such preconditions, and so he thought little of them. Yet, the ability to have a moral code requires an objective and unchanging standard that is immaterial, as Plato realized. The ability to live according to some aspects of the code, such as getting an education, requires the uniformity of nature. Does Confucianism account for any of this? No, like atheism it simply takes such things for granted. The very act of reasoning that Confucius used depended on deductive inference, and yet his worldview could not account for it either. Thus, Confucianism provides none of the necessary preconditions of intelligibility and therefore its presuppositions render it as folly.

When these factors are taken into consideration, Christians have nothing to fear from any system of immanent moralism. They are arbitrary due to the problem of authority, they are inconsistent in the fact that they prescribe as a solution the very problem itself (following the moral code), and they fail to meet the preconditions of intelligibility. Like Confucianism, Buddhism also is problematic. To that we now turn.

---

[32] Judaism has a non-arbitrary law code since it came from YHWH, but Judaism has nothing to change our nature to enable our following of the Law, nor does it have any means to provide justification. The Old Testament does teach about the God-initiated circumcision of the heart (regeneration) and justification via substitutionary atonement, but these fundamental Old Testament truths are all but ignored in modern Judaism. Only Christianity holds to them since they were fulfilled perfectly in the person of Jesus Christ.

Buddhism

Moving on to Buddhism, it is a religion that came out of Hinduism, and apparently rejected transcendent mysticism as the means to enlightenment. The founder was Siddhartha Gautama (563-483 B.C.) and he grew up in a Hindu environment (India) born to royalty.[33] He eventually renounced the luxury of his life, and even came to reject the world itself. Seeing a vision of four passing sights caused him to leave his life of royalty and seek true meaning. The four passing sights were 1) an old man nearing death, 2) a diseased and disfigured man, 3) a dead man's funeral procession, and 4) a shaven monk.[34] Seeing that life is suffering, he joined ascetic Hindus where he nearly abused himself to death.[35] When he realized that renouncing the world and trying to live as a monk did not cause enlightenment, he set out to study suffering in order to learn its meaning and to figure out how to avoid it. As he mediated under a tree, Mara (the evil one of Hinduism)[36] tempted him, and as he emerged victorious from that temptation, he reached enlightenment after forty-nine days, thus becoming the Buddha, or enlightened one. He also came to the conclusion of the Middle Way, which was a way between luxurious pleasure and suffering.

Once enlightened, the Buddha claimed there were no gods, which is quite strange since he came to this enlightenment after being tempted by a god. It is like using a boat to sail across a river. Once on land, the boat is discarded; therefore now there is no boat.[37] He claimed that his enlightening experience showed him that there is something wrong with the human race—suffering. Siddhartha did not ask people to believe what he said because he said it, but instead because they experienced it. Suffering is universal, and people know it through experience. They do not learn it from the gods, especially since there are no gods according to Siddhartha. Nor do they learn it from authoritative teachers, for he would admit that he had no authority. By knowing truth through experience, it becomes immanent rather than transcendent. Buddhism then is a *learn as you go* type of religion.[38]

Siddhartha denied the supernatural favoring atheism. To him, the chief end of man was to eliminate suffering by having the right experiences. He claimed that suffering comes from human desires, and therefore if a person can rid himself of

---

[33] Bresnan, 193.
[34] Corduan, 222.
[35] Bresnan, 200.
[36] Corduan, 222.
[37] I heard this one quite often in martial arts classes.
[38] Greg Bahnsen, "Types of Worldviews," *Series Two*.

desire then he can rid himself of suffering.[39] The primary means to be rid of desire is through perfect detachment, and the way to accomplish this is by following the Eightfold Path.[40] It is precisely this part of Buddhism that makes it moralistic. By adding moralism to the immanent nature of experience, Buddhism possesses an immanent moralistic religious foundation. In addition to following the Eightfold Path, a person must also believe the Four Noble Truths.[41] With the correct belief and actions in place, a person can eliminate desire thereby eliminating suffering. When a person reaches perfect detachment, they too become a Buddha or an enlightened one. Proper meditation through certain yogas and mantras is supposed to help, as is a rejection of the body as loathsome.

Of course, Buddhism did not remain as a simple pessimistic and self-centered attempt at self-extinction. By the time of Christ, some Buddhists revolted against the traditional beliefs set forth by Siddhartha and created what is called Mahayana Buddhism. They saw purpose in achieving enlightenment, but rather than entering a state of Nirvana, they would remain in the cycle of rebirth as a bodhisattva in order to help others achieve enlightenment.[42] The Mahayana schools eventually allowed for the existence of greater heavenly Buddhas that teach the bodhisattvas and rule over certain heavenly realms. This would allow for this type of Buddhism to mesh well with the popular polytheistic religions of both China and Japan. The vast majority of Buddhists fall under Mahayana beliefs. Those who hold to the original teachings of Siddhartha are known as Therevada Buddhists. Ultimately, both forms of Buddhism are easy to refute, because at their core they still hold to the immanent moralistic principles founded by Siddhartha Gautama, and thus they both suffer the same weaknesses.

PIA and the Argument from Truth and Folly

What should the Christian's response be to the Buddhist? By now, it should be obvious; we use the PIA technique. As with the other religions, we can spot arbitrariness and inconsistency simply by reminding the Buddhist of some of the teachings of Siddhartha . For example,[43] if a Zen Buddhist claims that a person must meditate on the sound of one hand clapping in order to help break free from attachment, the Christian should ask, "Who says so?" If he responds that the Buddha

---

[39] Zimmer, 467.
[40] Tennent, *Christianity at the Religious Roundtable*, 91.
[41] Bresnan, 224.
[42] Zimmer, 535.
[43] This example also comes from Greg Bahnsen's afore-cited lecture.

said so, the Christian can rightly respond with, "Buddha said not to believe something because he said it, and thus by his own standard you have not given me a valid reason to believe it." Perhaps he will appeal to the Zen authorities, but once again Siddhartha claimed there are no authorities other than experience.[44] If the Buddhist concedes and then argues that it should be believed by experiencing it, the Christian can simply say he has never experienced it and thus he has no reason to believe it. At that point, the Buddhist may tell the Christian that he "ought to" or "should" experience it, but the Christian can claim to see no reason to do so since it may just be a waste of time. In other words, the Buddhist cannot justify at all what he is asking people to do in order to come to Buddhist conclusions.

Buddhism asks people to shut off the mind and brain in order to have an experience, and they recommend eastern meditation as a tool since its primary goal is to empty the mind and create detachment. Suicide would be less work to achieve Buddhist goals. Suffering can end if life ends. In fact, with no life, there is no desire, and with no desire there is no suffering. Perhaps wars to annihilate the species can accomplish the goal too. Since there are apparently other ways to end suffering, why does anyone need Buddhist ideas? Of course, the Buddhist will argue for life-affirming activities to achieve the goal of ending suffering, but once again, on what authority is life-affirming activities deemed to be greater than suicide? On Siddhartha's authority? These points reveal the inconsistent and contradictory nature of Buddhism. It is arbitrary since people are told to believe something and act on it because Buddha did so and said so, but in the same breath it is inconsistent due to contradiction. Being tempted by a god to conclude there are no gods, and being told to listen to Buddha when he said not to listen to him are pretty big inconsistencies.

Some of the same problems of Confucianism exist in Buddhism too. A Confucian will reject Buddhism because he arbitrarily accepts Confucius's teachings. The Taoist then rejects both since its founder Lao Tzu said to follow the way or the Tao. Next comes the Shinto believer telling people to follow the Kami, or gods of Japan. Following any of these options makes one guilty of arbitrariness since none of these people have any real authority. Instead, you have the arbitrary opinion of Siddhartha in disagreement with the arbitrary opinions of every other teacher of all other forms of immanent moralism.

In terms of its inconsistency, Siddhartha claimed that man does not have a soul (anātman),[45] but then told his followers to be careful not to build up bad karma,[46]

---

[44] Bresnan., 213.
[45] Ibid., 219-220.
[46] Ibid., 231.

which itself is a transcendent property of souls and reincarnation. Knowing that such an idea was foolish, Siddhartha likened our existence to a flickering candle that passes on a flame to another candle. Thus, when dealing with an unanswerable weakness of his philosophy, Siddhartha resorted to a metaphor. The metaphor cannot explain how life flickers from one body to a new one if there is not a soul. Instead, it merely asserts that it does. Thus, Buddha's answer to inconsistency is to be arbitrary.

If he is right, and there is no soul, and somehow our lives flicker into new babies, but our memories die with the old body, then why care about bad karma? Eat, drink, and live the hedonistic life since that bad karma is going to travel onto someone else. Also, the ultimate goal of Buddhism is Nirvana, which is extinction. Supposedly when enlightenment is reached and there is perfect detachment, then the flickering stops and a person becomes extinct and can no longer suffer. Well, if there is no soul, then death would lead to extinction anyway, and Nirvana would be achieved without the Eightfold Path. Therefore, what use does it truly have? The baby that you flicker onto is not truly you, and thus when the body dies, extinction is already attained. Truly, Buddhism is so wrought with contradictions that it is powerless in accomplishing its stated goals.

Both Buddhism and Confucianism demonstrate that religions of immanent moralism have too big of a problem with arbitrariness and inconsistency. There is no authority in these religions to justify their moral code, and the inconsistencies are horrific. Even the consequences have proven to be more negative than positive. For example, Confucianism was used to create an oppressive caste-system in Japan during the Tokugawa Shogunate, which led to a society with zero chance of vertical social mobility. Buddhists are not known for their scientific advancements since science itself depends upon an attachment to this world and a thirst for discovery. When the goal of one's religion is detachment, science makes little sense. Nineteenth Century sociologist, Max Weber, made strong arguments that the religious worldviews of the Far East (Hinduism and the variety of immanent moralistic options) created societies incapable of groundbreaking scientific advancement and industrial revolutions.[47] Yet, the Protestant societies of Europe, with their Christian worldview understood the world in such a way that all of these advancements came from them.[48]

Finally, Buddhism cannot account for the preconditions of intelligibility. It provides no authoritative explanation for the uniformity of nature, logic, moral

---

[47] Max Weber, *Sociology of World Religions: Introduction.*

[48] Max Weber, *The Protestant Ethic and the Spirit of Capitalism*, Translated by Talcott Parsons, (New York: Charles Scribner's Sons, 1958), 1904-1905.

absolutes, the reliability of the mind, etc. In fact, Siddhartha argued that reality is an endless and circular chain of cause and effect, with no first cause. Therefore, nothing is, nor can, be permanent. This was his way to remove an absolute being, since by definition no being can be permanent in this endless chain of cause and effect. Of course, he seems to imply that the endless chain itself is permanent, which contradicts his entire attempt to say that nothing is permanent. Besides the fact that observable and scientific evidence (entropy) demonstrates the universe not to be endless and eternal, Siddhartha also has not proven anything, or provided any preconditions. He simply asserted that things flow in a never ending sequence, which assumes the uniformity of nature, but it by no means accounts for it. The only way to account for it is with an absolute sovereign being who sustains it. Yet, he developed his very idea of the endless uniform chain in an attempt to deny such a being. So his system is guilty of the worst kind of contradiction; if it is true, then it is false.

Truly, a Christian apologist would not have to try with difficulty to confound the Buddhist. The argument from folly shows it to be devastated by all parts of PIA. The argument from truth always demonstrates that Christianity alone is the necessary precondition of intelligibility and is free from arbitrariness and inconsistency.

Conclusion

Christians are not stuck in a Mexican standoff when faced with other religions. Hopefully, it was clearly demonstrated that religions of transcendent mysticism and immanent moralism fail to meet the preconditions of intelligibility just as bad as atheism and secular dualism. Referring back to the martial arts analogy, these two religions represent weak fighters. Transcendent mysticism is akin to a fighter who attempts to use telekinesis to win a fight. Since telekinesis is not real, the opponent can walk right up and finish the fight with no effort. Religions of immanent moralism are like the fighter who only knows how to do two punches. They may be good at their two punches, but someone with powerful kicks and many punches can easily defeat them.

These two categories of religion are so fundamentally flawed that it was easy to evaluate them in a single chapter and defeat them with the PIA. The bigger problem is posed by the third category of religion, namely, Biblical Counterfeits. They will be dealt with in the next and final chapter.

Chapter Eleven

Biblical Counterfeits

Introduction

In the previous chapter, two of the broad categories of religious thought were evaluated and found to be wanting. In this final chapter of this book, the final category of religious worldviews will be judged. It is here that we finally come to the biblical counterfeits. These types of religions are problematic since they borrow bits and pieces, or large portions, of the biblical worldview and create false and damning faiths. As such, they can meet some of the preconditions of intelligibility, though not all. These types of religions fall heaviest when their inconsistency and arbitrariness is displayed.

Continuing with the martial arts analogy, these religions represent the fighter that joined the school you learned everything from. Imagine that you are from the most comprehensive school in the world, with the greatest fighting science, and the most efficient use of techniques. Well, these biblical counterfeits are like someone that trained in the same place, learned many of your techniques and principles, but then deviated and attempted to open his own school all the while proclaiming his school to be the most comprehensive school in the world. He is dangerous because he knows enough of your techniques to put up a blow-for-blow fight. I have seen this before in training. However, one thing I observed time and time again is the counterfeits often deviate from the most important and fundamental principles of the martial art system. As a result, they lose the ability to stand against their former teachers and classmates, and often get humiliated in combat.

It is the same with the biblical counterfeits. They may have stolen some lofty ideas from the Bible (monotheism, sovereignty of God, ex nihilo creation, uniformity of nature, etc.), but they deviate from some of the most important fundamental truths (Trinity, divinity of Christ, universal depravity of man, the need of a Savior, monergistic salvation, sufficiency of the Bible, etc.), and as a result, they are unable to stand against the PIA technique. They might be able to falsely advance attacks from scripture against the truth, but ultimately, they are not consistent with what the scripture teaches, and they reject certain truths of the biblical worldview that are necessary to meet the preconditions of intelligibility. In short, when they attempt to challenge the school from which they stole their ideas, they end up humiliated. The goal of this chapter is to demonstrate this.

In dealing with the biblical counterfeits, there are three subcategories that the Christian apologist must be aware of. First, there are unitarian counterfeits that believe in a single God, but deny the Trinity. Islam, Judaism, Unitarians, and the Jehovah Witnesses are examples of this type of counterfeit. Second, there are polytheistic counterfeits. They possess a biblical-like view of God since they borrow certain ideas about God from the Bible, but the ultimate reality within their view consists of more than one god. Mormonism is the chief example of this type of counterfeit, as it speaks of God with a Christian vocabulary and claims to believe the Bible. Finally, there are Pseudo-Messianic counterfeits in which a group claims their leader is a savior serving that function in the place of Christ. Examples include the Moonies from Korea and the Branch Davidians in Texas in the early 1990s.

As long as the Christian apologist knows how to deal with the broad categories, he can deal with the variety of false faiths that come from them. Ultimately, all religions possess the same problems that every other non-Christian worldview does. They cannot meet the preconditions of intelligibility, and are arbitrary, inconsistent, and have had predominantly negative consequences in history. In short, they are obliterated before the PIA technique. The Christian would do well to study about the more prevalent counterfeits (i.e., Mormonism, Islam, etc.) in order to be ready for dialogue/debate, but even merely listening to their story provides enough information to refute them. In this chapter, basic elements of their stories of will be given in order to provide a context for the PIA technique. If the reader desires more detail about these faiths, there are other books dedicated to these counterfeits that should be consulted.[1] With that, it is time to move into the refutations.

I will begin with the unitarian counterfeits by using Islam as the case study, and then will briefly apply the refutation to other counterfeits of the same vein.

Unitarian Counterfeits

A unitarian counterfeit is one that denies that God is a Trinity. In fact, adherents of such faiths believe that it is contradictory to see unity and plurality work together without contradiction. By way of reminder, the philosophical inadequacy of unitarian

---

[1] Dr. Walter Martin's *Kingdom of the Cults* is an excellent single volume for this purpose.

conceptions of God were addressed in chapter two of this book where it was demonstrated that the doctrine of the Trinity makes it possible for God to possess personal attributes, and it clears up the one and many problem of philosophy. Unitarian deities cannot be absolute personalities that are distinct from creation, and as such no unitarian God could ever be sovereign. In other words, the claims that unitarian religions make concerning God (that he is personal, above creation, and sovereign over the universe) are philosophically impossible if the one God were unitarian rather than Trinitarian. It is suggested that the reader review those pages of chapter two prior to moving forward.

There are a number of unitarian counterfeits, such as Unitarian Universalism, Judaism, Jehovah Witnesses, and Islam. Islam is the single largest of these types of religions, and it is perhaps the greatest direct counterfeit to Christianity. Interestingly enough, critics of presuppositional apologetics often appeal to Islam as the counterexample to Christianity that will undermine a presuppositional defense of the Christian faith. It is claimed that Islam could make the same worldview arguments that Christians make. After all, Islam claims a personal god, it is monotheistic, and it claims to possess a holy book that is special revelation from the personal god. This is why Islam is the greatest direct counterfeit to Christianity. The Christian must be able to demonstrate that Islam is indeed a counterfeit that cannot meet the necessary preconditions of intelligibility, and that it suffers from arbitrariness, inconsistency, and many negative consequences. When the internal critique (argument from folly) is made of Islam, it is unable to stand as a coherent worldview, but instead is just as groundless and hopeless as atheism.

As with the other religions discussed thus far, a brief summary of the historical background and doctrine of Islam would benefit my readers. The religion was founded by Muhammad (570-632) roughly 600 years after the birth of Christ. Islamic apologists will immediately dismiss the notion that Muhammad founded Islam, but instead they will claim that it was the religion of Adam, Abraham, and Jesus, and that Muhammad simply was the final prophet of this religion.[2] Muhammad was born in the violent polytheistic Arab culture that was divided by tribal lines.

His personal life was one of much tragedy. For example, his father died right after Muhammad's birth, his mother died when he was six years old, his grandfather died when he was eight years old, and thus he lived until adulthood with his uncle Abu.[3]

---

[2] John L. Esposito, *Islam: The Straight Path*, 3rd ed. (Oxford University Press, USA, 1998), 4.
[3] James White, *What Every Christian Needs to Know About Qur'an.* (Bethany House Publishers, 2013), 21.

Abu ran a caravan that traveled to Palestine, Syria, and Persia, thus bringing Muhammad into contact with Jews and Christians. When he was twenty-five years old, Muhammad married a forty-year old rich widow named Khadijah, had three sons with her, but all three sons died. After this, Muhammad became deeply religious, often meditating in the caves of Mecca.

It was at this time, in the year 610, that he began to receive revelations. He apparently suffered from epilepsy (or worse) because his revelations often caused him to fall to the ground in convulsions while foaming at the mouth.[4] Muhammad concluded that these were demonic attacks,[5] but Khadijah convinced him to listen to the revelations believing they were from God.[6] The messenger claimed to be the angel Gabriel, and for the next twenty-years Muhammad received these revelations still bearing the symptoms of epileptic seizures. Gabriel commanded him to recite, resulting in the Qur'an being the written down records (or surahs) of the recitations. Muhammad claimed to be a new and final prophet of the true religion of Islam with the mission of restoring the original religion of the true God. In a haphazard manner, Islam blended Jewish and Christian ideas with Arabic ones. Initially, Muhammad's new religion was not well received in Mecca, and not long after Khadijah died, he was forced to flee Mecca in 622.

This moment in Muhammad's life is called the Hijra, which means flight, and it is the official start date of the Islamic calendar. Muhammad ended up over 200 miles north of Mecca at the city of Yathrib, where he became a successful man due to his political shrewdness and ability to mediate disputes between the tribal leaders.[7] He became the leader of the city and united it under himself by politically marrying women from the tribal families. Yathrib became an Islamic city united under Muhammad and was renamed Medina, meaning "City of the Prophet." After Khadijah's death, Muhammad married twelve other women, but still had no surviving sons. Due to the fact that Muhammad married for his own political power and elevated social status, it is reasonable to question that his first marriage to Khadijah also was a strategic move for him, since she was wealthy. In fact, only one of his marriages gained him no social advancement—his favorite marriage—and yet this marriage was quite disturbing. His favorite wife was Aisha, the daughter of his

---

[4] Winfried Corduan, *Neighboring Faiths: A Christian Introduction to World Religions* (IVP Academic, 1998), 79.

[5] Esposito, *Islam*, 7.

[6] White, *What Every Christian Needs to Know About Qur'an*. 23-24.

[7] Esposito, *Islam*, 8.

friend Abu Bakr, however, he married and consummated the marriage with her when she was only nine years old.[8] It seems that the prophet was also a pedophile.

It was in Medina that Muhammad first tried to spread the faith to Jews and Christians. As a result there are many favorable statements about Judaism and Christianity in the parts of the Qu'ran that were written early on. Perhaps the goal was to win these other religions over to Islam through flattery. In fact, the Qu'ran claims that previous revelation from Allah is found in the Torah, Psalms of David, and the Gospels of Jesus. This appeal to prior revelation will be a weakness in Islam, much like it is for Mormonism.[9]

As it became clear that the Christians and Jews rejected Muhammad as a prophet, he became upset with them and had later revelations that condemned them and encouraged their killing if they would not convert.[10] The Jews in particular offended Muhammad since they publically debated him, scoffed when he could not produce signs or prophecies, and ultimately ridiculed him. He would later carry out an annihilation of Jews in the Arabian Peninsula.[11]

After his position was secure in northern Arabia, he waged war against the Meccan caravans to lead them into a larger war. After winning a series of major battles, Muhammad conquered Mecca in 630 and made it the capital of Islam. All of the idols in the Kaba were destroyed, and the worship site was dedicated to Allah alone.[12] Muhammad proceeded to weld all of the Arab tribes into a theocracy with himself as the head of the society. Two years later, he died. However, following his death, the Arabs, now united under Islam, turned their constant inward fighting outward and proved to be a nearly unstoppable force. The Persian Empire fell, as did much of the Byzantine Empire, Egypt, North Africa, and Spain. It would not be until Charles Martel defeated the Islamic invaders at Tours that the westward spread of Islam was halted. After that time, Islamic civilization dominated much of the world until the Crusades.

Doctrinally, Islam has five dominant doctrines and a sixth less emphasized one.[13] First, there is only one god, Allah. The word Allah simply means, "The God." Second, God has sent many prophets to guide men, but Muhammad is the last and

---

[8] White, *What Every Christian Needs to Know About the Qur'an. 37.*

[9] Mormonism will be discussed shortly.

[10] Surah 4:48

[11] Mark A. Gabriel, *Islam And The Jews: The unfinished battle*, First ed. (Charisma House, 2003), 107–117.

[12] Sydey N. Fisher and William Ochsenwald, *The Middle East: A History, Volume 1*, Fifth ed. (McGraw Hill, 1997), 32-35.

[13] Greg Bahnsen, "Types of Worldviews," *Series Two.*

greatest of them, being called the seal of the prophets. Third, although there are four inspired books (Torah, Psalms, Gospels, and Qu'ran) the Qu'ran is the most important. In fact, Muslims believe that the Jews and Christians are "people of the book," that corrupted their revelation thus necessitating the Qu'ran in order to fix it. Fourth, Islam focuses heavily on intermediary deities such as angels, demons, and jinn through a complex angelology. Fifth, they believe in a final day of judgment in which all men will be resurrected and sent to either heaven or hell based on their works.[14] Heaven is a place of sensuous delight for males, as they will be served by women for all eternity. The sixth, and less emphasized, doctrine is that of hismet or fate. In Islam, this means that there is absolutely no free will, or any real autonomous volition, but Allah controls everything from the movements of leaves to every decision and word that every person speaks. There is little in common between this view of fate, and the compatiblism of scriptural (Calvinistic) Christianity.[15]

There are five pillars of belief and practice that all Muslims are to obey. First, a person must recite the creed, "There is no god but Allah, and Muhammad is his prophet." Second, a Muslim must pray five times a day facing Mecca. Third, alms giving is required by those who are in a position to give. Fourth, all Muslims must observe the month-long fast of Ramadan. Fifth, all able-bodied Muslims are to make a pilgrimage to Mecca at least once in their lives.[16] These five pillars demonstrate Islam to be a moralistic religion that focuses on works-righteousness. Like the doctrines, there is a sixth less emphasized pillar of Islamic practice that is highly pervasive. Jihad, or holy war, is the obligation of all Muslims against infidels, or nonbelievers.

Muslim apologists often claim Christians make more out of this than we should since jihad primarily refers to spiritual war within the individual Muslim. Although this is true, and this internal war is called greater jihad, the Islamic apologists cannot make light of what is called lesser jihad, which is physical warfare against all non-Muslims. It is pervasive throughout the Qu'ran and the Hadiths, and even a minimal knowledge of world history can attest to the historic interpretation of Muslims regarding the duty and necessity to spread Islam by the sword. Often liberals in the West get deceived in their vain political correctness and buy into the claims of what Dr. Mark Gabriel calls the "nice Islam of the West."[17] As result, they deny that Islam is a violent religion.

---

[14] Fisher and Ochsenwald, *The Middle East*. 78-79.
[15] Arminians demonstrate either dishonesty or ignorance when they liken Calvinism to Islam.
[16] Esposito, *Islam*, 88-92.
[17] Gabriel, *Islam And The Jews*, 51–55.

There have been many death threats in recent years against non-Muslims who speak offensive things against Islam. The terrorist attacks against the West are dubbed as radical Islam, but if such were true, then up until a century ago, much of Islamic civilization was radical Islam. Today, when an Imam claims that Muslims must defend themselves from a particular satanic threat, he can call for a holy war against that threat. Often, the threat can be a single person, and the Imam can place a ban on that individual thus charging all Muslims with the duty of killing that individual should they run into him. A famous example in recent history is found in Salman Rushdie. He wrote a book that spoke of the "Satanic Verses"[18] in the Qur'an where Allah allowed polytheistic worship alongside him, and as a result Muslims put a ban on Rushdie for exposing this truth. This ban is still in effect against Rushdie.

Given this short history and explanation of Islam, my readers now know more than enough to refute this biblical counterfeit with the PIA technique. Even though Muslims have the Qur'an as their holy book, and we have the Bible as ours, we are not in an even standoff, for the Islamic worldview cannot meet the preconditions of intelligibility, nor can it escape arbitrariness and inconsistency. To that we now turn.

PIA & Argument from Truth and Folly

In refuting Islam, the route that will be taken here is to first evaluate it from the scriptures. Most refutations thus far focused heavily on the argument from folly, but when it comes to biblical counterfeits, the argument from truth accomplishes more than it does against non-counterfeits. Against every other worldview, the argument from truth demonstrates that Christianity passes the PIA, but against biblical counterfeits it does much more than this. It also exposes more problems with the counterfeits since they often claim to accept the revelatory status of the Bible. Thus, showing where the Bible disagrees with the counterfeit actually helps to demonstrate inconsistency. In the end, both the arguments from truth and folly serve as an internal critique and effectively destroy these worldviews.

Any biblical counterfeit that awards the Bible with the status of divine revelation will always run into a prodigious problem. In Islam, the Qur'an claims to be a confirmation of the earlier revelations: Torah, Psalms, and Gospels. [19] By Muhammad making this appeal early on as an attempt to win the Christians and Jews over to himself, he really created a problem for Islam, since the Qur'an claims to confirm these prior revelations. However, these prior revelations claim that future

---

[18] Timothy C. Tennent, *Christianity at the Religious Roundtable: Evangelicalism in Conversation with Hinduism, Buddhism, and Islam* (Baker Academic, 2002), 145.

[19] Gabriel, *Islam And The Jews*, 38.

revelation has to be confirmed instead by past revelation.[20] There already exists a major conflict between the two revelations as to the determination of what constitutes true divine revelation. That alone is a major conflict, and every additional detailed conflict that can be shown between the Bible and Qur'an only compiles the number of inconsistencies Muhammad created for his religion by appealing to the Bible as revelation.

It would take an entire book itself just to show all the places where the Bible contradicts the Qur'an, but here a few of the larger examples can be highlighted. Muhammad taught a moralistic means to get right with Allah,[21] but the Bible teaches of salvation by grace[22] and condemns all moralistic attempts at being right with God.[23] There are many large theological contradictions such as this. For example, the Qur'an claims that it is wrong to worship Jesus or to call Him the Son of God since God supposedly cannot have a Son.[24] The Qur'an unequivocally denies the deity of Jesus Christ. In fact, the Qur'an claims that all Trinitarians are truly polytheists.[25] Muhammad clearly did not understand the doctrine of the Trinity, for it is a total belief in the existence of only one God, but that the one God exists as Three Persons. Jesus' divinity does not mean there is more than one God, but instead it confirms that God became a man to redeem His elect. The Bible teaches these truths in many places, as found in chapter one of this book.

Redemption is a larger problem for Muhammad. Allah commands men to obey the Qur'an, but if it is true that all men have failed, then how does man's nature change to enable him to obey? Muslims deny original sin,[26] thus what is their explanation for the universality of sin?[27] How does Allah deal with past guilt of past law breaking?[28] Like religions of immanent moralism, Islam offers no coherent story

---

[20] Deuteronomy 13:1-4.

[21] Surah 36:54.

[22] Ephesians 2:8-10.

[23] Galatians 1:8-9.

[24] Surah 2:116.

[25] Surah 5:76

[26] Esposito, *Islam*, 27.

[27] Finitude of creation is the explanation often given, but this creates many problems. Ultimately, this would mean people go to hell because they were prebuilt as finite beings, and the problems that exist in the world exist due to poor workmanship by Allah. Creation was not "good" in a biblical sense since death happened apart from sin due to Allah's apparent inability to create a world free of death and sin. Furthermore, how will there be sinlessness in Paradise if man's finitude still exists? These are problems that Muhammad did not think through.

[28] Apparently, all one has to do is repent and past guilt is forgiven. However, this renders Allah to be unholy, unjust, and no different than a liberal judge that allows a child molester to go free just because he says he is sorry.

of redemption. Instead, a man tries harder, and if he has more good deeds than wicked, the wicked ones do not matter and the person is saved from wrath.

Imagine the trouble any human would have (including a Muslim) with the following scenario. Someone raped and murdered[29] his mother in front of him, but then for the next five years served as a nurse and saved one hundred lives. Later the culprit was arrested for the previous rape and murder, but the judge acquitted him due to the good deeds outweighing the bad. How would a person feel if this happened? He would declare such a judge to be unjust. Yet, this is no different than Allah's scale of justice. No matter how many good deeds one does, objective guilt still exists for the bad deeds, and by definition, it is unjust to allow the guilty to go free when no restitution or payment for the crime has been made.

Within Christianity, regeneration changes the nature of those who are elect in order to enable them to obey God, and Christ's substitution on the cross allows for the full wrath and punishment to be inflicted upon Christ for the sins of the elect. The incarnation of God via the virgin birth allows for a human (Jesus) to be born without Adam's sin and the sin nature, to earn perfect, human righteousness, and then to switch accounts with sinners taking the punishment for their sin and yet giving them the credit of His righteousness! This is why God is both the just (punishes sin) and the justifier (declares sinners righteous). Only in Christianity does redemption exist and make sense. Islam certainly is lacking in this regard and contradicts the Bible blatantly. In fact, Surah 35:18 declares no one can bear another's burden for him, but instead, each person must bear his own burden. Yet, since forgiveness is given even with no payment for sin, Muslims technically do not even bear their own burden (logically speaking).

There are other embarrassing contradictions between the Qur'an and the Bible as well. One example is that Surah 19:28 claims Mary the mother of Jesus was the sister of the high priest Aaron. The root of this mistake is simple to see. Mary's name in Hebrew is Miriam, which was the name of Aaron and Moses' sister. The two Miriam's lived 1,400 years apart from each other and were from completely different tribes as the former was from Levi and the latter from Judah. In an oral culture like Muhammad's, one can see why a mistake like this could be made. However, Muslim

---

[29] I am purposely choosing a heinous crime in an attempt to illustrate the absolute lack of justice in the notion of God letting sin go unpunished with no atonement. After all, if a crime like this repulses us, imagine how much more so a perfect and holy God is repulsed by sin. Due to God's holiness, the white lie from our lips is more repulsive to Him than rape and murder is to us. We must never lose sight of just how serious sin is to God. This example was meant to stir hatred of the sin in the hearts of my readers so that they can in some limited way understand that God's hatred of sin is infinitely greater than theirs.

apologists cannot tolerate the notion of their perfect revelation having errors. Thus, they claim that Muhammad meant that Mary was a woman like Miriam. The text is clear. Muhammad thought the two Miriams were the same person.

An error similar in kind is found in the crucifixion of Jesus. Since Islam has no place for Christian redemption, and since Muslims do not want to believe that a prophet of Allah would be crucified, the Qur'an claims that a Jesus look-alike was crucified instead but people confused him for Jesus.[30] Also, it would be an embarrassment if Muhammad's bones were still in the ground, but a lesser prophet like Jesus (according to the Qur'an) was still alive via the Resurrection. In fact, this embarrassment is unavoidable due to a number of teachings from the Qur'an that make little sense if Jesus truly was the lesser prophet. In the book *Kingdom of the Cults*, this point is stated as follows:

> It is interesting to compare Jesus and Muhammad according to the Qur'an. Jesus did miracles (Surah 3:49; 5:110), but Muhammad did not (Surah 13:8: "thou art a warner [of coming divine judgment] only"; also 6:37; 6:109; 17:59 and 17:90-93); Jesus was sinless (Surah 3:46), but Muhammad sinned and needed forgiveness (Surah 40:55: "ask forgiveness of thy sin"; 42:5: "ask forgiveness for those on earth"; 47:19 "ask forgiveness for thy sin"; 48:2: "that Allah may forgive thee of thy sin"). Jesus was called "the Messiah" and was even born of a virgin (3:45-47)! Yet Muhammad is supposed to be the greatest of the prophets.[31]

The list of discrepancies can go on for pages. It suffices to say that the Qur'an has just been refuted with the very biblical revelation that it claims to accept. However, the Muslims will not allow it to end so easily. When the Muslim claims to honor the Law, Psalms, and Gospels, what he really means is that he honors these revelations as corrected by the Qur'an. In fact, it is quite deceptive to call the Qur'an a continuation of these revelations when it is used by Muslims to go back and change the meaning of the previous revelations.

Their justification of this comes from their claim that the Christians and Jews have corrupted the Scriptures, and the Qur'an is needed to correct such corruptions. At this point, the Christian has the right to ask what manuscript evidence exists to support the "revisions." Are there any ancient copies of the Torah, Psalms, and

---

[30] Surah 4:157. Also note that Surah 19:33 contradicts this since it has Jesus say that he would die and be raised again.

[31] Walter Martin, *The Kingdom of the Cults*, Revised Updated and Expanded Anniversary ed. (Bethany House Publishers, 1997), 623.

Gospels that contradict the more recent copies, thus proving through manuscripts that the texts were corrupted? On the contrary, the manuscripts overwhelmingly support the Bible as it is. The Muslim has no manuscripts to go back to as proof of the corruption. The purpose of appealing to manuscript evidence is not to argue him into the kingdom with evidence, but instead it is designed to demonstrate the arbitrary nature of his claim. His mere assertion of biblical corruption does not constitute an argument, but instead, it is only an unjustified opinion.

Muslims often argue that the Qur'an is superior to the Bible because it has no textual variants, whereas there are tens of thousands of variants in Bible manuscripts.[32] Muslims declare the variants to be conflicts, but to do so is highly deceptive. They cannot show any of the variants to be conflicts, since most of them are spelling errors. And the ones that do show a conflict do not actually affect any Christian doctrines. In fact, due to comparing the thousands of manuscripts against each other to check them, Christians can prove that the manuscripts agree on 98.33% of the words and thus we have 98.33% of the original autograph.[33] That is fantastic support for the integrity of the Bible.

The Muslims, in contrast, claim they have no variants and that every copy of the Qur'an is identical to every other copy of the Qur'an. This is not as much of a strength as they would hope. The third Caliph,[34] Uthman, ordered all manuscripts of the Qur'an to be turned into his government on the pain of death. When all of the manuscripts were turned in, his people selected which ones they thought were correct and burned all variants. This is an indisputable historical fact from Islamic sources.[35] This is why they have no variants. Therefore, they have no ability to go back and check their Qur'an against older manuscripts to make sure it is accurate. Instead, they have a single textual tradition surviving due to the decision made by a crooked politician to burn all others. If Christians wanted only one variant, it would not be difficult to accomplish.[36] If on pain of death every Christian was ordered to turn in all Bibles, and all accept the ESV were burned, then it could be said that the Bible

---

[32] This is not only true of their apologists, but also of many lay Muslims. In personal interactions with Muslim friends and Muslims encountered during street witnessing, I have come across variations of this argument.

[33] James White, *The King James Only Controversy: Can You Trust Modern Translations?* Bethany House Publishers, 2009), 66.

[34] Esposito, *Islam*, 21.

[35] White, *What Every Christian Needs to Know About Qur'an*. 258-263. James White interacts with many primary sources in his book that enlighten his readers concerning the Uthmanic Revision of the Qur'an.

[36] Greg Bahnsen, "Types of Worldviews," *Defending the Christian Worldview Against All Opposition, Series One and Series Two.*

has no variant readings. Would anyone truly think this would make the Bible more trustworthy? No. Why then would it be any different for the Qur'an?

Having no way of knowing what the variant Qur'an texts ever said, there is no evidence for the Qur'an's reliability. This fact renders Muslims guilty of arbitrariness. It is utterly arbitrary for them to say the Christian text is corrupt when it has thousands of manuscripts as evidence to test its reliability but then to declare their text to be perfect when it has absolutely no manuscript evidence. Their demand that the Qur'an is the corrective revelation for the Bible is arbitrary due to the fact that they have no rational reason to claim this other than the mere assertion of it. They do not have an uncorrupted and unbroken, unified Qur'an. Instead, they merely removed the possibility to ever find out if it is an accurate record of what Muhammad truly said since they have nothing to check it against. A Muslim could never rationally offer the same assurance that the Christian can concerning the reliability of his special revelation from God. People make mistakes during the copying process, and therefore, the thousands of manuscripts help us to determine where the copying errors were made. Truly God has preserved the text of the Bible masterfully and has left us the proof to demonstrate it. This certainly is not the case with Islam.

Therefore, when refuting the Qur'an from the Bible, it is easy to show the various contradictions between the two. This is not a problem for us Christians since we do not claim that the Qur'an is inspired. In fact, on the contrary, it is at best the whim of a pedophiliac speaking from the influence epileptic seizures, and it is at worst a text inspired directly by Satan. When comparing texts, it is clear that the symptoms Muhammad experienced while receiving his revelations are an almost identical match with some cases of demonic possession in the New Testament. A perfect example is found in Luke 9:38-42:

> And behold, a man from the crowd cried out, "Teacher, I beg you to look at my son, for he is my only child. And behold, a spirit seizes him, and he suddenly cries out. It convulses him so that he foams at the mouth, and shatters him, and will hardly leave him. And I begged your disciples to cast it out, but they could not." Jesus answered, "O faithless and twisted generation, how long am I to be with you and bear with you? Bring your son here." While he was coming, the demon threw him to the ground and convulsed him. But Jesus rebuked the unclean spirit and healed the boy, and gave him back to his father.

If the physical experience of Muhammad's revelations from Allah actually matches demonic possession in the New Testament, then it stands to reason that the Qur'an is nothing more than a Satanic revelation to a demon possessed man. This is not a difficult idea for Christians since 2 Corinthians 11:14 teaches that Satan disguises himself as an angel of light. Muhammad claimed to be visited by an angel of light, but his physical actions from such encounters suspiciously line up with the visitations of the angels of darkness.

Summing up the argument from truth, Islam cannot stand against the Bible. The Qur'an contradicts the Bible in many places, thus undermining Muhammad's appeal to the books of the Jews and Christians. Given that the Bible provides the only worldview that meets the preconditions of intelligibility, any contradiction from the Qur'an is just one more reason to reject it. Comparing it to the Bible demonstrated both its inconsistency and arbitrariness. Yet, this is only the tip of the iceberg. We have yet to apply the argument from folly to the Qur'an. Truly, the argument from folly tears to tatters any notion that the Qur'an is a word from God.

Thus, Christians can easily dismantle Islam with an internal refutation as well. There are certain contradictions within the Qur'an, thus making it not only contradictory with previous revelation, but also within itself. The most important contradiction comes from Surah 6:103, which reads, "No vision can grasp Him, but His grasp is over all vision. He is above all comprehension, yet is acquainted with all things."[37] In other words, Allah is so transcendent that nothing in human experience can be likened to him. He cannot be grasped nor comprehended. Although the Bible describes God in a similar manner, it also makes it clear that God is immanent and makes Himself known as far as a creature can possibly know Him. The Qur'an only focuses on the transcendent nature of Allah, and in fact its rejection of immanence is its basis for rejecting the incarnation of Christ as being impossible.

Why is this problematic for the Qur'an? If nothing in human experience can be likened to Allah, and if nothing in human experience can comprehend him, then what is the Qur'an? The Qur'an is human words of a human language, attempting to describe Allah and his revelation in nothing other than human experience. This is the worst kind of contradiction imaginable: "The Qur'an cannot be true if the Qur'an is true," or, "If the Qur'an is true, then it is false."[38] This is an inescapable dilemma for the Muslim apologist. The Qur'an cannot be a revelation of God based upon its own criteria. If what it says about Allah is true, then what it claims about itself (i.e.,

---

[37] Esposito, *Islam*, 22. I took the quotation of the Qur'an from this source, not the argument that follows.

[38] Greg Bahnsen, "Types of Worldviews."

revelation of Allah) cannot be true. Even calling Allah by the masculine pronoun "him" is relating the deity to the human experiences of personality, masculinity, and categorization. Human language is part of human experience and comprehension. Therefore, if nothing in human language can be said of Allah since human language is an aspect of human experience, then nothing that the Qur'an says about Allah can be a fair comparison to him. By the Qur'an's own claim that there cannot be any revelation in human language that can accurately tell humans about Allah, and yet the Qur'an is just that, a revelation in human language telling humans about Allah, it defeats itself. This contradiction destroys the credibility of the entire Muslim worldview.

There are many smaller contradictions as well. A good example is the Qur'an's treatment of the Jews. Prior to Muhammad turning on them, the Qur'an has many favorable statements regarding the Jews. Surah 2:47 speaks of the favor Allah bestowed upon them in the past; Surah 5:20-21 speaks of Allah sending them prophets in the past; and Surah 2:62 claims Jews and Christians are saved as long as they do good works. After the Jews rejected Muhammad, the Qur'an's revelation shifts dramatically. Surah 4:46 and 5:78 claimed the Jews were cursed due to disbelief; Surah 2:91 and 5:70-71 reversed the praise of the prophets being sent to the Jews by saying they killed the prophets; and Surah 3:85 reversed the earlier declaration concerning the salvation of Jews and Christians by claiming salvation only exists in Islam. In fact, Surah 5:60 declares that Allah turned the Jews into monkeys and pigs as part of his curse against them, a doctrine that Muslims claim was literally fulfilled.[39] The point behind these texts is simple. On one hand, the Jews are favored of God and can be saved by good works on their own terms, but then on the other hand, they are cursed of God and cannot be saved unless they are Muslims. These are contradictions. The Qur'an cannot keep its story straight because rather than being a revelation from God, it is nothing more than the twenty-year record of Muhammad shifting his policies during his attempts to solidify power underneath him.

Of course, Muslim apologists do have an answer for this. However, their answer is just one more reason to reject Islam. They answer with an interpretive scheme called *nasikh*, which is a form of progressive revelation. *Nasikh* is the idea that Allah revealed the truth to Muhammad one step at a time and later on changed his position on various matters due to various circumstances. Under this principle, the newer revelation cancels out the older revelation that it contradicts. The nullified revelation is then referred to as *mansookh*. Thus, when interpreting conflicting passages of the

---

[39] Gabriel, *Islam And The Jews*, 92.

Qur'an, a dedicated Muslim will always accept the later revelation as authoritative (*nasikh*) and the earlier as disregarded (*mansookh*). Most of the later revelations occurred in Medina, whereas the previous revelations took place in Mecca. With that said, if a passage that was revealed to Muhammad in Medina contradicts one revealed in Mecca, the interpreter is obligated to live by the precept of the Medina revelation.[40]

Mark Gabriel illustrates this principle of *nasikh* by appealing to Surah 2:106 and 16:102. The former reads, "Whatever a Verse (revelation) do we abrogate or cause to be forgotten, we bring a better one or similar to it. Know you not that Allah is able to do all things?"[41] The latter says, "And when we change a Verse (of the Qur'an) in place of another—and Allah knows best what He sends down …"[42] These Qur'anic passages are blatant admissions that Allah changes his mind and strikes down his own previous revelation.

The implications of this are staggering. How can the Qur'an be the perfect word of Allah that is eternal and from heaven (as Muslims claim), but then at the same time, Allah has to correct himself within it? Truly, this is nothing more than mental gymnastics to deal with the fact that their book is riddled with contradictions. This principle of Islamic progressive revelation is the Muslims attempt to make the contradictions disappear, but in return they sacrifice the immutability of their deity. In fact, it is better to say that *nasikh* is not progressive revelation at all, for if it were, it would be additive. Instead, it is nothing more than contradiction and annulment, which subtracts from revelation.[43]

Who would trust his eternal soul to a deity that cannot even make up his mind on the words designed to guard the soul? *Nasikh* is far different than Christian concepts of progressive revelation. In the biblical view, God revealed His truth over time, but the newer revelation did not contradict nor abrogate the older. At times, later events within salvation history fulfilled the older revelation thus rendering parts of it inapplicable (since they were fulfilled), but it was not contradicted by the new revelation nor was it struck down. The older revelation is still the Word of God reflecting His immutable nature and character.

Truly, no one can legitimately claim that Islam and Christianity represent the clashing of two equal worldviews, with either one having an equal chance at being correct. Instead, it is a clash between the true worldview of Christ and the arbitrary

---

[40] Ibid., 45–47.
[41] Ibid., 47.
[42] Ibid.
[43] Martin, *The Kingdom of the Cults*, 621.

and inconsistent worldview of Islam. The internal contradictions and arbitrariness of the Qur'an render it moot before the *I* and *A* of the PIA.

As if the internal refutation was not enough, the external deficiencies of Islam add insult to injury. The lack of manuscript evidence is one major embarrassment, as has already been addressed. Additionally, Muslims claim that Islam is the original religion of Adam, yet no archeological dig has ever uncovered any scroll, building, or artifact that demonstrates any aspect of Islam to predate Muhammad. Supposedly Abraham, the prophets, and Jesus were Muslims, but there are no ancient texts close to their time that remotely hints such. Moses wrote the closest text about Abraham to his time, and it contradicts Islamic theology. The Jewish prophets left behind their writings, and once again, Islamic theology is absent. The closest texts to Jesus' time are the New Testament documents, and once again, there is not a single trace of Islam there. In fact, the secular statements of Josephus, Tacitus, Pliny, and Seutonius all agree with many of the New Testament's statements concerning the ministry of Jesus, yet the Islamic understanding of Jesus is totally absent in these. The truth be told, even the monotheists in Arabia that predated Muhammad were not Islamic in their doctrine and thinking. [44] All of the known facts of history contradict Muhammad's claims concerning the past, whereas the details of the Bible continue to be confirmed again and again by archeological digs.

Of course, Islam fairs even worse when it comes to meeting the preconditions of intelligibility. Can Islam account for the uniformity of nature? Not really. Its god cannot exist due to the contradictions ascribed to him in the Qur'an. Even worse, the unitarian conception of God is bound by creation rather than being lord over it. For example, if the attributes of love and personality belong to Allah, then as attributes there can never be a time where Allah did not have these attributes, especially if he is immutable. Yet, love is an attribute of persons and is relational. Who did Allah love prior to creation? He could love no one until he actually first created angels and man. This means that he could not possess the attribute of love until there was a creation. If such were true, then Allah's attributes are dependent upon creation, thus proving him not to be distinct from it. If he depends on creation, then how can he be sovereign over it, thereby guaranteeing the uniformity of nature? A god that is not distinct from the creation cannot be relied upon to make it uniform. Thus, the one and many problem of philosophy discussed in chapter two destroys all unitarian counterfeits.

Can Islam account for the laws of logic? The numerous contradictions in the Qur'an speak against its god being the author of logic. Furthermore, if logic is

---

[44] Corduan, *Neighboring Faiths*, 79.

reflective of God's perfect mind, and as His image bearers we attempt to imitate this immaterial function of God, then would not God have to be immanent in order for His creatures to access logic? The transcendent descriptions of Allah would make this impossible. Since humans cannot experience Allah, they could not participate in a function derived from Allah's mind. Therefore, in Islam, logic would have to come from a different source than Allah, thus proving that Islam cannot account for the laws of logic.

Concerning absolute morality, Islam still has problems. Although Islam has a moral code, it does not line up with the previous revelation of the Old and New Testaments on many points, thus showing it to be contradictory. For example, does Islam have an explanation for the bloody sacrificial rites of the Old Testament and the need of cleanness in order to have the localized presence of God in the community via the Tabernacle and Temple? It seems as though it is not even addressed in Islam, yet in the previous revelation of the Jews, it demonstrated the holiness of God and sinfulness of man, along with the need of divinely prescribed redemption through atonement. Did God somehow forget these moral realities when Muhammad was born? Another problem for Islam is much of its moral standards are rightly viewed as oppressive and barbaric by non-Muslims.[45] Furthermore, Allah is an arbitrary character that can change his mind frequently as the surahs concerning the Jews demonstrated. In the Christian worldview, moral goodness is such because it is reflective of God's nature. Therefore, it is unchanging and is certainly not arbitrary.

What about Islam's consequences? It is true at the peak of Islamic civilization that literature, art, and science did advance. However, it can be argued that it happened as a result of the similarity between the way Christians, Muslims, and Jews view the world. Although Muslims cannot account for the uniformity of nature, they recognize its existence thus enabling them to do science. Although Muslims cannot account for the laws of logic, they still use them to survive in this fallen world. Apart from the good that Islamic civilization brought, the evil is far greater. The sword spread from Arabia all of the way to India, to Eastern Europe, to North Africa, and to Western Europe. In the process millions upon millions have died. Even today, terrorism finds its greatest tenants in radical Islam. Many of the nearly 250 million Muslims that surround Israel are, for the most part, dedicated to the annihilation of

---

[45] This is not to say that a majority opinion of man decides what is right or wrong, but the conscience that all men have as a result of our status as broken image bearers of God does for the most part cause man to revile certain evils. Many of Islam's "moral" practices cause such revulsion. Although unbelievers cannot justify their moral disgust with Islam, Christians can, since our God and the Bible provide the precondition for absolute morality.

the Jewish people. Politically correct liberals can deceive themselves all they want, but the documentation that exists within the laws and newspapers of these nations speaks volumes.

In short, Islam fails when an internal critique is performed. It is highly arbitrary, blatantly inconsistent, lacking in external evidence, fails to account for the preconditions of intelligibility, and is full of negative consequences. The Christian is by no means in any type of impasse with the Muslim. Where Islam fails, Christianity completely succeeds.

What about other unitarian counterfeits? Although they may teach different details than Islam, they all still have the same fundamental problems. Whether we are talking about adherents of Judaism, Jehovah Witnesses, or Unitarian Universalists, they cannot stand against the one and many problem. Therefore, their conceptions of God are all dependent upon creation for the attribute of personality. Thus, the basic precondition of personhood is lacking. Furthermore, not being distinct from creation then renders their god unable to keep nature uniform since he cannot be sovereign over it.

They may claim they believe in a god that is sovereign, personal, and distinct from creation, but their rejection of the Trinity makes these beliefs impossible to sustain without a self-refuting contradiction. As such, their conception of ultimate reality cannot account for logic, or morality either. Once again, if the Christian knows how to refute one unitarian, then he can refute all variants. Of course, it is a good idea to learn about some of the details of the variants so that arbitrariness and inconsistency can be pointed out as well.

For example, Jehovah Witnesses claim their one god Jehovah is perfect, and he declares that it is wrong to lie. Furthermore, they claim to believe the Bible (their version) is the word of God. Yet, even in their version of the Bible, Deuteronomy 18:20-22 teaches that the false prophet must die, and that a false prophet is someone who prophesies in the name of God, and yet, the prophecy does not come to pass. The governing group for the Jehovah Witnesses is the Watchtower Bible and Tract Society and they claim themselves to be prophets. The Watchtower is known for its numerous predictions concerning the return of Christ, and yet it has always been wrong. The Watchtower predicted Christ's return and that the end of human government would happen in 1874, then 1914, and then1975.[46] In 1925, it predicted that Abraham, Isaac, and Jacob, and the prophets would return in 1925 and live in a

---

[46] Ron Rhodes, *Reasoning from the Scriptures with the Jehovah's Witnesses*, Updated and Exp. (Harvest House Publishers, 2009), 343–350.

house in San Diego.[47] Therefore, by their own standard, the Jehovah's Witnesses are false prophets.[48] Thus, if their theology is true, then it is false. Everything that comes out of the Watchtower's press should be rejected if it's own standard is true!

On the issue of lying, they are known for their dishonesty in proof texting. One example, from many, is their misuse of the *New Encyclopedia Britannica* in an attempt to undermine the doctrine of the Trinity. The Watchtower writes:

> The *New Encyclopedia Britannica* says: "Neither the word Trinity, nor the explicit doctrine as such, appears in the New Testament, nor did Jesus and his followers intend to contradict the Shema in the Old Testament: 'Hear, O Israel: The Lord our God is one Lord' (Deut. 6:4). . . . The doctrine developed gradually over several centuries and through many controversies. . . . By the end of the 4th century.... the doctrine of the Trinity took substantially the form it has maintained ever since."- (1976), Micropaedia, Vol. X, p. 126.[49]

A simple reading of this quotation would lead one to believe that the Trinity is a non-biblical doctrine according to the *New Encyclopedia Britannica*. However, a reader with a keen eye and mind would notice with suspicion that there are ellipses throughout the quotation. Ellipses are not always a sign of deceit, but nevertheless, it usually is a good idea to see what was omitted. In this particular case, the Watchtower portrayed the *NEB* in a false manner.[50] Below is the full quote from the *NEB* to illustrate this point:

> Trinity, in Christian doctrine, the unity of Father, Son, and Holy Spirit as three persons in one Godhead.

> Neither the word Trinity nor the explicit doctrine appears in the New Testament, nor did Jesus and his followers intend to contradict the Shema

---

[47] Ibid.

[48] Jehovah Witnesses attempt to escape this problem by claiming the prophets and apostles made mistakes too. However, they cannot show a single example from Scripture of any of them committing a false prophecy. Thus, their answer does not work. By the standard set forth in Deuteronomy 18:20-22, they are false prophets.

[49] Martin, *The Kingdom of the Cults*, 405.

[50] I am indebted to a member of my church, Brian Orr, who wrote on this subject for his thesis paper in Bible College. When I reviewed his thesis and noticed the deliberate deceit of the Watchtower Bible and Tract Society, I wanted to ensure that all of the readers of this book see their deceitful proof texting of secular sources. There are many more examples than just this one. The more examples one reads, the more indignant one will become at their blatant lies.

in the Hebrew Scriptures: "Hear, O Israel: The Lord our God is one Lord" (Deuteronomy 6:4). The earliest Christians, however, had to cope with the implications of the coming of Jesus Christ and of the presumed presence and power of God among them—i.e.,, the Holy Spirit, whose coming was connected with the celebration of the Pentecost. The Father, Son, and Holy Spirit were associated in such New Testament passages as the Great Commission: "Go therefore and make disciples of all nations, baptizing them in the name of the Father and of the Son and of the Holy Spirit" (Matthew 28:19); and in the apostolic benediction: "The grace of the Lord Jesus Christ and the love of God and the fellowship of the Holy Spirit be with you all" (2 Corinthians 13:14). Thus, the New Testament established the basis for the doctrine of the Trinity.

The doctrine developed gradually over several centuries and through many controversies. Initially, both the requirements of monotheism inherited from the Hebrew Scriptures and the implications of the need to interpret the biblical teaching to Greco-Roman religions seemed to demand that the divine in Christ as the Word, or Logos, be interpreted as subordinate to the Supreme Being. An alternative solution was to interpret Father, Son, and Holy Spirit as three modes of the self-disclosure of the one God but not as distinct within the being of God itself. The first tendency recognized the distinctness among the three, but at the cost of their equality and hence of their unity (subordinationism); the second came to terms with their unity, but at the cost of their distinctness as "persons" (modalism). It was not until the 4th century that the distinctness of the three and their unity were brought together in a single orthodox doctrine of one essence and three persons.

The Council of Nicaea in 325 stated the crucial formula for that doctrine in its confession that the Son is "of the same substance [homoousios] as the Father," even though it said very little about the Holy Spirit. Over the next half century, Athanasius defended and refined the Nicene formula, and, by the end of the 4th century, under the leadership of Basil of Caesarea, Gregory of Nyssa, and Gregory of Nazianzus (the Cappadocian Fathers), the doctrine of the Trinity took substantially the form it has maintained ever since. It is accepted in all of the historic confessions of Christianity, even though the impact of the Enlightenment decreased its importance.[51]

It is clear that it misrepresented what the *NEB* wrote in such a manner that no word less than lie can be used to describe their actions. So what is the point? The point is it claims that lying is a sin, but its "prophet" organization seems to have no problem with lying to convince people of its false doctrines. This is just one example of inconsistency. A close study of the Jehovah's Witnesses cult reveals that this is normative for them. When one adds to it the weight of the one and many problem, thus causing their entire conception of the divine to fall apart; there is nothing left for them to stand on.

Unitarian Universalists will fail on philosophical grounds. In addition to their conception of God being unable to meet the preconditions of intelligibility, they also vary from one group to another in their beliefs. Their ultimate authority changes from one group to the next, and none of them truly rely on Scripture as the rule and authority in life. The easiest way to dispute these people is to deal with them on philosophical grounds showing them that they are arbitrary, inconsistent, and they have no right on their worldview to rely on logic or reason.

Judaism does not fare much better. Adherents of Judaism may object to the charge of being a biblical counterfeit by claiming that the Old Testament revelation came first, and therefore Christianity depends upon its conception of God. This is true, but two points must be kept in mind.

First, Judaism as it is currently practiced (in all of its forms) is based upon rabbinical tradition and teaching that emerged after the destruction of Jerusalem in A.D. 70.[52] Thus, its doctrinal understanding, religious forms, and combined worldview are more representative of a body of tradition that is a few hundred years younger than Christianity and the New Testament doctrines. Second, the Old Testament does not present itself as complete revelation and the prophets clearly understood that complete revelation would come with the Messiah. Therefore, it is in the Christian worldview that we have the complete special revelation from YHWH to man, mediated through His Messiah, Jesus. It is for this reason that the Christian worldview meets the preconditions of intelligibility and stands against the PIA technique, whereas Judaism fails certain portions of the test.

---

[51]"Trinity (Christianity) -- Britannica Online Encyclopedia," http://www.britannica.com.ezproxy.liberty.edu:2048/EBchecked/topic/605512/Trinity (accessed October 26, 2011).

[52] Corduan, 53.

Comparatively speaking, Jews may be the most difficult to deal with for no other reason than they possess two-thirds of God's divine revelation. They have loads of external archeological evidence to support their special revelation, and within the Old Testament there is not inconsistency and arbitrariness. Yet, Judaism forfeits these strengths due to its dedication to the aforementioned rabbinical tradition, which puts it at great odds with the Old Testament revelation. Jews operate without the Temple and sacrifice, priest and prophet, and ultimately without their Davidic king mediating the covenant with YHWH. As a result, their practice is often in contradiction with Old Testament revelation, thus demonstrating Judaism to be arbitrary. Their beliefs often disagree with what the Tanakh teaches, showing them to be arbitrary since they trust the opinions of men who lack authority instead of the oracles of God that possess all authority for life and practice.[53] As such, they focus on good works rather than the need for the redemption that the Old Testament points them to. Finally, their unitarian understanding of YHWH is beset with the problems elucidated above and also is unbiblical since God's Triune nature is strongly hinted in the Old Testament.[54]

The bottom line is that it does not matter what the unitarian variant is. The one and many problem renders their god as a contradiction, their doctrines and standards end up being arbitrary, and a closer inspection reveals inconsistency. The Christian simply needs to listen to their story as they themselves offer the rope by which their worldview ultimately gets hanged.

Polytheistic Counterfeits

With unitarian counterfeits now dealt with, we can turn to polytheistic biblical counterfeits. Mormonism is the most prevalent and successful polytheistic counterfeit in the world. Most of us have experienced Mormons knock on our doors as they sought to spread their Latter-Day-Saint religion. Often, the Mormon evangelists will readily admit that their faith stands or falls upon Joseph Smith. With that being the case, Christians have every right to evaluate the man and his story. Therefore, the basic story of Mormonism will be laid out below, and then the PIA technique will be applied to it. Just like every other false worldview, Mormonism

---

[53] Key examples are found in the rampant liberalism found in Reformed and Conservative Judaism. Many are pro-choice, favor gay marriage, and advocate the intermarriage between Jews and unconverted Gentiles (this is no problem for Jews, like myself, who are Christians since the wall has been torn down between the two groups—Ephesians 2:14—but from the Old Testament covenant-people perspective, this was forbidden). If you add to this the manner in which Yom Kippur is observed, it does not obey the specific details set forth in books of Moses.
[54] See the footnotes in chapter two's discussion of the Trinity.

proves itself incapable of meeting the preconditions of intelligibility, and it is both arbitrary and inconsistent. With that said, let us consider the story of this large, polytheistic cult known as the Latter Day Saints.

Since the Mormons invite us to challenge their prophet, the basic story of his life is a good place to start. Concerning the man himself, before he founded his new religion, he was tried and convicted of being a peep-stone diviner. This can be found in the indisputable County Records of Bainbridge, NY.[55] In the 1800s, peep-stone lookers were charlatans, or conmen, that would put supposed magic stones in their hat, and look into the hat while holding it over the ground. They would claim to see what was under the ground through this.[56] Thus, people who were easily deceived would pay these types to tell them where to dig for wells, hidden treasure, and so on. The state rightly considered this profession to be nothing more than fraud, and so it was illegal in New York.

Many Mormons are unaware of the fact that Joseph Smith was a convicted fraud, but of those that are aware, their argument is that whatever he did prior to his call from God was irrelevant.[57] They are correct to say that his conviction as a conman does not prove Mormonism false, but it certainly raises the possibility, and even the probability, that Mormonism was simply his next con. Since Mormons trust their soul in Joseph Smith's keeping, it should be a sobering thought that before the man was a prophet he was convicted of being a conman.

As with the religions previously discussed, often one of the best methods of refutation is a simple repetition of the story in order to look for inconsistencies. After all, liars can hardly ever keep their story straight.

Joseph Smith was born in the year 1805 in the State of Vermont but settled with his family in New York when he was eleven years old. His family held membership with the Presbyterian Church,[58] but Joseph Smith strayed clear of biblical Christianity claiming to be perplexed and confused due to the existence of many denominations. According to his story, he was in the woods praying at age fourteen, and God the Father and Jesus Christ appeared to him, with the Father telling him to listen to the Son. Allegedly, God told Joseph Smith to join no church since all of the

---

[55] Greg Bahnsen, "Types of Worldviews." Series One.

[56] Martin, *The Kingdom of the Cults*, 184.

[57] This argument actually is false. Joseph Smith claimed to receive his first vision in 1820, yet he was found guilty of money-digging in a court of Law in 1826. So he had already received his call as a prophet, and still worked as a conman for at least six years.

[58] Joseph Smith, "Joseph Smith History 1:7," *Pearl of Great Price* (The Church of Jesus Christ of Latter-day Saints, 1981), 48

churches were corrupt and that the Christian creeds were abominable.[59] This then supposedly justified him staying clear of the church of his family.

In September of 1823, he claimed to have another vision, in which an angel named Maroni gave him his commission as God's prophet and told him that there was a book written on golden plates that records the history of the former inhabitants of America.[60] This book also was supposed to contain the fullness of the gospel in it since it possessed the gospel delivered by Jesus Christ to the American inhabitants in the distant past. Being told these gold plates were nearby, Joseph Smith claimed to have found them in a stone box, but he was forbidden from taking them with him. Therefore, he returned to the same spot for four years perhaps to study them, and then in 1827 he was permitted to take them with him for safe keeping. Around this time, he eloped with Emma Hail of Harmony, Pennsylvania. He moved into his father-in-law's house, and it was there that he copied the alphabetical characters from the plates and began translating them.[61]

Word of his story spread, and a New York farmer by the name of Martin Harris proposed to publish the book that Smith was writing, but only if it could be verified that the plates were genuine and that they were being correctly translated. Joseph Smith gave copies on paper of the characters he copied from the plates along with their translation and claimed it was the language of Reformed Egyptian. According to the Mormon story, Martin Harris had the characters and translation confirmed by a professor in New York City named Charles Anthon, in which the professor identified the characters as Egyptian, Chaldean, Babylonian, Assyrian, and Arabic.[62] The story must be interrupted at this point to clarify one point. When rumors began to spread that Dr. Anthon confirmed Smith's plates, the professor made public statements that he never saw the plates, nor confirmed the writing, and that Reformed Egyptian did not exist.[63] Apparently, Joseph Smith was lying.

In 1829, a former schoolteacher named Oliver Cowdery became the amanuensis for Smith as he did the translating. Of course, it is highly convenient that he was not allowed to see the plates, but instead Smith hung a sheet up and was by himself on the other side reading off the translation as Cowdery wrote it down.[64] Not long after this, they went out into the woods to pray, and another vision occurred in which John

---

[59] Ibid, Joseph Smith History 1:19-20, 49-50.

[60] The Testimony of the Prophet Joseph Smith, *The Book of Mormon* (The Church of Jesus Christ of Latter-day Saints, 1981)

[61] Smith, "Joseph Smith History 1:55-65," *Pearl of Great Price*, 55-57

[62] Ibid, Joseph Smith History 1:64, 56.

[63] Martin, *The Kingdom of the Cults*, 197–199.

[64] Ibid., 187.

the Baptist sent them, from heaven, the Aaronic priesthood. Apparently this now allowed them to understand the Scriptures and prophesy. Later on, Peter, James, and John conferred the Melchizedek priesthood on them[65] at the banks of a river.[66] In 1830, the *Book of Mormon* officially went on sale, and then on April 6, the Mormon Church was incorporated as a church of six members. Within a month's time, however, the church grew to forty members. Due to Smith's poor reputation as an immoral man in New York, he relocated his church to Ohio.

The Mormons did missionary work among the Indians of Kirtland, Ohio, and during this time Smith published the revelation of the Doctrines and Covenants. In Kirtland, Mormon numbers grew dramatically, yet the majority of the population considered his religion to be a hoax, and they viewed him as being greatly immoral due to his recent claim that God now allowed polygamy.[67] During this time, he revised the King James Version of the Bible of its alleged errors, and he declared in prophecy that God chose Jackson County, Missouri as the land of promise and the city of Zion. Taking this prophecy seriously, the Mormons moved to that county, specifically in Independence, Missouri, but this did not last since mobs attacked them there.[68] Apparently, this forced God to choose a different city of God in western Missouri. Smith's followers began to fight battles against the settlers in western Missouri, thus causing the state militia to get involved, which ended up in Smith and some of his followers being imprisoned. They escaped prison and fled eastward to Illinois where Smith settled in the city of Nauvoo, Illinois in 1839. Preferring to be called the "general," he created a small army called the Nauvoo legion to protect them from outside violence. However, a small anti-Mormon newspaper, the *Nauvoo Expositor*, published an unfavorable article against the Mormons, and Smith ordered that his Nauvoo legion destroy the printing press[69] and that all copies of the article be burned.[70]

Smith's criminal actions led to a complaint to the State governor, which then led to the arrest of Joseph Smith. Even though he was released, he was soon rearrested with his brother Hyrum. While in jail in Carthage, Illinois, on the night of June 27, 1844, a mob attacked the facility and killed Joseph Smith and his brother. Greg Bahnsen believed that this event above all allowed the Mormon Church to be a

---

[65] Smith, "Joseph Smith History 1:68-74," *Pearl of Great Price*, 57-58.

[66] The Bible makes it clear that only Jesus Christ is the priest in the order of Melchizedek (cf. Hebrews 7:17).

[67] Martin, *The Kingdom of the Cults*, 188–189.

[68] Greg Bahnsen, "Types of Worldviews." Series One.

[69] Apparently, the army was not just for defensive purposes.

[70] Martin, *The Kingdom of the Cults*, 190.

success.[71] While alive, it was difficult to take Smith seriously, but now he was a martyr, and people tend to have soft hearts for martyrs. Also, just prior to this, authorities were on the verge of proving the "golden plates" were really counterfeiting plates that he was producing counterfeit money with, but the investigation was closed with his death. It would have been one more proof that the man was still a con artist and Mormonism was simply his biggest con. Instead of the truth being exposed, people now had a martyr who was presented by Mormons as a hero who died as the true prophet of God. Now, nearly two centuries later, young men show up to our doors wearing white shirts and black ties, telling us this false story again and again with tears in their eyes, moving people with their sincerity.

Doctrinally speaking, Mormonism is a polytheistic faith that has nothing to do with biblical Christianity. Mormons may be surprised to hear this truth, and sadly some Mormons do not even know what their religion truly teaches. However, it is not difficult with their three sacred books (*Book of Mormon, Pearl of Great Price,* and *Doctrine and Covenants*) to point out their many polytheistic passages. Their doctrine is that there are many gods, but they only worship one god, thus making it classifiable as henotheism. Biblical Christianity, in contrast, believes that only one God exists.

With a brief, general story of Mormonism now presented, it is time to ask the question, "How does it hold up against the PIA technique?" To that we now turn.

PIA & Argument from Truth and Folly

As with Islam, the process for refuting Mormonism is going to be accomplished in three steps: 1) biblical refutation; 2) internal refutation; 3) external refutation. The biblical refutation will be the argument from truth, since Mormonism will be disputed from the teachings of the Bible—the only teachings that can provide for the preconditions of intelligibility. The internal and external refutations comprise the argument from folly, demonstrating that within the framework of Mormonism itself, it cannot be true. Weaved into this will be arguments demonstrating a total failure of Mormonism against the PIA technique.

First, we will begin with the biblical refutation. Mormons claim to accept the Bible as revelation from God, but they also believe that Jesus revealed truth via special revelation to the Indians of America, and that this revelation is the *Book of Mormon.* As with Islam, Christians would do well then to hold them to the fact that

---

[71] Greg Bahnsen, "Types of Worldviews." Series One.

hey claim to believe the Bible. The Bible provides for us the standard by which to udge their added "revelation."

Since Deuteronomy 18:15-22 makes it clear that true revelation from God will be ulfilled, Joseph Smith's revelation is disqualified since his prophecies were not ulfilled, such as Jackson County, Missouri being Zion. Furthermore, Galatians 1:9 ays that if anyone preaches a different gospel than the biblical one, that person is accursed. Well, it is an indisputable fact that Mormonism's gospel is far different rom the biblical counterpart. We are supposed to judge new revelation by the tandard of past revelation since God will not and cannot contradict Himself. This is a huge problem for Mormonism.

Mormon theology says there are many gods,[72] they are refined matter rather than spirit,[73] and that they marry and have sex and produce souls for the planets they ule.[74] The Bible makes it clear there is only one God,[75] He is spirit,[76] that He does not marry or have sexual relations, and that He is from everlasting to everlasting.[77] Mormons also believe that Adam was a god, and in particular, he is the god of the earth.[78] They also claim that Jesus and Satan are brothers.[79] Simply put, there are a most of points where Mormon doctrine contradicts the Bible. Thus, by the standard of he Bible, Mormonism is to be rejected. Also, by Mormonism's appeal to the Bible is revelation, it proves itself to be inconsistent since it has two revelations in contradiction.

Of course, Mormons will not fall this easily, but instead they will reveal what they eally mean when they say they believe the Bible. Like Muslims, when they claim hat the Bible is divine revelation, they mean that they accept the Bible when it is properly translated and interpreted according to their standard (i.e., Smith's evisions). They claim that when this is done, the Bible does not contradict the Mormon revelations. How convenient.

The Christian has the right to demand of them to prove that they have a proper ranslation of the Bible. Do they have documentary evidence to support their view of vhat the Bible really teaches? In fact, they blatantly rewrote parts of the Bible. For xample, in Genesis 50 it strongly implies that Joseph Smith would one day

---

[72] *Book of Mormon*; Abraham 4:1.

[73] *Doctrine and Covenants* 130:22.

[74] Martin, *The Kingdom of the Cults*, 222.

[75] Isaiah 44:6.

[76] John 4:24.

[77] Isaiah 40:28.

[78] *Journal of Discourses,* 1:50.

[79] *Pearl of Great Price*, Moses 4:1-4.

appear.[80] These are not mistranslations of Hebrew words, but they are blatant additions. These are major differences that the Mormon Inspired Bible has, and Mormons claim that these are the original verses, whereas our translations have been corrupted over the centuries to omit them.

If they seek to advance that claim, where is the manuscript evidence to support it? No archeological dig has ever unearthed any ancient manuscripts of Bible books that have anything that even resembles a single one of these differences expressed in the Mormon Bible. This proves then, that they are additions that Joseph Smith added in the 1800s. Otherwise, there should be manuscript evidence. Their response is to insist that you must trust their version anyway because God revealed it to Joseph Smith, and therefore, it must be true. This amounts to nothing more than arbitrariness since they have no justification for their insistence.

They lean on Article 8 of their faith to get them out of the bind that the Bible causes them. It reads, "We believe the Bible to be the word of God as far as it is translated correctly; we also believe the Book of Mormon to be the word of God."[81] The Book of Mormon is not held to the same standard since Joseph Smith sees it as the word of God due to its infallible translation. Thus, they can arbitrarily reject what the Bible truly says, and believe the false additions that Smith added to it and all the while ignore the external manuscript evidence. Because of their commitment to Article 8, they will always read the Bible through the lens of the Book of Mormon.

This lens causes them to ignore that their new revelation does not harmonize at all with the old revelation. A plurality of material gods each ruling their own planet is far different than the single immaterial God ruling the universe and heaven above. The teaching that men will become gods and receive their own planet differs greatly from the redeemed receiving resurrection bodies and inheriting the New Earth with Christ. The teaching that women who engage in celestial marriage will have the joy of bearing children for all eternity is totally contradictory to the New Testament teaching that there is no marriage at the resurrection. The material gods of Mormonism undergo change, whereas the immaterial God of the Bible is immutable. The point of all of this is simple. Mormon doctrine even contradicts the parts of the Bible that Joseph Smith left intact. Through and through, the Mormon faith is inconsistent, and it must be rejected. It contradicts the Scriptures, and with

---

[80] "Joseph Smith Translation: Genesis 50:24-38 -- LDS.org,"
https://www.lds.org/scriptures/jst/jst-gen/50?lang=eng (accessed March 24, 2014).
[81] Articles of the Faith -- LDS.org
https://www.lds.org/scriptures/pgp/a-of-f/1?lang=eng (accessed March 24, 2014).

Deuteronomy 13, 18, and Galatians 1:9, Christians can discern that Mormonism is the product of a false prophet.

When the Mormon attempts to flee from this by claiming the Bible has been corrupted throughout the ages, and therefore Christians do not truly have inspired revelation, the Christian needs to point out the obvious. As Bahnsen so eloquently put it,

> ...the Mormons' faith comes down to them believing a story about a man who had plates that no one else was allowed to see, in a language that no one else knows, and he translated it in an infallible way. Their faith is not arrived at through an examination of two sacred texts that can be objectively studied, but instead it comes down to the word of Joseph Smith against the massive amounts of manuscript evidence and translational consensus that we have for the Bible. It really is nothing more than the choice of believing a story that a conman told rather than believing the text of the Bible that can be publically verified.[82]

In other words, the Mormons believe what they are told without justification, thus making them guilty of arbitrariness. Thus, a biblical criticism of Mormonism shows it to be folly.

An internal critique is just as damning. One only needs to look at the *Book of Mormon* itself to find its many holes. According to *Mormon 9:32*, the plates were written in Reformed Egyptian. Linguists have long insisted that no such language exists, and so Mormons are forced to arbitrarily believe their text in spite of the evidence. In 9:32, the text admits that Reformed Egyptian is not a human language (even though it has a human culture's name). Prior to this, Martin Harris wanted to know if the plates were authentic, and Smith told him the writing was in Reformed Egyptian, which sounds an awful lot like the name of a human language. Chances are Smith soon discovered Reformed Egyptian did not exist, and so he added this disclaimer in 9:32. This was convenient for Smith since it now made his claim non-falsifiable since scholars could not compare it to other manuscripts in order to determine authenticity. After all, it is a "heavenly" language, meaning there was no expert on earth other than Joseph Smith that could verify the text. Thus, it all comes down to taking a single man's word for it, a man who was a convicted conman.

Another problem comes just one verse later. In 9:33, Smith says that Hebrew would have been a more perfect script to write in, but the gold plates were not large

---

[82] Greg Bahnsen, "Types of Worldviews." Series One.

enough for the Hebrew script, and so God used Reformed Egyptian instead. Why could not God just make bigger plates? Is their god that impotent? In addition to this, there are no historical records of any ancient civilization writing things down on metal plates, yet the Mormons claim that in 600 B.C. the entire Old Testament was written on brass plates. Truly, the story does not comport with itself, and it disagrees with known facts of history.

Mormons also claim that Joseph Smith translated these plates infallibly by using two ancient Jewish artifacts, the *urim* and *thummim*.[83] How he had these items is a mystery in and of itself, since even Jewish scholars are not exactly sure what these items were in the Old Testament. Even worse, he made the translation behind closed sheets so that no one could see what he was truly doing. His followers simply wrote down what he verbally said to them.

Seeing the suspicious nature of this, Mormons are quick to say after Smith finished translating, he took the plates to Dr. Anthon in New York City for verification of the text and translation. There are two prodigious problems with this. First, Dr. Anthon vehemently denied that this occurred once rumors reached him that Mormons were claiming this.[84] Second, and far worse, 9:32 says this Reformed Egyptian language was a heavenly tongue, and 9:34 says that no human on earth knows it. If this is the case, how in the world could have Dr. Anthon known the language in the first place in order to confirm it? The whole idea of sending plates to a human expert that cannot possibly know the language makes absolutely no sense. Instead, it seems that Joseph Smith was inventing stories and was forced to backtrack his account too many times and in the process left some really big inconsistencies.

Another internal problem with the *Book of Mormon* is the fact that there have been many changes or revisions to it. Supposedly the original edition was an inspired translation. If that were the case, why would there be the necessity for newer versions? In fact, some Mormons go to libraries in search for older copies of their books so that they can walk out with them and destroy the unfavorable evidence. The older copies are becoming a rarity, but fortunately some Christians guard their copies well. It is not hard to find the many changes between the older copies and the newer ones. Some Christians have done well to pull out an old 19th century copy and compare verses with Mormons at the parts where changes have been made. When an explanation is demanded, often the only response given is an exhortation to blindly trust Joseph Smith and to pray (without doubting) that God will show that the *Book of Mormon* is true.

---

[83] Smith, "Joseph Smith History 1:59-62," *Pearl of Great Price*, 55-56
[84] Martin, *The Kingdom of the Cults*, 197–199.

On an external level, Mormonism is wrought with difficulties as well. Apart from no manuscript evidence to support its favorable claims of itself or its claims against the Bible, there also are a host of archeological difficulties. The *Book of Mormon* lists numerous ancient cities with descriptions, and yet not a single one of them has ever been discovered anywhere in the Americas. The book also mentions languages and writing, metallurgical technology, animals (like the horse), weapons (chariots and swords), metal coins as currency, and many other things that did not exist in the Americas prior to the European invasions begun in 1492. Yet, according to Smith these were present in the ancient Americas. Smith made these claims before archeology came to maturity, but once it did, the *Book of Mormon's* claims were falsified.[85] The Bible, in contrast, has been vindicated through archeological finds again and again. As an example of this, Smith tried to claim the American Indians were descendents of Jews, but modern DNA research shows this clearly is not the case. The Bible claims Arabs and Jews are descended from a single man, something that has been supported by modern DNA research. The list can truly go on and on for external evidence, but the point has been made. Mormonism was a conman's best con, nothing more.

Summing up Mormonism then, a simple telling of its story shows it to be inconsistent and arbitrary. There was no objective means to test anything that Smith said, and so his followers believed him blindly. His life was one of consistent run-ins with the law, thus showing that his nature never changed much between his time as a peep-stone looker and a prophet. Additionally, a comparison between the *Book of Mormon* and the Bible demonstrates massive contradictions, thereby showing the Christian that Mormonism is heretical and showing the Mormon that he has a problem since he claims to believe the Bible. Internally, the *Book of Mormon* is its own worst enemy for numerous reasons: it contradicts itself concerning the plates, it contains descriptions of cities and items that were non-existent in the Americas, and

---

[85] Another example of Joseph Smith's blunders was the *Book of Abraham* fraud. Joseph Smith claimed to have acquired an ancient Egyptian document that was written by Abraham during his time in Egypt. Smith then translated the hieroglyphs and this became of the Book of Abraham in *The Pearl of Great Price*. The Egyptian document was believed to have been destroyed in the Great Chicago Fire of 1871, thus making his claim difficult to falsify. Well, fragments of the document were recovered in 1966 in a museum. Once looked at by Egyptologists, it was determined that the document pertained to Egyptian funerals and had nothing to do with what Joseph Smith claimed. This definitively proved that Joseph Smith fraudulently produced the *Book of Abraham*—a book canonized as inspired by the Latter-day Saints. Anyone today can see the facsimiles of the document in the *Pearl of Great Price* and then compare them to the fragments found in 1966. They are the same.

its revisions undermine its claim of infallibility. Externally, archeology and DNA research deals a deathblow to the claims that Smith made.

And worst of all, nothing in Mormonism accounts for the preconditions of intelligibility. There is nothing in it to account for the uniformity of nature since a more powerful god could always undermine the earth's god (Adam) and change the laws. The laws of logic have no ultimate transcendent mind that they are derived from in Mormonism since its gods are material and are subject to change, whereas the biblical God is immaterial (logic also is immaterial) and God is immutable, thus making logic trustworthy.

Concerning consequences, the consequences of Mormonism are not as bad as that of atheism, evolution, Islam, or many other worldviews, but the confusion that it brings to people concerning the truth is nevertheless a major negative consequence of this religion. Ultimately, Mormonism is a tool of Satan designed to lead tens of millions of people straight to hell.

Years ago, some Mormon missionaries were invited to my house during our weekly Bible Study. After much questioning and answering, they were completely refuted at all possible levels. My friend Jim asked a telling question. He asked, "Why should I worship your god? Point me to the god at the beginning of the chain of gods so that I can evaluate him." The Mormons could not answer this since they have no idea how this works even according to their own worldview. The problems that they would have to face in the case of an infinite regression of gods is too much for them to bear. If there is no infinite regression, then how did the first god become god? You would think these are important questions that Joseph Smith would have had to figure out if he was going to offer a new religion, but clearly he did not think it through. The Bible Study ended with both Mormons crying, claiming to be filled with the tears of the Holy Spirit, and as they walked out of my house, the older of the two said, "I don't care if you have one-thousand facts that disprove the *Book of Mormon*, I still believe and know it is true." That is stubborn arbitrariness at its worst, yet it is the only way for any Mormon to remain a Mormon when confronted with the truth.

Any polytheistic biblical counterfeit will have the same basic problems concerning the PIA technique. Ultimately, the god that they choose to worship cannot be the ultimate absolute of all existence, but instead he must be derivative of some other ultimate absolute. At that point, the ultimate absolute often becomes impersonal like all other unbelieving worldviews. If your ultimate absolute is not an absolute personality, distinct from creation, with total sovereignty, and is a unity of plurality, then your ultimate absolute cannot account for the preconditions of intelligibility. This then leads to unavoidable arbitrariness and inconsistency, as it is impossible to truly have a coherent worldview when your ultimate presupposition cannot provide the preconditions of intelligibility. In the case of Mormonism, the dubious nature of Joseph Smith, the numerous contradictions and lies, and the external evidences that expose its mythical status, all make it extremely easy to cast down this false prophet and his false religion.

Pseudo-Messianic Counterfeits

Not much needs to be said concerning Bahnsen's third category of biblical counterfeits. There have been numerous cases in history where an individual founds a religious movement with "Christian" undertones, only to later declare himself as the mediator between God and man. Often, the leader convinces his cult that he is a savior functioning in the place of Christ, as if there was something lacking in Christ's work. In some cases, the leader eventually declares that he is Jesus Christ and that the second coming has occurred through him.

Some of the more prominent examples in the last few generations are Jim Jones and his People's Temple cult, David Koresh and his Branch Davidian cult, and Sun Myung Moon and the Unification Church, otherwise called the Moonies. Although each of these variants is quite different from the others, they all center on a single leader misusing the Bible to gain total obedience and loyalty from their cult members. They hold such power over their followers, that in the case of Jim Jones and David Koresh, the majority of their followers committed suicide at the command of their alleged saviors.

I recommend that Christians do some research of these types of movements in order to gain a decent understanding of them. Ultimately refuting them is not difficult. Their leaders are sinful men lacking in exhaustive knowledge and divine authority, thus resulting in their futility since ultimately their words can carry no more weight than anyone else's. Since they often claim to use the Bible, they are open to charges of inconsistency as their doctrines always contradict the Scripture. Their leaders often are beset with moral sin (often sexual), and they possess none of the righteous characteristics of the Messiah Jesus. Therefore, following these men is without justification (arbitrary). As with other religious worldviews, the Christian merely needs to listen to their story, perform the internal critique (argument from folly), and then offer them the only worldview that makes sense of everything (argument from truth). Hopefully it is clear to the Christian by now that this is how to deal with all worldviews.

Conclusion

In our journey through the biblical counterfeits, hopefully it was made clear that refuting these worldviews is no more difficult than addressing atheism, paganism, or any other so-called knowledge raised against God. In fact, with biblical counterfeits, Christians have an extra angle of attack since the counterfeits already claim to accept the Bible. This makes the argument from truth blend seamlessly with the argument from folly since the truth of Scripture demonstrates an inconsistency in the biblical counterfeits' worldview, as they tend to teach doctrines in opposition to the very Scripture they claim to believe in.

For Christians, often these counterfeits represent the most frustrating opposition. They often claim the name of Christ, but then teach abominable lies about Him. In the process, millions of people are inoculated against the power of His name. They have such misconceptions concerning the Savior, that when they hear the real gospel, it does not sound as great to them since they learned of a different Jesus altogether. Satan has done his greatest damage to the church through the biblical counterfeits.

As soldiers of Jesus Christ, you must be ready to "make a defense to anyone who asks you for a reason for the hope that is in you."[86] Yet, in so doing you must in your "hearts honor Christ the Lord as holy."[87] Only by resting solidly on true biblical and systematic theology can you honor the true Jesus in your heart as holy. Only with a detailed understanding of true doctrine can you stand steadfast against the false doctrines of the biblical counterfeits. Saints, let this be a call and reminder that always being ready to make a defense, first and foremost, means that you must always be "ready in season and out of season" to proclaim the truth and "reprove, rebuke, and exhort"[88] those who oppose Christ and His truth. Apologetics cannot be divorced from sound theology and dealing with the cults proves this point cogently.

---

[86] 1 Peter 3:15.
[87] Ibid.
[88] 2 Timothy 4:2.

Conclusion

It was my honor and privilege to offer for your consideration a presuppositional approach to apologetics. I do hope that the presentation was clear, fair, and persuasive. If so, then you the reader have found in this one volume both an explanation of biblical apologetics and examples of it in action. You have been given both knowledge and application, or better put, orthodoxy and orthopraxy. As Christians, we are called to preach the gospel to all nations, and in the process we will surely have to give a defense for the hope that is in us. Many Christians do this already, but just as I did in the past, they do not lean upon what the Bible has to say about defending the faith. It is my prayer that this book convicts all Christians not only to engage in apologetics, but also to engage in it in the right way.

Truly, presuppositional apologetics is what the evangelical world needs. As the New Atheists gain a greater following, as pagan religions continue to gain more adherents and respect in the West, as people's natural outlook now presupposes postmodernism, and as more people tend to see Christianity as a joke due to the lack of truth being proclaimed from the pulpits, we true Christians need to build our worldview firmly on the right foundation of God's Word. As the old hymn goes, "All other ground is sinking sand." We need to be committed to the Scriptures, and more importantly, we need to be committed to honoring God in all that we do. Namely, we must strive to be biblical people, doing biblical things, in the biblical way.

Presuppositional apologetics is the biblical way to do apologetics. As such, it can no longer remain the sole possession of Reformed theologians. It must branch out and take Evangelicalism by storm. Evangelicalism is in great trouble since more and more of it is being torn apart by savage wolves. This makes the work of unbelievers even easier in dismissing the truth. If evangelical churches would only rise up and teach their people systematic theology, biblical theology, and biblical apologetics, then the sheep would be better equipped to do the work of the ministry. They would think Christ's thoughts after Him. They would cast down every lofty opinion raised against Christ. Namely, they would live and act like Christians.

Stephen Feinstein

Bibliography

Andrews, Edgar. *Who Made God? Searching for a Theory of Everything*. EP Books, 2009.

Aristotle and Louise Ropes Loomis. *On Man in the Universe*, Classics Club Edition edition. (Walter J. Black, n.d.),

Bahnsen, Greg L. *Always Ready: Directions for Defending the Faith*. Edited by Robert R. Booth. Covenant Media Press, 1996.

_____. *Van Til's Apologetic*. P & R Publishing, 1998.

_____. *Presuppositional Apologetics Stated and Defended*. American Vision, 2010.

Behe, Michael J. *Darwin's Black Box: The Biochemical Challenge to Evolution*. 2nd ed. Free Press, 2006.

Book of Mormon. Church of Jesus Christ of Latter-day Saints, 1981

Bresnan, Patrick. *Awakening: An Introduction to the History of Eastern Thought, 2nd Ed*. Prentice, 2002.

Brown, Walter T., and Walt Brown. *In the Beginning: Compelling Evidence for Creation and the Flood*. 7th ed. Center for Scientific Creation, 2001. Chan, Wing-tsit. *A Source Book in Chinese Philosophy*. Princeton University Press, 1969.

Coppedge, James F. *Evolution: Possible or Impossible?* Zondervan Publishing House, 1973.

Corduan, Winfried. *Neighboring Faiths: A Christian Introduction to World Religions*. IVP Academic, 1998.

Craig, William Lane., John M. Frame, Kelly James Clark, and Paul D. Feinberg. *Five Views on Apologetics*. Ed. Steven B. Cowan and Stanley N. Gundry. Grand Rapids, MI: Zondervan Pub. House, 2000.

Darwin, Charles. *The Origin of the Species*, 6th edition. Macmillan Publishing Co., 1927.

Dawkins, Richard. *The God Delusion*. Transworld Publishers, 2006.

Doctrine and Covenants. Church of Jesus Christ of Latter-day Saints, 1981

Esposito, John L. *Islam: The Straight Path*. 3rd ed. Oxford University Press, USA, 1998.

Fisher, Sydney N. and William Ochsenwald. *The Middle East: A History, Volume 1*. Fifth ed. McGraw Hill, 1997.

Frame, John M. *Apologetics to the Glory of God: An Introduction*. P & R Publishing, 1994.

Gabriel, Mark A. *Islam And The Jews: The Unfinished Battle*. First ed. Charisma House, 2003.

Gould, Stephen Jay. "Evolution's Erratic Pace," *Natural History*, Vol. 5, 1977.

_____. "The Return of Hopeful Monsters," *Natural History*, vol. 86, 1977.

Hoyle, Fred and N. Chandra Wickramasinghe, *Evolution From Space: A Theory of Cosmic Creationism*. New York: Simon and Schuster, 1981.

Lewin, Roger . "Evolution Theory under Fire," *Science*, Vol. 210, 1980.

Lewis, C. S. *Mere Christianity*. HarperSanFrancisco, 2001.

Lisle, Jason. *Ultimate Proof of Creation*. New Leaf Publishing Group/Master Books, 2009.

Martin, Thomas R. *Ancient Greece: From Prehistoric to Hellenistic Times*. 1St ed. Yale University Press, 1996.

Martin, Walter. *The Kingdom of the Cults*. Revised Updated and Expanded Anniversary ed. Bethany House Publishers, 1997.

McDowell, Josh. *The New Evidence That Demands A Verdict Fully Updated To Answer The Questions Challenging Christians Today*. Rev Upd. Thomas Nelson, 1999.

Mortenson, Terry, and Thane H. Ury, eds. *Coming to Grips with Genesis: Biblical Authority and the Age of the Earth*. New Leaf Publishing Group, 2008.

Bibliography

Murray, Eden "Inadequacies of Neo-Darwinian Evolution as a Scientific Theory," *Mathematical Challenges to the Neo-Darwinian Interpretation of Evolution,* editors Paul S. Moorhead and Martin M. Kaplan, 1967.

Pearl of Great Price. Church of Jesus Christ of Latter-day Saints, 1981

Plato et al. *Essential Dialogues of Plato.* New York: Barnes & Noble, 2005.

Plato, *Timaeus.* Penn State Hazleton

http://www2.hn.psu.edu/faculty/jmanis/plato/timaeus.pdf

Pratt, Jr. Richard L. *Every Thought Captive: A Study Manual for the Defense of Christian Truth.* P & R Press, 1979.

Rhodes, Ron. *Reasoning from the Scriptures with the Jehovah's Witnesses.* Updated and Exp. Harvest House Publishers, 2009.

Robertson, A.T. *Word Pictures in the New Testament,* Vol.V c1932, Vol.VI c1933 by Sunday School Board of the Southern Baptist Convention. Oak Harbor: Logos Research Systems, 1997.

Staff, Holman Bible Editorial, ed. *HCSB Study Bible, Brown/Tan Duotone Simulated Leather.* Holman Bible Publishers, 2010.

Schaeffer, Francis A. *The Complete Works of Francis A. Schaeffer: A Christian Worldview.* Crossway Books, 1985.

Tennent, Timothy C. *Christianity at the Religious Roundtable: Evangelicalism in Conversation with Hinduism, Buddhism, and Islam.* Baker Academic, 2002.

Til, Cornelius Van. *Defense of the Faith:* P & R Publishing, 1969.

_____. *Defense of the Faith:* P & R Publishing, 1980.

_____. *A Survey of Christian Epistemology,* In Defense of the Faith, vol.2: P & R Publishing, 1969.

Transcript of Greg Bahnsen and Edward Tabash Debate, http://www.foranswer.org/Top_Ath/Bahnsen_Tabash.pdf.

Trinity (Christianity) -- Britannica Online Encyclopedia," http://www.britannica.com.ezproxy.liberty.edu:2048/EBchecked/topic/605512/Trinity.

Weber, Max. *Sociology of World Religions: Introduction.*

_____. *The Protestant Ethic and the Spirit of Capitalism*, Translated by Talco Parsons, Charles Scribner's Sons, 1958.

White, James. *The King James Only Controversy: Can You Trust Moder Translations?* Bethany House Publishers, 2009.

White, James. *What Every Christian Needs to Know About the Qur'an.* Bethan House Publishers. 2013.

Wilt, Ben. *Ultimate Apologetics.* Answers in Genesis, 2009.

Zimmer, Heinrich Robert and Joseph Campbell, *Philosophies of India.* Princeto University Press, 1969.

Zuckerman, Solly. *Beyond the Ivory Tower.* Taplinger Publishing Co., 1970.

Scripture Index

General Index

Stephen Feinstein is available for speaking engagements and public appearances.

For more information contact:

Stephen Feinstein
C/O Advantage Books
P.O. Box 160847
Altamonte Springs, FL 32716

info@ advbooks.com

To purchase additional copies of this book or other books published by Advantage Books call our order number at:

407-788-3110 (Book Orders Only)

or visit our bookstore website at:
www.advbookstore.com

Longwood, Florida, USA
"we bring dreams to life"™
www.advbookstore.com

Made in the USA
Monee, IL
14 August 2023

41012635R00164